GLOBAL ECONOMIC STUDIES

GLOBALIZATION

TRADE AGREEMENTS, GLOBAL HEALTH AND UNITED NATIONS INVOLVEMENT

GLOBAL ECONOMIC STUDIES

Additional books in this series can be found on Nova's website
under the Series tab.

Additional E-books in this series can be found on Nova's website
under the E-book tab.

GLOBALIZATION

TRADE AGREEMENTS, GLOBAL HEALTH AND UNITED NATIONS INVOLVEMENT

MARILYN G. MASSARI

AND

KARL J. LUTZ

EDITORS

Nova Science Publishers, Inc.

New York

For permission to use material from this book please contact us:
Telephone 631-231-7269; Fax 631-231-8175
Web Site: http://www.novapublishers.com

NOTICE TO THE READER

The Publisher has taken reasonable care in the preparation of this book, but makes no expressed or implied warranty of any kind and assumes no responsibility for any errors or omissions. No liability is assumed for incidental or consequential damages in connection with or arising out of information contained in this book. The Publisher shall not be liable for any special, consequential, or exemplary damages resulting, in whole or in part, from the readers' use of, or reliance upon, this material. Any parts of this book based on government reports are so indicated and copyright is claimed for those parts to the extent applicable to compilations of such works.

Independent verification should be sought for any data, advice or recommendations contained in this book. In addition, no responsibility is assumed by the publisher for any injury and/or damage to persons or property arising from any methods, products, instructions, ideas or otherwise contained in this publication.

This publication is designed to provide accurate and authoritative information with regard to the subject matter covered herein. It is sold with the clear understanding that the Publisher is not engaged in rendering legal or any other professional services. If legal or any other expert assistance is required, the services of a competent person should be sought. FROM A DECLARATION OF PARTICIPANTS JOINTLY ADOPTED BY A COMMITTEE OF THE AMERICAN BAR ASSOCIATION AND A COMMITTEE OF PUBLISHERS.

Additional color graphics may be available in the e-book version of this book.

LIBRARY OF CONGRESS CATALOGING-IN-PUBLICATION DATA

Globalization : trade agreements, global health and United Nations involvement / editors, Marilyn G. Massari and Karl J. Lutz.
    p. cm.
 Includes bibliographical references and index.
 ISBN 978-1-61470-327-3 (hardcover : alk. paper) 1. United States--Commercial treaties. 2. Balance of trade--United States. 3. United States--Commercial policy. 4. World health. 5. United Nations. I. Massari, Marilyn G. II. Lutz, Karl J. III. Title: Globalisation.
 HF1455.G57 2011
 382'.973--dc23
                          2011022200

Published by Nova Science Publishers, Inc. † New York

CONTENTS

PREFACE

This book presents current research in the study of globalization, with a particular focus on global health programs, trade agreements and United Nations involvement. Topics discussed include trade agreements and their impact on the U.S. economy; U.S. trade deficit and the impact of changing oil prices; free trade agreements; centers for disease control and prevention global health programs; the 2009 influenza pandemic; United Nations assistance mission in Afghanistan; the United Nations Human Rights Council and the United Nations Convention on the Rights of the Child.

Chapter 1- The United States is in the process of considering a number of trade agreements. In addition, the 111th Congress may address the issue of trade promotion authority (TPA), which expired on July 1, 2007. These agreements range from bilateral trade agreements with countries that account for meager shares of U.S. trade to multilateral negotiations that could affect large numbers of U.S. workers and businesses. During this process, Congress likely will be presented with an array of data estimating the impact of trade agreements on the economy, or on a particular segment of the economy.

An important policy tool that can assist Congress in assessing the value and the impact of trade agreements is represented by sophisticated models of the economy that are capable of simulating changes in economic conditions. These models are particularly helpful in estimating the effects of trade liberalization in such sectors as agriculture and manufacturing where the barriers to trade are identifiable and subject to some quantifiable estimation. Barriers to trade in services, however, are proving to be more difficult to identify and, therefore, to quantify in an economic model. In addition, the models are highly sensitive to the assumptions that are used to establish the parameters of the model and they are hampered by a serious lack of comprehensive data in the services sector. Nevertheless, the models do provide insight into the magnitude of the economic effects that may occur across economic sectors as a result of trade liberalization. These insights are especially helpful in identifying sectors expected to experience the greatest adjustment costs and, therefore, where opposition to trade agreements is likely to occur.

This chapter examines the major features of economic models being used to estimate the effects of trade agreements. It assesses the strengths and weaknesses of the models as an aid in helping Congress evaluate the economic impact of trade agreements on the U.S. economy. In addition, this chapter identifies and assesses some of the assumptions used in the economic models and how these assumptions affect the data generated by the models. Finally, this chapter evaluates the implications for Congress of various options it may consider as it assesses trade agreements

Chapter 2- Petroleum prices rose sharply in the first half of 2008, at one time reaching more than $140 per barrel of crude oil. Since July, however, petroleum prices and import volumes have fallen at a historically rapid pace; in January 2009, prices of crude oil fell below $40 per barrel. At the same time the average monthly volume of imports of energy-related petroleum products fell slightly. The sharp rise in the cost of energy imports added an estimated $28 billion to the nation's trade deficit in 2007 and $120 billion in 2008. The fall in the cost of energy imports combined with the drop in import volumes as a result of the slowdown in economic activity reversed the trend of rising energy import costs and sharply reduced the overall costs of U.S. energy imports for 2008 and for the first two months of 2009. Beginning in March 2009, the import price of petroleum products rose each month through September 2009, the most recent period for data. This report provides an estimate of the initial impact of the changing oil prices on the nation's merchandise trade deficit.

Chapter 3- Free trade areas (FTAs) are arrangements among two or more countries under which they agree to eliminate tariffs and nontariff barriers on trade in goods among themselves. However, each country maintains its own policies, including tariffs, on trade outside the region.

In the last few years, the United States has engaged or has proposed to engage in negotiations to establish bilateral and regional free trade arrangements with a number of trading partners. Such arrangements are not new in U.S. trade policy. The United States has had a free trade arrangement with Israel since 1985 and with Canada since 1989, which was expanded to include Mexico and became the North American Free Trade Agreement (NAFTA) effective in January 1994.

U.S. interest in bilateral and regional free trade arrangements surged, and the Bush Administration accelerated the pace of negotiations after the enactment of the Trade Promotion Authority in August 2002. U.S. participation in free trade agreements can occur only with the concurrence of the Congress. In addition, FTAs affect the U.S. economy, with the impact varying across sectors.

The 111th Congress and the Obama Administration face the question of whether and when to act on three pending FTAs—with Colombia, Panama, and South Korea. Although the Bush Administration signed these agreements, it and the leaders of the 110th Congress could not reach agreement on proceeding to enact them. In addition, the Trade Promotion Authority (TPA) expired on July 1, 2007, meaning that any new FTAs agreed to would not likely receive expedited legislative consideration, unless the authority is renewed. While expressing some support for the agreements, President Obama and his Administration have indicated that outstanding issues remain for each of them which need to be addressed before he would send implementing legislation to Congress. The Administration had not indicated a timeline for this process.

In the meantime, on November 14, 2009, President Obama committed to work with the current and prospective members the Trans-Pacific Strategic Economic Partnership Agreement (TPP). The TPP is a free trade agreement that includes nations on both sides of the Pacific. The TPP, which originally came into effect in 2006, currently includes Brunei, Chile, New Zealand, and Singapore. Besides the United States, Australia, Peru, and Vietnam have also expressed interest in joining.

FTAs could raise some important policy issues, if the 111th Congress considers implementing legislation and as it monitors ongoing negotiations as part of its oversight responsibilities: Do FTAs serve or impede U.S. long-term national interests and trade policy objectives? Which type of an FTA arrangement meets U.S. national interests? What should U.S. criteria be in choosing FTA partners? Are FTAs a substitute for or a complement to U.S. commitments and interests in promoting a multilateral trading system via the World Trade Organization (WTO)? What effect will the expiration of TPA have on the future of FTAs as a trade policy strategy?

In the last few years, the United States has considered bilateral and regional free trade areas (FTAs) with a number of trading partners. Such arrangements are not new in U.S. trade policy. The United States has had a free trade arrangement with Israel since 1985 and with Canada since 1989. The latter was suspended when the North American Free Trade Agreement (NAFTA) that included the United States, Canada, and Mexico, went into effect in January 1994.

U.S. interest in bilateral and regional free trade arrangements surged, and the Bush Administration accelerated the pace of negotiations after the enactment of the Trade Promotion Authority in August 2002. U.S. participation in free trade agreements can occur only with the concurrence of the Congress. In addition, FTAs affect the U.S. economy, with the impact varying across sectors.

The 111th Congress and the Obama Administration face the question of whether and when to act on three pending FTAs—with Colombia, Panama, and South Korea. Although the Bush Administration signed these agreements, it and the leaders of the 110th Congress could not reach agreement on proceeding to enact them. In addition, the Trade Promotion Authority (TPA) expired on July 1, 2007, meaning that any new FTAs agreed to would not likely receive expedited legislative consideration, unless the authority is renewed. While expressing some support for the agreements, President Obama and his Administration have indicated that outstanding issues remain for each of them which need to be addressed before he would send implementing legislation to Congress. The Administration had not indicated a timeline for this process.

In the meantime, on November 14, 2009, President Obama committed to work with the current and prospective members the Trans-Pacific Strategic Economic Partnership Agreement (TPP). The TPP is a free trade agreement that includes nations on both sides of the Pacific. The TPP, which originally came into effect in 2006, currently includes Brunei, Chile, New Zealand, and Singapore. Besides the United States, Australia, Peru, and Vietnam have also expressed interest in joining.

FTAs could raise some important policy issues if the 111th Congress considers implementing legislation and as it monitors ongoing negotiations as part of its oversight responsibilities: Do FTAs serve or impede U.S. long-term national interests and trade policy objectives? Which type of an FTA arrangement meets U.S. national interests? What should U.S. criteria be in choosing FTA partners? Are FTAs a substitute for or a complement to U.S. commitments and interests in promoting a multilateral trading system via the World Trade Organization (WTO)? What effect will the expiration of TPA have on the future of FTAs as a trade policy strategy?

This report will monitor pending and possible proposals for U.S. FTAs, relevant legislation and other congressional interest in U.S. FTAs.

Chapter 4- A number of U.S. agencies and departments implement U.S. government global health interventions. Overall, U.S. global health assistance is not always coordinated. Exceptions to this include U.S. international responses to key infectious diseases; for example, U.S. programs to address HIV/AIDS through the President's Emergency Plan for AIDS Relief (PEPFAR), malaria through the President's Malaria Initiative (PMI), and avian and pandemic influenza through the Avian Flu Task Force. Although several U.S. agencies and departments implement global health programs, this chapter focuses on funding for global health programs conducted by the U.S. Centers for Disease Control and Prevention (CDC), a key recipient of U.S. global health funding.

Congress appropriates funds to CDC for its global health efforts through five main budget lines: Global HIV/AIDS, Global Immunization, Global Disease Detection, Malaria, and Other Global Health. Although Congress provides funds for some of CDC's global health efforts through the above-mentioned budget lines, CDC does not, in practice, treat its domestic and global programs separately. Instead, the same experts are mostly used in domestic and global responses to health issues. As such, CDC often leverages its own resources in response to global requests for technical assistance in a number of areas that also have domestic components, such as outbreak response; the prevention and control of injuries and chronic diseases; emergency assistance and disaster response; environmental health; reproductive health; and safe water, hygiene, and sanitation.

President Barack Obama has indicated early in his Administration that global health is a priority and that his Administration would continue to focus global health efforts on addressing HIV/AIDS. When releasing his FY2010 budget request, President Obama indicated that his Administration would increase investments in global health programs and, through his Global Health Initiative, improve the coordination of all global health programs. The President requested that in FY2011, Congress appropriate $353 million to CDC for global health programs—an estimated 5% increase over FY2010 enacted levels. From FY2001 to FY2010, Congress made available more than $3 billion available to CDC for global health programs.

CDC also partners in programs for which it does not have specific appropriations, such as global efforts to address tuberculosis (TB) and respond to pandemic influenza. In addition, the State Department and the U.S. Agency for International Development (USAID) transfer funds to CDC for its role as an implementing partner in U.S. coordinated initiatives, including PEPFAR, PMI, and the Neglected Tropical Diseases (NTD) Initiative.

There is a growing consensus that U.S. global health assistance needs to become more efficient and effective. There is some debate, however, on the best strategies. This chapter explains the role CDC plays in U.S. global health assistance, highlights how much the agency has spent on global health efforts from FY2001 to FY2010, and discusses how funding to each of its programs has changed during this period. For more information on U.S. funding for other global health efforts, including those implemented by USAID, the Department of Defense (DOD), and the Global Fund to Fight AIDS, Tuberculosis, and Malaria (Global Fund) and debates about making U.S. global health assistance more efficient, see CRS Report R40740

Chapter 5- On June 11, 2009, in response to the global spread of a new strain of H1N1 influenza ("flu"), the World Health Organization (WHO) declared the outbreak to be an influenza pandemic, the first since 1968. The novel "H1N1 swine flu" was first identified in California in late April. Since then, cases have been reported around the world.

When the outbreak began, U.S. officials adopted a response posture under the overall coordination of the Secretary of Homeland Security. Among other things, officials established a government-wide informational website (http://www.flu.gov), released antiviral drugs from the national stockpile, developed new diagnostic tests for the H1N1 virus, and published guidance for the clinical management of patients and the management of community and school outbreaks.

Several federal emergency management authorities have been invoked for the response to the pandemic, including a presidential declaration of a national emergency, and a declaration by the Secretary of Health and Human Services (HHS) of a public health emergency. Among other things, these authorities have allowed federal officials to make certain unapproved drugs available to patients with severe cases of influenza, and to ease certain requirements on hospitals to aid them in caring for surges in the volume of patients.

Federal health officials have purchased millions of doses of H1N1 pandemic flu vaccine, approved through the routine licensing process used for seasonal flu vaccines. A voluntary nationwide vaccination program is underway, largely coordinated by state and local health officials and carried out through public clinics, private health care providers, schools, and others. The Secretary of HHS has implemented waivers of liability and an injury compensation program in the event of unforeseen vaccine safety problems. Allocation schemes were developed to give priority for limited vaccine doses to those in high-risk groups. However, there have been a number of problems associated with shortfalls of actual (versus predicted) vaccine availability, and charges that vaccine would not be available for most of the individuals in designated priority groups until after the peak of pandemic virus transmission had passed. Some Members of Congress and others have questioned the adequacy of federal activities to improve the capacity for and timeliness of flu vaccine production.

To address the outbreak, the Obama Administration requested $2 billion in FY2009 emergency supplemental appropriations, and transfer authority for an additional amount of almost $7 billion from existing HHS accounts. On June 26, the President signed P.L. 111-32, the Supplemental Appropriations Act, 2009, which provided $1.9 billion immediately and an additional $5.8 billion contingent upon a presidential request documenting the need for, and proposed use of, additional funds. The President has subsequently asked for most of the contingent amount. A balance of almost $1.3 billion remains available.

This report provides a synopsis of key events in the H1N1 pandemic response, followed by information about selected federal emergency management authorities and actions taken by DHS, HHS, and state and local authorities. It then lists congressional hearings held to date; discusses appropriations and funding for pandemic flu preparedness and response activities; summarizes U.S. government pandemic flu planning documents; and lists sources for additional information. An Appendix describes the WHO process to determine the phase of an emerging flu pandemic

Chapter 6- Since its establishment in 1945, the United Nations has been in a constant state of transition as various international stakeholders seek ways to improve the efficiency and effectiveness of the U.N. system. Recent controversies, such as corruption of the Iraq Oil-For-Food Program, allegations of sexual abuse by U.N. peacekeepers, and instances of waste, fraud and abuse by U.N. staff, have focused renewed attention on the need for change and improvement of the United Nations. Many in the international community, including the United States, have increased pressure on U.N. member states to implement substantive reforms. The 111th Congress will most likely continue to focus on U.N. reform as it considers appropriate levels of U.S. funding to the United Nations and monitors the progress and implementation of ongoing and previously- approved reform measures.

In September 2005, heads of U.N. member states met for the World Summit at U.N. Headquarters in New York to discuss strengthening the United Nations through institutional reform. The resulting Summit Outcome Document laid the groundwork for a series of reforms that included establishing a Peacebuilding Commission, creating a new Human Rights Council, and enlarging the U.N. Security Council. Member states also agreed to Secretariat and management reforms including improving internal U.N. oversight capacity, establishing a U.N. ethics office, enhancing U.N. whistle-blower protection, and reviewing all U.N. mandates five years or older.

Since the World Summit, U.N. member states have worked toward implementing these reforms with varied degrees of success. Some reforms, such as the creation of the Human Rights Council and the Peacebuilding Commission, have already occurred or are ongoing. Other reforms, such as mandate review and U.N. Security Council enlargement, have stalled or not been addressed. U.N. member states disagree as to whether some proposed reforms are necessary, as well as how to most effectively implement previously agreed-to reforms. Developed countries, for example, support delegating more power to the Secretary-General to implement management reforms, whereas developing countries fear that giving the Secretary-General more authority may undermine the power of the U.N. General Assembly and therefore the influence of individual countries.

Congress has maintained a significant interest in the overall effectiveness of the United Nations. Some Members are particularly interested in U.N. Secretariat and management reform, with a focus on enhanced accountability and internal oversight. In the past, Congress has enacted legislation that links U.S. funding of the United Nations to specific U.N. reform benchmarks. Opponents of this strategy argue that tying U.S. funding to U.N. reform may negatively impact diplomatic relations and could hinder the United States' ability to conduct foreign policy. Supporters contend that the United Nations has been slow to implement reforms and that linking payment of U.S. assessments to progress on U.N. reform is the most effective way to motivate member states to efficiently pursue comprehensive reform.

Chapter 7- The most serious challenge facing Afghans and Afghanistan today remains the lack of security. Recent moves by the Taliban and other insurgents to reestablish control of some areas of the country have slowed the pace and extent of economic development and the expansion of the Afghan government, an essential part of the peacebuilding process in Afghanistan. On December 1, 2009, the Obama Administration laid out its strategy for Afghanistan in response to a battlefield assessment from General McCrystal and reemphasized an earlier commitment to civilian efforts in cooperation with the United Nations. The December 1 policy announcement was a follow-on to a March 2009 Obama Administration statement that identified Afghanistan as a top national security priority. It also highlighted the unsatisfactory status of progress to date and need to find a way forward. Congress has focused on Afghanistan as a critical concern during the first session of the 111th Congress.

The United Nations has had an active presence in Afghanistan since 1988. Since the Bonn Agreement of December 2001, international donor activity and assistance has been coordinated primarily through the United Nations Assistance Mission in Afghanistan (UNAMA), though there are other coordinating institutions tied to the Afghan government.

Most observers agree that continued, substantial, long-term development is key, as is the need for international support, but questions have been raised about aid effectiveness (funds required, priorities established, impact received) and the coordination necessary to achieve sufficient improvement throughout the country.

The international recovery and reconstruction effort in Afghanistan is immense and complicated and, in coordination with the Afghan government, involves U.N. agencies, bilateral donors, international organizations, and local and international non-governmental organizations (NGOs). The international community and the Afghan government have sought to establish coordinating institutions and a common set of goals in order to use donor funds effectively.

The international donor community has put great emphasis on Afghan "ownership"— meaning leadership and control—of reconstruction and development efforts by the country itself. Although the Afghan government is taking on an increasingly central role in development planning and the management of aid funds, the international community remains extensively involved in Afghan stabilization, not only in diplomacy and development assistance, but also in combating insurgents and addressing broader security issues. The coordinated aid programs of the United States and its European allies focus on a wide range of activities from strengthening the central and local governments of Afghanistan and its security forces, to promoting civilian reconstruction, reducing corruption, and assisting with elections.

This report examines the central role of UNAMA in Afghanistan. It discusses the obstacles the organization faces in coordinating international efforts and explores related policy issues and considerations for the 111th Congress. This report will be updated as events warrant.

Chapter 8- On March 15, 2006, the U.N. General Assembly passed a resolution replacing the Commission on Human Rights with a new Human Rights Council (the Council). The U.N. Secretariat and some governments, including the United States, view the establishment of the Council as a key component of comprehensive U.N. reform. The Council was designed to be an improvement over the Commission, which was widely criticized for the composition of its membership when perceived human rights abusers were elected as members. The General Assembly resolution creating the Council, among other things, increased the number of meetings per year and introduced a "universal periodic review" process to assess each member state's fulfillment of its human rights obligations.

One hundred seventy countries voted in favor of the resolution to create the Council. The United States, under the George W. Bush Administration, was one of four countries to vote against the resolution. The Administration maintained that the Council structure was no better than the Commission and that it lacked mechanisms for "maintaining credible membership." It initially stated that it would fund and support the work of the Council. During the Council's first two years, however, the Administration expressed concern with the Council's focus on Israel and lack of attention to other human rights situations. In April 2008, the Bush Administration announced that the United States would withhold a portion of its contributions to the 2008 U.N. regular budget equivalent to the U.S. share of the Human Rights Council budget. In June 2008, it further announced that the United States would engage with the Council "only in matters of deep national interest."

The Barack Obama Administration participated as an observer in the 10th regular session of the Human Rights Council (held in March 2009). The Administration stated that it furthers the United States' interest "if we are part of the conversation and present at the Council's proceedings." At the same time, however, it called the Council's trajectory "disturbing," particularly its "repeated and unbalanced" criticisms of Israel. In March 2009, the Obama Administration announced that it would run for a seat on the Council. The United States was elected as a Council Member by the U.N. General Assembly on May 12, 2009, and its term began on June 19, 2009.

Since its establishment, the Council has held 12 regular sessions and 12 special sessions. The regular sessions addressed a combination of specific human rights abuses and procedural and structural issues. Six of the 12 special sessions addressed the human rights situation in the Occupied Palestinian Territories and in Lebanon. Other special sessions focused on the human rights situations in Burma (Myanmar), Darfur, Sri Lanka, and Democratic Republic of the Congo.

Congress maintains an ongoing interest in the credibility and effectiveness of the Council in the context of both human rights and broader U.N. reform. In the Omnibus Appropriations Act, 2009 (Division H, the Department of State, Foreign Operations, and Related Programs Appropriations Act, 2009 of P.L. 111-8), for example, Congress prohibited U.S. contributions to support the Council unless (1) the Secretary of State certifies to the Committees on Appropriations that funding the Council is "in the national interest of the United States" or (2) the United States is a member of the Council. A similar provision was included in Division J of the Consolidated Appropriations Act, 2008 (P.L. 110-161). Withholding Council funds in this manner would be a largely symbolic policy action because assessed contributions finance the entire U.N. regular budget and not specific parts of it. This chapter will be updated as events warrant.

Chapter 9- U.S. ratification of the United Nations (U.N.) Convention on the Rights of the Child (hereafter referred to as CRC or the Convention) may be a key area of focus during the 111th Congress, particularly if the Barack Obama Administration seeks the advice and consent of the Senate. CRC is an international treaty that aims to protect the rights of children worldwide. It defines a child as any human being under the age of 18, and calls on States Parties to take all appropriate measures to ensure that children's rights are protected— including the right to a name and nationality, freedom of speech and thought, access to healthcare and education, and freedom from exploitation, torture, and abuse. CRC entered into force in September 1990, and has been ratified by 193 countries, making it the most widely ratified human rights treaty in the world. Two countries, the United States and Somalia, have not ratified CRC. The President has not transmitted CRC to the Senate for its advice and consent to ratification.

Despite widespread U.S. support for the overall objectives of the Convention, some past and current policymakers have raised concerns as to whether it is an effective mechanism for protecting children's rights. The Clinton Administration signed the Convention in February 1995, but did not submit it to the Senate primarily because of strong opposition from several Members of Congress. The George W. Bush Administration opposed CRC and expressed serious political and legal concerns with the treaty, arguing that it conflicted with U.S. laws regarding privacy and family rights. The election of President Barack Obama in 2008 has focused renewed attention on the possibility of U.S. ratification. The Administration has stated that any decision to pursue ratification of CRC will be determined through an interagency policy review. Perhaps more than other human rights treaties, CRC addresses areas that are usually considered to be primarily or exclusively under the jurisdiction of state or local governments, including education, juvenile justice, and access to healthcare. Some of these conflicting areas will likely need to be resolved by the executive branch and the Senate before the United States ratifies the Convention.

The question of U.S. ratification of CRC has generated contentious debate. Opponents argue that U.S. ratification would undermine U.S. sovereignty by giving the United Nations authority to determine the best interests of U.S. children. Some are also concerned that CRC could interfere in the private lives of families, particularly the rights of parents to educate and discipline their children. Moreover, some argue that CRC is an ineffective mechanism for protecting children's rights. They emphasize that countries that are widely regarded as abusers of children's rights, including China and Sudan, are party to the Convention. Supporters of U.S. ratification, on the other hand, hold that CRC's intention is not to circumvent the role of parents but to protect children against government intrusion and abuse. Proponents emphasize what they view as CRC's strong support for the role of parents and the family structure. Additionally, supporters hold that U.S. federal and state laws generally meet the requirements of CRC, and that U.S. ratification would strengthen the United States' credibility when advocating children's rights abroad.

This report provides an overview of CRC's background and structure and examines evolving U.S. policy toward the Convention, including past and current Administration positions and congressional perspectives. The report also highlights issues for the 111th Congress, including the Convention's possible impact on federal and state laws, U.S. sovereignty, parental rights, and U.S. family planning and abortion policy. It also addresses the effectiveness of CRC in protecting the rights of children internationally and its potential use as an instrument of U.S. foreign po

In: Globalization
Editors: M. G. Massari and K. J. Lutz, pp. 1-23

ISBN: 978-1-61470-327-3
© 2012 Nova Science Publishers, Inc.

Chapter 1

TRADE AGREEMENTS:
IMPACT ON THE U.S. ECONOMY[*]

James K. Jackson

ABSTRACT

The United States is in the process of considering a number of trade agreements. In addition, the 111th Congress may address the issue of trade promotion authority (TPA), which expired on July 1, 2007. These agreements range from bilateral trade agreements with countries that account for meager shares of U.S. trade to multilateral negotiations that could affect large numbers of U.S. workers and businesses. During this process, Congress likely will be presented with an array of data estimating the impact of trade agreements on the economy, or on a particular segment of the economy.

An important policy tool that can assist Congress in assessing the value and the impact of trade agreements is represented by sophisticated models of the economy that are capable of simulating changes in economic conditions. These models are particularly helpful in estimating the effects of trade liberalization in such sectors as agriculture and manufacturing where the barriers to trade are identifiable and subject to some quantifiable estimation. Barriers to trade in services, however, are proving to be more difficult to identify and, therefore, to quantify in an economic model. In addition, the models are highly sensitive to the assumptions that are used to establish the parameters of the model and they are hampered by a serious lack of comprehensive data in the services sector. Nevertheless, the models do provide insight into the magnitude of the economic effects that may occur across economic sectors as a result of trade liberalization. These insights are especially helpful in identifying sectors expected to experience the greatest adjustment costs and, therefore, where opposition to trade agreements is likely to occur.

This chapter examines the major features of economic models being used to estimate the effects of trade agreements. It assesses the strengths and weaknesses of the models as an aid in helping Congress evaluate the economic impact of trade agreements on the U.S. economy. In addition, this chapter identifies and assesses some of the assumptions used in the economic models and how these assumptions affect the data generated by the

---

[*] This is an edited, reformatted and augmented version of CRS Report RL31932, dated November 10, 2009.

models. Finally, this chapter evaluates the implications for Congress of various options it may consider as it assesses trade agreements.

BACKGROUND

Congress plays a direct role in formulating and implementing U.S. international trade policies. During the 108th, 109th, and 110th Congresses, this role gained increased importance as the United States negotiated an unprecedented number of trade agreements. The 111th Congress may also address the issue of trade promotion authority (TPA), which expired on July 1, 2007. Under this authority, Congress grants the President the authority to enter into certain reciprocal trade agreements [1]. Currently, the United States is involved in multilateral negotiations in the Doha Development Agenda under the auspices of the World Trade Organization (WTO). On a regional level, the United States signed an agreement on the Dominican Republic-Central America-United States Free Trade Agreement (CAFTA-DR), and has at times been involved with countries in southern Africa. In addition, the United States has pursued bilateral trade agreements with Malaysia, the United Arab Emirates, and Thailand. It has concluded agreements with Australia, Bahrain, Canada, Chile, Dominican Republic, Israel, Jordan, Mexico, Morocco, Oman, Peru, and Singapore, and the five countries of the Central American Common Market (Guatemala, Honduras, Nicaragua, El Salvador, and Costa Rica) [2]. The United States has signed free trade agreements with South Korea, Columbia, and Panama, but Congress has not enacted legislation to approve and implement these agreements. The Bush Administration concluded agreements with Panama, Peru and Colombia, separately from Ecuador and Bolivia, the other members of the proposed Andean-U.S. Free Trade Agreement.

Building a broad-based public consensus on international trade issues often has proven to be difficult, especially as certain industries and labor groups within the economy have been adversely affected by international competition. Based on previous experiences with international trade agreements, Members of Congress and the public may view these agreements with varying degrees of support and opposition. While few critics are likely to oppose outright all of the trade agreements being negotiated, critics will oppose some aspects of the agreements, because certain groups within the economy will incur a disproportionate share of the adjustment costs associated with each trade agreement. Economists and others have developed economic models that utilize advanced techniques to assess the economic impact of trade agreements on the economy as a whole and on specific sectors within the economy. To help Congress evaluate the potential economic effects, this chapter examines a sampling of these studies and offers an assessment of the estimates they have generated.

AN OVERVIEW OF THE MAJOR AGREEMENTS

Multilateral Agreements

In November 2001, trade7 ministers from 142 member countries of the World Trade Organization met in Doha, Qatar to launch the 4th WTO ministerial. The Doha meeting succeeded primarily by agreeing to begin a new round of multilateral trade negotiations [3] These negotiations are intended to build on agreements reached under the Uruguay Round of negotiations on trade in agriculture and trade in services, part of the WTO's already-established work program. For the United States, the chief goal of the negotiations is to improve market access in agricultural trade, primarily by eliminating agricultural export subsidies; easing tariffs and quotas; and reducing other forms of trade-distorting domestic support. In addition, the United States hopes to expand negotiations on trade in services and to reduce tariffs on industrial goods.

Selected CRS Products on Trade Issues

CRS Report 98-840, *U.S.-Latin America Trade: Recent Trends and Policy Issues*, by J. F. Hornbeck.

CRS Report RL30981, *Panama: Political and Economic Conditions and U.S. Relations*, by Mark P. Sullivan.

CRS Report RL31356, *Free Trade Agreements: Impact on U.S. Trade and Implications for U.S. Trade Policy*, by William H. Cooper.

CRS Report RL31772, *U.S. Trade and Investment Relationship with Sub-Saharan Africa: The African Growth and Opportunity Act*, by Vivian C. Jones.

CRS Report RL31870, *The Dominican Republic-Central America-United States Free Trade Agreement (CAFTA-DR)*, by J. F. Hornbeck.

CRS Report RL32540, *The Proposed U.S.-Panama Free Trade Agreement*, by J. F. Hornbeck

CRS Report RL32593, *Thailand: Background and U.S. Relations*, by Emma Chanlett-Avery.

CRS Report RL33445, T*he Proposed U.S.-Malaysia Free Trade Agreement*, by Michael F. Martin.

CRS Report RL33653, *East Asian Regional Architecture: New Economic and Security Arrangements and U.S. Policy*, by Dick K. Nanto.

CRS Report RL33951, *U.S. Trade Policy and the Caribbean: From Trade Preferences to Free Trade Agreements*, by J. F. Hornbeck.

CRS Report RL34108, *U.S.-Peru Economic Relations and the U.S.-Peru Trade Promotion Agreement*, by M. Angeles Villarreal.

CRS Report RL34330, *The Proposed U.S.-South Korea Free Trade Agreement (KORUS FTA): Provisions and Implications,* coordinated by William H. Cooper.

CRS Report R40502, *The Trans-Pacific Strategic Economic Partnership Agreement*, by Ian F. Fergusson and Bruce Vaughn.

A framework agreement on future negotiations was concluded in Geneva on August 1, 2004, but a new deadline for the completion of the talks was not set and the talks stalled in 2005. This framework was viewed hopefully, because it provides a blueprint for future negotiations on agriculture, non-agricultural market access, services and trade facilitation. The 6th Ministerial, which occurred in Hong Kong in December 2005, was seen by many as the last opportunity to settle key negotiating issues that could produce an agreement by 2007, the de facto deadline for the negotiations before the U.S. trade promotion authority expired. On April 21, 2006, WTO Director-General Pascal Lamy announced that WTO negotiators would not meet the April 30, 2006, deadline for reaching an agreement on a framework for further negotiations and that he had committed negotiators to six weeks of continuous talks to reach an agreement. Trade negotiators failed to reach an agreement during talks in Geneva from June 30-July 1, 2006, and the talks were indefinitely suspended. On January 1, 2007, however, Lamy announced that the talks were back in "full negotiating mode." Chairs of the agriculture and industrial market access negotiating groups offered draft modalities texts on July 17, 2007, that are serving to keep the differing parties to the negotiations engaged in the talks despite criticism from nearly all quarters over the texts.

Regional Trade Agreements

Free Trade Area of the Americas (FTAA)

At the second Summit of the Americas in April 1998, 34 nations of the Western Hemisphere agreed to initiate formal negotiations to create a Free Trade Area of the Americas by 2005 [4]. The negotiations initiated efforts in five areas (market access, agriculture, services, investment, and government procurement), but the negotiations have stalled. The United States and Brazil attempted to broker a compromise by moving the negotiations away from a comprehensive, single undertaking toward a two-tier framework comprising a set of "common rights and obligations" for all countries, combined with voluntary plurilateral arrangements with country benefits related to commitments. This approach, however has proved elusive and five of the participants—Brazil, Argentina, Uruguay, Paraguay, and Venezuela—have blocked an effort to restart the negotiations.

U.S.-Southern African Customs Union Free Trade Agreement

In November 2002, the Bush Administration announced that it was pursuing negotiations for a free trade agreement with the Southern African Customs Union (SACU), comprised of Botswana, Namibia, Lesotho, South Africa, and Swaziland [5]. These negotiations reflect congressional interest in strengthening U.S. trade with Africa as expressed in the African Growth and Opportunity Act (P.L. 106-200). U.S. negotiators hope to gain reductions in tariffs and in non-tariff barriers in such areas as telecommunications, financial services, legal services, and the movement of personnel. The Southern African members had pressed for increased market access for goods not already covered by the Africa Growth and Opportunity Act, especially for textiles and apparel, footwear, and agricultural products. After six rounds of talks, negotiations stalled and the December 2004 deadline for concluding the talks passed. The talks were deadlocked over differing views over the objectives of the talks and what sectors should be included for negotiation. Currently, the United States and SACU are continuing talks for a Trade, Investment, and Development Cooperation Agreement, which may lead to an eventual FTA. The United States has signed Trade and Investment Framework Agreements with Ghana, Liberia, Mauritius, Mozambique, Nigeria, Rwanda, and South Africa, as well as several regional groups. Also, the United States has signed Bilateral Investment Treaties with several Sub-Saharan African countries, including: Cameroon, Republic of the Congo (Brazzaville), Democratic Republic of the Congo (Kinshasa), Mozambique, and Senegal.

The Enterprise for ASEAN Initiative

On October 26, 2002, President Bush announced that the United States had begun negotiations with the Association of Southeast Asian Nations (ASEAN) under the Enterprise for ASEAN Initiative (EAI) [6]. The initiative offered the prospect of bilateral trade agreements with the 10 ASEAN members (Brunei, Cambodia, Indonesia, Laos, Malaysia, Myanmar (Burma), Philippines, Singapore, Thailand, and Vietnam). Since the EAI was announced, the United States concluded FTAs with Singapore and initiated agreements with Thailand and Malaysia. The United States concluded a Trade and Investment Framework Agreement (TIFA) with ASEAN in August 2006. In addition, the United States has expressed interest in joining the Trans-Pacific Strategic Partnership Agreement (TPP), which currently includes Brunei, Chile, New Zealand, and Singapore. Australia, Peru, and Vietnam have also expressed interest in joining the agreement. Two-way trade between the United States and ASEAN reached $182 billion in 2008.

U.S.-Andean Free Trade Agreement

The Bush Administration initiated talks with the four Andean countries—Colombia, Peru, Ecuador, and Bolivia—in November 2003 to reduce and eliminate barriers to trade and investment [7]. Negotiations began in May 2004, but the talks failed to reach a conclusion. As a result, Peru decided to continue negotiating with the United States without Colombia or Ecuador, and concluded a bilateral agreement in December 2005, referred to as the U.S.-Peru Trade Promotion Agreement. Separate talks continued with Colombia and concluded successfully on February 27, 2006. Prospects for FTAs with Brazil, Argentina, Ecuador, Bolivia, and Venezuela appear unlikely.

Central American Free Trade Agreement—Dominican Republic

The Bush Administration signed an agreement with the five Central American Common Market nations—Costa Rica, El Salvador, Guatemala, Honduras, and Nicaragua—on August 5, 2004 [8]. President Bush signed the agreement into law on August 2, 2005 (P.L. 109-53). All countries except Costa Rica and the Dominican Republic have ratified the agreement. As of July 1, 2006, the United States had implemented the agreement for El Salvador, Honduras, Nicaragua and Guatemala will did so for Costa Rica after it had adopted the necessary regulatory and legal framework.

Many supporters have viewed the Dominican Republic-Central American Free Trade Agreement (CAFTA) as a stepping stone toward completing a Free Trade Area of the Americas. U.S. negotiators hope to assist U.S. firms and workers by reducing tariffs on U.S. merchandise exports, and by reducing barriers to e-commerce, services, and intellectual property trade. The U.S. also hopes to use the agreement to improve the participants' commitment to the World Trade Organization's General Agreement on Trade in Services (GATS) and to define better the rules on transparency. The Central American participants are aiming to deepen their already strong trade relationship with the United States and to improve access for their textile and apparel products to the U.S. market.

Completed Bilateral Trade Agreements

U.S.-Australian Free Trade Agreement

The United States and Australia concluded a bilateral free trade agreement on February 8, 2004. The agreement was signed by the President on August 3, 2004 (P.L. 108-286) and took effect January 1, 2005. For the United States, the agreement lowered Australian tariffs on most U.S. exports of manufactured goods and agricultural products and will ensure nondiscriminatory treatment in most areas of bilateral trade in services, government procurement, foreign investment, and improved protection for intellectual property rights. For Australia, the agreement lowers tariffs on U.S. imports of Australian beef, dairy, cotton, and peanuts, but provides no change in access to sugar producers. Various U.S. agricultural interests, including beef, dairy, and sugar producers, opposed the negotiations, because of Australia's large, and competitive, agricultural sector. At $14 billion in 2004, Australia is the 15th-largest market for U.S. exports and, at $7 billion, Australia is the 30th-largest importer to the United States.

U.S.-Bahrain Free Trade Agreement

On September 14, 2004, the United States and Bahrain concluded negotiations for a free trade agreement [9]. The President signed the agreement into law on January 11, 2006 (P.L. 109-169). The Administration views the agreement as a first step toward an eventual Middle East Free Trade Area by 2013. Bahrain has a Bilateral Investment Treaty with the United States and a Trade and Investment Framework Agreement. The agreement will eliminate tariffs on all consumer and industrial product exports to Bahrain and eliminate tariffs on 98% of all U.S. agricultural products with a 10-year phase out for the remaining items. Textiles and apparel trade will be duty free if the product contains either U.S. or Bahrainian yarn. U.S. services providers will have among the highest degree of access to service markets in Bahrain of any U.S. FTA to date in such areas as audiovisual, express delivery, telecommunications, computer and related services, distribution, healthcare, and services incidental to mining, construction, architecture, and engineering. U.S. financial services and life and medical insurance providers will also have access to Bahrain's economy.

U.S.-Chile Free Trade Agreement

On June 6, 2003, the United States and Chile signed a bilateral free trade agreement [10]. The agreement was signed by the President on September 3, 2003 (P.L. 108-77), and became effective on January 1, 2004. For the United States, trade with Chile accounts for less than one percent of U.S. overall trade, but the agreement is significant because it is the first such agreement with a South American country. The main U.S. objectives were accomplished by gaining market access and reduced tariff rates for U.S.-made goods. In time, all goods traded between the two countries will receive duty-free access. Under the agreement, 85% of bilateral trade in consumer and industrial products is eligible for duty-free treatment, with other product tariff rates being reduced over time. About 75% of U.S. agricultural exports will enter Chile duty-free within four years and all duties will be fully phased out within 12 years after implementation of the agreement. For Chile, 95% of its exports gain duty-free status immediately and only 1.2% fall into the longest 12 year phase out period. Other critical issues that were resolved include environment and labor provisions, more open government procurement rules, increased access for services trade, greater protection of U.S. investment and intellectual property.

U.S.-Moroccan Free Trade Agreement

President Bush signed the United States-Morocco Free Trade Agreement (P.L. 108-302) on August 3, 2004. The agreement entered into force on January 1, 2006, after the Moroccan parliament ratified the agreement and King Mohammed VI signed it [11]. The agreement is intended to strengthen economic ties between the United States and Morocco and to show support for Morocco's position as a moderate Arab state. Morocco's agriculture sector is highly protected and should offer opportunities for U.S. business investment and U.S. exports. In particular, U.S. trade officials expect that reductions in Morocco's 20% tariff rate called for by the agreement should increase U.S. exports to the country, especially exports of such items as wheat, soybeans, feed grains, beef, and poultry. Business leaders also expect that the agreement will increase U.S. investment in Moroccan telecommunications and tourism as well as in the fields of energy, entertainment, transport, finance, and insurance. U.S. exports of information technology products, construction equipment, and chemicals are expected to benefit. Morocco is looking for increased access to the U.S. market, especially for Morocco's citrus products, textiles, and apparel goods.

U.S.-Oman Free Trade Agreement

The Bush Administration notified Congress in November 2004 that it would begin negotiations on a free trade agreement with the United Arab Emirates (UAE) and Oman. Talks began on March 8, 2005, with the UAE and on March 12, 2005, with Oman. The President signed an agreement with Oman on January 19, 2006. The Senate passed implementing legislation on June 29, 2006 (S. 3569), and the House passed the legislation (H.R. 5684) on July 20, 2006. Following the House action, the Senate re-passed the implementing legislation under the House number on September 19, 2006, and it became P.L. 109-283, when President Bush signed the law on September 26, 2006.

U.S.-Peru Trade Promotion Agreement (PTPA)

On January 16, 2009, President Bush signed a proclamation to implement the U.S.-Peru Trade Promotion Agreement as of February 1, 2009 [12]. The Agreement eliminates duties on 80% of U.S. exports of consumer and industrial products to Peru. An additional 7% of U.S. exports will receive duty-free treatment within five years of implementation. Remaining tariffs will be eliminated ten years after implementation. The United States has extended duty-free treatment to imports from Peru under the Andean Trade Preference Act, which is set to expire on December 31, 2009. The PTPA is expected to have a small effect on the U.S. economy, because U.S. trade with Peru accounts for a small percent of total U.S. trade. The dominant import from Peru is copper, followed by petroleum and other oils and related products. The leading U.S. export item to Peru is petroleum oils and related products, followed by wheat and meslin.

U.S.-Singapore Free Trade Agreement

On September 4, 2003, President Bush signed the U.S.-Singapore Free Trade Agreement (P.L. 108-78) into law [13]. This agreement is the first of its kind for the United States with an Asian country and sparked a debate over whether the United States should pursue such bilateral agreements or pursue greater liberalization of trade relations through regional or multilateral forums. Both Singapore and the United States had few remaining restrictions on their overall trade activities, so the economic impact of this particular FTA is expected to be small for the United States. Nevertheless, the agreement eliminates, with a phase-in period, tariffs on all goods traded between the two countries, covers trade in services, and protects intellectual property rights.

The areas that are affected the most are U.S. exports of chewing gum and distilled spirits and imports of textiles and apparel. Industry analysts expect that U.S. textile and apparel producers will experience few direct economic effects from this agreement, but there has been a sharp division of views among industry representatives regarding the agreement's rules of origin governing trade in apparel goods. Apparel producers argue that the rules of origin on apparel are restrictive and have been made worse through the agreement by additional complications and burdens that discourage trade in apparel. The AFL-CIO opposed the agreement, because it argued that the agreement would not sufficiently protect core worker rights.

In the area of services, the agreement should improve U.S. market access across a broad range of sectors. U.S. banks, insurance companies, and securities and financial services companies are looking to expand in Singapore's market. The agreement also liberalizes controls over express delivery service and such professional service providers as lawyers, engineers, and architects. In addition, the agreement eases restrictions on telecommunications services, e-commerce, foreign investment, intellectual property rights, and government procurement.

Signed Bilateral Trade Agreements Requiring Congressional Approval

U.S.-Colombia Free Trade Agreement

On February 6, 2006, the United States and Colombia announced that they had concluded negotiation of a free trade agreement. The agreement is comprehensive and would eliminate tariffs and other barriers in goods and services trade between the two countries. Similar to the U.S.-Peru FTA, the U.S.-Colombia agreement would eliminate duties on 80% of U.S. exports of consumer and industrial products to Colombia immediately upon implementation. An additional 7% of U.S. exports would receive duty-free treatment within five years and all remaining tariffs would be eliminated within ten years of implementation. Implementing legislation has not been introduced in the Congress.

U.S.-South Korea Free Trade Agreement

The Bush Administration notified Congress on February 3, 2006, of its intent to begin formal negotiations on a free trade agreement with South Korea. On February 12, 2007, the negotiators had completed the seventh round of talks. For U.S. negotiators, the most difficult part of the talks is in contending with South Korea's well-protected agricultural sector, non-tariff barriers in the automotive and other manufacturing sectors, and status of products made at the Kaesong industrial complex, an industrial zone in North Korea set up by South Korean manufacturers. For the South Koreans, major sticking points are U.S. protection of textiles and apparel producers.

U.S.-Panama Free Trade Agreement

The Bush Administration began formal negotiations with Panama on April 25, 2004, in Panama City, Panama [14]. The negotiations progressed quickly and an agreement was signed on June 28, 2007. The United States sought reductions in tariffs and other barriers to U.S.

industrial, agricultural, and consumer goods, and wanted to define rules for services trade, investment, government procurement, intellectual property rights, and dispute resolution mechanisms. U.S. labor groups have challenged Panama's labor conditions, laws, enforcement efforts, and the language of the FTA. Panama is seeking to solidify its access to U.S. markets for agricultural goods, textiles and apparel, but already receives considerable benefits from the Caribbean Basin initiative's (CBI) unilateral trade preferences of the United States and is among the largest recipients of U.S. foreign direct investment in Latin America.

Pending Bilateral Trade Agreements

U.S.-Malaysia Free Trade Agreement

Negotiations with Malaysia began on March 8, 2006; the fifth round of the talks occurred during the week of February 5, 2007 [15]. The United States is seeking the removal of import licensing restrictions on motor vehicles, removal of government procurement restrictions, increased protection for intellectual property rights (IPR), liberalized financial services, and negotiations on a broad range of services.

U.S.-Thailand Free Trade Agreement

The United States and Thailand began formal negotiations on a free trade agreement on June 28, 2004, in Hawaii. The Administration argues that the agreement will be comprehensive and seek to liberalize trade in goods, agriculture, services, investment, and intellectual property rights. In particular, the Administration said that the agreement will promote U.S. exports, primarily benefitting U.S. farmers and the auto and auto parts industries, will protect U.S. investment, and will advance the Enterprise for ASEAN Initiative. Other issues that likely will be negotiated include government procurement, competition policy, environment and labor standards, and customs procedures. The United States is Thailand's largest market, which accounts for 20% of Thailand's exports.

U.S.-United Arab Emirates Free Trade Agreement

The Bush Administration notified Congress in November 2004 that it would begin negotiations on a free trade agreement with the United Arab Emirates (UAE) and Oman. Talks began on March 8, 2005, with the UAE and on March 12, 2005, with Oman. Worker protection issues have presented a major hurdle, because the UAE relies heavily on guest workers and it places restrictions on the right to strike or organize. The Administration hopes that an agreement will build on agreements that have been signed with other nations in the area (Israel, Jordan, Morocco, Bahrain, and Oman) and will encourage a movement toward more open trade and more investment.

TRADE LIBERALIZATION AND THE GAINS FROM TRADE

Nations pursue trade liberalization to achieve a number of national objectives. Economists argue, however, that free trade, or the international trade of goods and services free from restrictions and barriers, provides nations with a broad group of economic benefits [16]. These benefits are categorized as one-time, or static, benefits, which include gains for consumers and gains for producers, and dynamic benefits that accrue over time and can positively affect the long-term rate of growth of a country. While it is not always possible to measure these effects precisely, most economists believe that the net effect of international trade on the national economy as a whole is positive, i.e., that the total gains exceed the total costs.

Table 1. Major Components of U.S. Gross Domestic Product
(Expressed as percent share of total GDP; billions of US dollars)

	1990-94	1995-99	2000-2004	2005-2008	2009-I	2009-II	2009-III	2008
Gross domestic product	100.00	100.00	100.00	100.00	100.00	100.00	100.00	$14,441.4
Personal consumption	66.76	67.32	69.60	69.83	70.45	70.66	70.98	10,129.9
Gross private domestic investment	14.36	16.59	16.29	16.36	11.92	11.03	11.04	2,136.1
Change in private inventories	0.36	0.62	0.20	0.17	-0.90	-1.25	-1.03	-34.8
Net exports of goods and services	-0.92	-1.71	-4.27	-5.34	-2.67	-2.40	-2.71	-707.8
Exports	9.91	10.97	9.92	11.48	10.65	10.56	10.93	1,831.1
Goods	7.02	7.83	6.98	7.95	6.98	6.91	7.26	1,266.9
Services	2.89	3.14	2.94	3.53	3.67	3.64	3.67	564.2
Imports	10.83	12.67	14.19	16.82	13.32	12.95	13.64	2,538.9
Goods	8.85	10.61	11.88	14.13	10.64	10.32	11.00	2,126.4
Services	1.98	2.06	2.31	2.69	2.68	2.63	2.64	412.4
Government consumption	19.81	17.80	18.38	19.15	20.31	20.70	20.68	2,883.2
Federal	8.19	6.38	6.40	7.09	7.81	8.04	8.14	1,082.6
State and local	11.62	11.42	11.98	12.06	12.50	12.66	12.54	1,800.60

Source: Department of Commerce, Bureau of Economic Analysis.

Production Gains

International trade is one among a number of forces that determine the complex makeup of jobs, industries, wages, and products in the economy. For the United States, international trade alone does not determine economic expansions or contractions, the level of income, the level of national output, the overall wage rate, or even have much of an impact on the distribution of income [17]. Table 1 shows the major components of U.S. Gross Domestic Product (GDP), the broadest measure of the output of goods and services during a year averaged over five-year periods.

Table 1. Major Components By convention, these components are comprised of the household sector, or personal consumption, business investment, or gross private domestic investment, changes in inventories, the government sector, and the net export sector, or the net of U.S. exports of goods and services and the imports of goods and services. As the data indicate, U.S. exports of goods have accounted for 7% to 8% of total U.S. GDP over the past 18 years. In 2008, such exports accounted for $1.3 trillion, or about 7% of U.S. GDP. Trade liberalization, however, by reducing foreign barriers to U.S. exports and by removing U.S. barriers to foreign goods and services, helps to strengthen those industries that are the most competitive and productive and to reinforce the shifting of labor and capital from less productive endeavors to more productive economic activities.

Adjustment Costs

Economists have long recognized that the long-term production gains associated with greater specialization in the economy create a wide range of short-term adjustment costs as labor and capital are shifted from less efficient industries and activities into more efficient industries and activities. These adjustment costs are difficult to measure, but they are potentially large over the short run and can entail significant dislocations for some segments of the labor force, for some companies, and for some communities. In negotiating trade agreements, governments are most mindful of the adjustment costs involved and, at times, are constrained in their ability to fashion such agreements because of opposition by groups within the economy that will bear heavy costs from trade liberalization. These costs are especially acute for labor groups within the economy that lack advanced education and training skills that provide them with the means necessary to be redeployed in other sectors of the economy.

Consumption Gains

Economists generally agree that consumption gains for consumers comprise the largest long-term gains for an economy that arise from international trade and, therefore, from any reduction of trade barriers. Trade models attempt to estimate these effects indirectly. A change in trade policies should lead to changes in prices for traded goods and, therefore, in consumers' real incomes, as well as to changes in the efficiency of production, which will also improve a nation's overall economic welfare. Consumption gains mean that consumers benefit from international trade by having a broader selection of goods and services available to them at lower prices than are available from purely domestic production. Also, the wider array of product selection likely enhances consumer well-being, because the competition that arises from international trade also affects the quality of the goods and services that are available. In some cases, this means that consumers have a choice of different levels of quality and that they can acquire not only the particular type of good they desire, but also the level of quality they desire. Since international trade encourages specialization, the production gains from trade also mean that consumers are offered a greater selection of prices for the goods they consume. If consumers choose lower- priced goods, their real incomes rise, which allows them to consume an even broader assortment of goods and services, and it expands national incomes.

Economic Growth

In addition to the "static" gains from trade described above, a growing body of research suggests that trade potentially plays a dynamic role in the economy. The full range of these effects are difficult for trade models to capture because they extend beyond the estimation time-frame of the models. Research into dynamic trade models concludes that there are important feedback effects and channels through which trade can alter the structure of markets and the rate of economic growth over the long run. By stimulating trade and investment, trade liberalization could add to these feedback effects. The literature on dynamic trade models concludes that free trade, or trade liberalization, alters all participants' rate of economic growth through a number of channels, including improved access to specialized capital goods; human capital accumulation, learning-bydoing, and the transfer of skills; and the introduction of new products [18]. These activities alter the rate of economic growth by changing the incentives for firms to invest in research and development—technical change— which, in turn, leads to permanent changes in the rate of economic growth. In assessing this body of research, a U.S. International Trade Commission study asserted that, "formal empirical application of the new growth theory in a trade context has barely started," but that "the dynamic effects of trade policy changes can yield substantially larger estimates than those based on static models." [19]

ESTIMATING THE ECONOMIC IMPACT OF TRADE AGREEMENTS

Overview

Since the stakes involved in liberalizing trade are potentially very large for some groups and for some countries, economists have attempted to analyze the economic effects of removing barriers to trade in goods and services and to derive monetary values for those effects. Several different approaches are used to estimate the cost and effect of reducing barriers to trade in goods and services [20]. The most common approach uses sophisticated mathematical models of the U.S. economy to simulate the effects of trade liberalization. The three models used most often are: gravity models, partial equilibrium models, and general equilibrium models. Gravity models are based on the theory that large economies have a greater pull on trade flows than do smaller economies [21]. As a result, the size of an economy and its distance from trading partners are important factors in estimating the monetary value of changes in trading rules. Partial equilibrium models are used to measure the effects of trade restraints on a specific sector, rather then on the economy as a whole. Both gravity models and partial equilibrium models provide aggregate estimates of the effects of changes in trading rules and barriers, but they offer limited detailed information on the labor and sectoral effects of trade liberalization.

General equilibrium models, or computable general equilibrium (CGE) models, attempt to encompass all economic activity within an economy and attempt to estimate the economy-wide effects of changes in trade or economic policy. These models can offer comprehensive assessments of cross- and inter-industry linkages both worldwide and between regions of the world [22]. Such models attempt to mimic as closely as possible the real world economy through the use of an abstract mathematical representation of the environment in which relevant economic agents operate and of the decision-making process by which they make choices of consumption of goods, capital accumulation, etc [23]. These models incorporate assumptions about consumer behavior, market structure and organization, production technology, investment, and capital flows in the form of foreign direct investment. General equilibrium models use large sets of data that represent numerous countries and attempt to estimate economy-wide feedback effects from a change in trade policy in a given sector or industry and assess the impact of the change on employment, production, and economic welfare.

The Michigan Model and Estimates

One well-known and often-referenced general equilibrium model used frequently to analyze the economic effects of changes in trade policy is the model maintained by economists Drusilla Brown, Robert M. Stern, and Alan V. Deardorff at the University of Michigan [24]. In a recent study, Brown, Stern, and Deardorff used the model to estimate the economic effects on the United States of trade negotiations in the multi-country Doha Development Round and various proposed regional and bilateral trade agreements. In each scenario, the trio begin by using available data to develop a base estimate of the present level of trade. Next, they adjust the model to reflect some basic assumptions about how trade negotiations will reduce barriers to trade and then use these estimates to make an adjusted projection of major macroeconomic data. The difference between the initial set of data on the economy and the projected macroeconomic data that reflects anticipated changes in the economy as a result of trade negotiations gives rise to the numerical estimates of the effects of trade negotiations on trade, employment, industrial composition, and other macroeconomic data. One important drawback to the estimates derived by Brown, Deardorff, and Stern, and others is that the general equilibrium models used to derive most of the estimates of trade liberalization do not capture the adjustment costs that inevitably arise from trade liberalization. As a result, the data generated by the models represent the positive effects of changes in trade rules, but not the overall net effects—positive and negative—of trade liberalization. Using the technique described above, Brown, Stern, and Deardorff developed estimates of the impact on the U.S. economy of reaching an agreement on the various components of the Doha Development round. They adopted a number of key assumptions, including an assumption that the negotiations will result in a 33% reduction in the barriers to trade in agriculture, manufactures, and services, which is projected to give rise to a combined increase in economic activity of $164 billion in the U.S. economy, as indicated in Table 2 [25]. This and the other estimates used in this chapter that were derived by the Michigan model estimated a permanent change in economic activity between the "before" and "after" states of the economy and should not be considered either as an annual change in economic welfare or as an annual amount that can be accumulated over time. Brown, Stern, and Deardorff also projected the impact on the United States if all barriers to trade worldwide were removed unilaterally, which they estimate at $497 billion. With current U.S. gross domestic product (GDP) of over $13 trillion, the monetary gains for the U.S. economy associated with the above estimates of trade liberalization would be less than 1.5% and 4.5% of GDP, respectively.

Table 2. Estimated Economic Effects on the United States of a 33% Reduction in Barriers to Trade in Agriculture, Manufactures, and Services at the Doha Development Round (in $ U.S. billions)

Agricultural Protection	Manufactures Tariffs	Services Barriers	Combined
$-7.23	$36.52	$134.75	$164.04

Source: Brown, Drusilla K., Alan V. Deardorff, and Robert M. Stern, Multilateral, Regional, and Bilateral Trade-Policy Options for the United States and Japan. Research Seminar in International Economics, Discussion Paper No.490, The University of Michigan, December 16, 2002. Table 1.

A small decline in U.S. welfare in the agricultural sector reflects reductions in agricultural import tariffs, export subsidies, and production subsidies. In this formulation, these reductions produce offsetting effects in the agricultural sector itself, [26] but they induce slightly negative effects on other sectors in the economy as a result of changes in prices for agricultural goods and for the U.S. terms of trade (prices of exports relative to prices of imports). Gains in the manufacturing sector arise from reduced foreign tariffs on U.S. manufactured goods exports, which increases U.S. exports and domestic manufacturing output and improves production efficiency. These gains also represent a shift of capital within the economy from less productive activities into manufacturing areas that are more productive and capital flows from abroad in the form of foreign direct investment. The large gains indicated in the services sector reflect the relatively high level of foreign barriers U.S. exporters presently face in this sector and the high level of U.S. competitiveness in this sector.

In a process similar to that described above, Brown, Stern, and Deardorff estimate the impact on the U.S. economy of various regional and bilateral trade agreements, as indicated in Table 3.

As expected, bilateral trade arrangements would produce modest gains for the U.S. economy as a whole, given the smaller value of a bilateral trade relationship for the U.S. economy.

These arrangements are expected to be of greater importance to the trading partners because of the size of their trade with the United States relative to the size of their overall level of trade and the size of their respective economies. Trade agreements with Chile, Singapore, Australia, Morocco, and South Korea, for instance, are estimated to result in trade benefits for the U.S. economy of $4 billion, $17 billion, $19 billion, $6 billion and $30 billion, respectively.

A free trade agreement with the 21 nations that comprise the Asia-Pacific Economic Association Cooperation is projected to offer economic benefits of $244 billion for the United States and surpass those of the Doha round, most likely because free trade agreements tend to be more comprehensive in terms of the number of industrial and services sectors that are involved compared with the WTO negotiations. An agreement with ASEAN is projected to yield benefits of $13 billion, while a Free Trade Agreement of the Americas (FTAA) would give rise to an estimated $68 billion in economic benefits [27]. An agreement with the Southern African Customs union would be expected to yield $12.6 billion in trade benefits to the United States [28].

The Michigan model incorporates an input-output model for each economy in the model. Input- output accounts trace the flow of input commodities into the production processes of industries, the flow of intermediate goods between industries, and the flow of output from industries to final uses in the economy. This approach provides an estimate of the magnitude of employment effects that might be expected and a view of the possible job gains and losses across industrial sectors in the economy, as indicated in Table 4 and Table 5.

In the approach used by Brown, Stern, and Deardorff, it is assumed that job losses will be perfectly offset by job gains, so that the data in Table 4 and Table 5 are not projections of the job losses and job gains for each sector. Instead, the model provides an estimate of the relative magnitude of employment effects that might be experienced in various industries, thereby identifying those industries that are most vulnerable to increased competition as a result of trade liberalization.

According to this approach, global free trade, or trade without restrictions, would add jobs to the U.S. agricultural sector, but reduce jobs in textiles, apparel, retail trade, and services [29]. Similarly, completing the liberalization schedule of the Uruguay round of trade talks was shown to result in the largest gains in jobs in agriculture, with losses in textiles and apparel, although there would be job gains in services due to the more limited schedule of liberalization.

Table 3. Estimated Economic Effects on the United States of Free Trade Agreements with Various Trading Partners (in $ U.S. billions)

APEC FTA	ASEAN FTA	Free Trade Agreement of the Americas (FTAA)	Chile FTA	Singapore FTA	Korea FTA
$244.25	$12.98	$67.59	$4.41	$17.5	$30.1
SACU FTA	CAFTA	Australia FTA	Morocco FTA		
$12.61	$17.26	$19.39	$5.97		

Source: Brown, Drusilla K., Alan V. Deardorff, and Robert M. Stern, Multilateral, Regional, and Bilateral Trade-Policy Options for the United States and Japan. Research Seminar in International Economics, Discussion Paper No.490, The University of Michigan, December 16, 2002. Table 3. Updated estimates are from: Brown, Drusilla K, Kozo Kiyota, and Robert M. Stern, Computational Analysis of the Free Trade Area of the Americas (FTAA). Research Seminar in International Economics, Discussion Paper No. 508, the University of Michigan, revised February 5, 2005. Brown, Drusilla K, and Kozo Kiyota, and Robert M. Stern, Computational Analysis of the U.S. FTAs With Central America, Australia, and Morocco. Research Seminar in International Economics, Discussion Paper No. 507, Revised January 31, 2005. Brown, Drusilla K., Kozo Kiyota, and Robert M. Stern, Computational Analysis of the U.S. FTA With the Southern African Customs Union (SACU). Research Seminar in International Economics, Discussion Paper No. 545, May 31, 2006.

The Doha Round, with its focus on agriculture and services, would generate gains in the agricultural sector, but employment losses in textiles and apparel, retail trade, and services, although these losses would be one-third of those that might be experienced under global free trade.

As expected, free trade agreements with APEC, ASEAN, and a Free Trade Agreement of the Americas yield smaller changes in employment than either global free trade, or the Doha round of trade talks. Furthermore, the model simulation indicates that each bilateral trade agreement the United States has negotiated can be expected to have a small impact on the U.S. economy.

Table 4. Projected Sectoral Employment Effects (Job Gains and Losses) in the United States of Various Multilateral Trade Agreements (number of workers)

	Global free trade	Doha (one-third cut)	APEC FTA	ASEAN
Agriculture	278,658	91,966	394,420	27,259
Mining	5,794	1,912	-236	-68
Food	61,966	20,451	34,811	3,401
Textiles	-66,265	-21,870	-50,099	-19,570
Apparel	-157,229	-51,891	-107,610	-38,570
Leather	-28,829	-9,515	-24,769	-10,068
Wood	46,941	15,502	4,264	4,459
Chemicals	27,828	9,184	-545	-1,410
Mineral Prod.	-1,146	-378	-1,906	643
Metal	22,174	7,318	-1,483	5,261
Transp.	15,209	5,020	-1,587	1,518
Mach.	68,028	22,451	-10,699	-870
Other Manuf	30,096	9,933	-40,992	-23,864
Elec.	7,566	2,497	-419	846
Constr.	2,814	929	-11,377	2,876
Trade	-91,056	-30,051	-129,833	13,330
Services	-300,997	-99,339	105	18,333
Gov. Services	78,418	25,881	-52,047	16,495

Source: Brown, Drusilla K., Alan V. Deardorff, and Robert M. Stern, Multilateral, Regional, and Bilateral Trade-Policy Options for the United States and Japan. Research Seminar in International Economics, Discussion Paper No.490, The University of Michigan, December 16, 2002. Tables 2 and 4. Brown, Drusilla K., Kozo Kiyota, and Robert M. Stern, Computational Analysis of the Free Trade Area of the Americas (FTAA). Research Seminar in International Economics, Discussion Paper No. 508, the University of Michigan, Revised February 5, 2005. Tables 2 and 4.

Investment and Capital Flows

One drawback to the present state of development of general equilibrium models is that they still do not compare in complexity with the real economy, nor do they capture all of the potential economic effects that could arise from trade agreements. For instance, the Michigan model incorporates investment flows that reflect a shift of resources within the economy from less productive to more productive economic activities and a shift of resources across national borders in the form of foreign investment in the economy [30]. As a result of trade liberalization, inflows of foreign capital would be expected to increase as U.S. industries become more productive and, therefore, more profitable and attractive to foreign investors. By the same token, U.S. direct investment abroad would increase as trade liberalization improved the prospects of foreign economies. In some estimates, the flows of foreign capital comprise a large part of the overall economic gains that are derived within the models. The models, however, do not reflect the corresponding appreciation or depreciation of the dollar's exchange rate that would accompany such flows. These corresponding changes in the dollar's value could blunt or reinforce the positive trade effects the model associates with trade liberalization policies.

Table 5. Projected Sectoral Employment Effects (Job Gains and Losses) in the United States of Various Regional and Bilateral Trade Agreements (number of workers)

	FTAA	SACU	Australia	Morocco
Agriculture	-12,460	973	94	1,314
Mining	-3,251	27	504	-44
Food	-3,452	353	-756	542
Textiles	-6,028	-109	810	-32
Apparel	-16,804	-211	619	-129
Leather	620	202	207	-8
Wood	2,502	163	394	-10
Chemicals	2,883	127	1,555	-88
Mineral Prod.	957	76	539	29
Metal	2,024	33	1,957	-138
Transp.	2,970	369	1,741	-50
Mach.	21,830	1,230	6,229	-367
Other Manuf	2,148	77	653	-52
Elec.	-228	14	15	2
Constr.	-88	-13	-257	-57
Trade	1,991	-2101	-11,716	-1,140
Services	2,788	11	-2,188	-194
Gov. Services	1,597	-1221	-398	389

Source: Brown, Drusilla K., Alan V. Deardorff, and Robert M. Stern, Multilateral, Regional, and Bilateral Trade-Policy Options for the United States and Japan. Research Seminar in International Economics, Discussion Paper No. 490, The University of Michigan, December 16, 2002. Table 2 and 43. Brown, Drusilla K., Kozo Kiyota, and Robert M. Stern, Computational Analysis of the Free Trade Area of the Americas (FTAA). Research Seminar in International Economics, Discussion Paper No. 508, the University of Michigan, Revised February 5, 2005. Tables 2 and 4 Updated estimates are from: Brown, Drusilla K, Kozo Kiyota, and Robert M. Stern, Computational Analysis of the Free Trade Area of the Americas (FTAA). Research Seminar in International Economics, Discussion Paper No. 508, the University of Michigan, Revised February 5, 2005. Table 2. Brown, Drusilla K, and Kozo Kiyota, and Robert M. Stern, Computational Analysis of the U.S. FTAs With Central America, Australia, and Morocco. Research Seminar in International Economics, Discussion Paper No. 507, Revised January 31, 2005. Tables 7b and 8b. Brown, Drusilla K., Kozo Kiyota, and Robert M. Stern, Computational Analysis of the U.S. FTA With the Southern African Customs Union (SACU). Research Seminar in International Economics, Discussion paper No. 509, July 6, 2004. Table 3b.

Data on Barriers to Trade in Services

Another inherent problem associated with estimating the effects of trade liberalization is the dearth of information on barriers to trade in services. As Table 5 shows, the Michigan model and other general equilibrium models estimate that the largest gains from trade liberalization likely would arise from the liberalization of trade in services. This result conforms well with most notions of where additional benefits from trade liberalization may reside and from the dominating role of services in the U.S. economy. In developing their estimates of the benefits of liberalizing trade in services, Brown, Deardorff, and Stern use estimates developed by Bernard Hoekman [31] on the average gross operating margins of firms listed on national stock exchanges in 18 countries as a proxy for estimating barriers to services trade. Hoekman bases his estimates on a standard economic assumption that the prices firms charge should reflect their marginal costs.

Market restrictions, or barriers to entry by foreign firms, however, drive a wedge between market price and marginal cost so that firms operating in protected markets will generate higher than expected profits, or experience higher than average rates of return. Hoekman considers this wedge to be indicative of the magnitude of domestic barriers in services sectors. According to Hoekman's data, all U.S. service sectors except construction had profit margins above average, which would imply that all U.S. service sectors except construction have erected relatively high barriers to entry by foreign firms. As a result, the model simulation estimates large employment losses in this sector under global free trade and the Doha development round of trade negotiations.

This conclusion, however, does not conform well with the estimates of most studies on market openness. For instance, the Organization for Economic Cooperation and Development (OECD) concluded after analyzing the services sectors of the 30 member countries of the OECD that the U.S. services sector was among the very least restrictive [32]. Hoekman also offered a caution in using the estimates because, "In general, a large number of factors will determine the ability of firms to generate high (gross operating) margins, including market size (number of firms), the business cycle, the state of competition policy enforcement, the substitutability of products, fixed costs, etc." [33] In addition, Hoekman's estimates do not differentiate between industries that have high profit margins as a result of barriers and those that have high profit margins because they possess some sort of economic competitive advantage. Without better data on the extent and nature of barriers to trade in the services sectors, it will continue to be difficult to develop monetary estimates of the costs of those barriers and, therefore, estimates of the economic benefits that could accrue as a result of market liberalization. After reviewing various studies that have attempted to assign values to national barriers to services trade, Hoekman concluded,

> Summing up, although the data situation is not very good, quite a bit can be done by analysts to quantify the relative magnitude and distribution of the gains of increasing competition on services markets.. .The research clearly suggests that potential gains from liberalization may be very large. While this work is important and useful, the state of the data on barriers is such that, in the near term, policymakers will have to continue to rely primarily on rules of thumb in determining negotiating priorities [34]

Brown, Deardorff, and Stern make an assumption that the Doha Round of negotiations will result in a 33% reduction in barriers to trade in services, agriculture, and manufactured goods. While such an assumption is essential in order to run the economic model, it may not reflect realistically the outcome of the negotiations. In addition, it is not clear what a 33% reduction in the barriers to trade in services would look like, since the nature of this sector and the barriers it faces are substantially different from those that exist in the manufacturing and agricultural sectors and the barriers in the services sector do not lend themselves to a similar process of reciprocal exchange of market access.

Economic activities that comprise the services sector range from such business services as accounting, financial, and architectural activities to a broad range of consumer services that are not easily defined and categorized [35]. Anticipating the effects of liberalizing trade in these areas is difficult for most nations because they do not know the full extent of the barriers their exports face. In addition, nations are grappling with a subtle, but important, distinction in the services sector between liberalizing barriers to market access that involve eliminating discrimination in the treatment of foreign and domestic services providers and governmental activities that involve a range of regulatory and supervisory activities, especially in the areas of public health and safety, the environment, and clean water and air standards. Such issues become even more complicated in countries like the United States where regulatory responsibilities are shared by the federal, state, and local governments, and professional governing bodies.

IMPLICATIONS FOR CONGRESS

The United States currently is involved in negotiating an assortment of trade agreements. These agreements range from bilateral agreements with trading partners that account for very small shares of total U.S. trade to multinational trade agreements that could have a significant effect on certain U.S. workers, industries, and businesses. At some point, Congress may well be asked to consider legislation that implements these agreements. In doing so, it may consider a number of different, and perhaps conflicting, objectives and it will be presented with data and information that emphasize differing viewpoints on how the agreements will affect the economy and the nation.

Econometric modeling, aided by recent advances, can assist policymakers in analyzing the economic effects of trade agreements. These models are particularly helpful in exploring the effects of trade liberalization in such sectors as agriculture and manufacturing where the barriers to trade are identifiable and subject to some quantifiable estimates. In most cases, these barriers are represented by tariffs or quotas that can be adjusted on a reciprocal basis. Barriers to trade in the services sector, however, are proving to be more difficult to identify and, therefore, to quantify in an econometric model. Although progress is being made, it likely will be some time before the models can provide realistic estimates of the effects of trade liberalization in this sector. The models, however, do provide a sense of the magnitude of economic effects that can be expected to occur across sectors in the economy. This is especially helpful in identifying which sectors likely will experience the greatest adjustment costs.

There are drawbacks to using the econometric models. Such modeling is highly sensitive to the assumptions that are used to establish the parameters of the model and are hampered by a serious lack of comprehensive data in the services sector. Such shortcomings likely will not be as apparent in analysis of bilateral trade agreements between the United States and another trading partner, but they likely will become important when the analysis involves a large number of countries, such as in a regional or multilateral trade agreement. In addition, these models likely understate the adjustment costs that are inevitably involved in liberalizing trade and they may well understate the positive effects of trade liberalization over the long run, because such effects are beyond the time-frame of the estimates. As a result, it is possible that trade liberalization may have a larger positive impact on the U.S. economy over the long term than most economic models indicate. Nevertheless, even if the derived benefits from multilateral negotiations were twice as great as the most optimistic estimates indicate, except for unilateral reductions in trade barriers in all countries, the overall impact on the U.S. economy is expected to be modest, at best, relative to the size f the U.S. economy. The effects on the economy from liberalizing trade on a bilateral basis through the proposed bilateral free trade arrangements will yield especially minor gains for the U.S. economy as a whole.

Congress may choose to reject any trade agreement in favor of maintaining the status quo, or it may choose to circumvent the arduous task of negotiating multilateral trade agreements and unilaterally remove all barriers to U.S. trade. While unilaterally removing all trade barriers would please economic purists, it is unlikely given the issues it would raise and the prospects that it would leave U.S. negotiators with few bargaining chips during trade negotiations. Such an action likely would engender a public backlash, particularly from those labor and trade groups that would be most directly affected by such a policy. In addition, the task of demonstrating the benefits of liberalizing trade is complicated by the fact that the short term adjustment costs associated with trade liberalization are difficult to equate clearly with the benefits that accrue slowly over time. This means that it is difficult to demonstrate conclusively at the early stages of negotiations that the long-term benefits of trade liberalization will outweigh the short-term adjustment costs.

Given these prospects, it seems likely to assume that policymakers will weigh the benefits of greater trade liberalization against the anticipated dislocations for workers and industries and determine whether to accept or reject each agreement on the basis of a broad set of factors. While such analyses cannot forecast every outcome, they can aid policymakers in assessing which industries and sectors likely will experience the highest adjustment costs and, therefore, which industries and groups may need assistance in receiving training or other assistance. Often, Congress has addressed trade-induced changes through trade adjustment assistance for workers and firms displaced as a result of trade agreements and trade liberalization. Such assistance has often been promoted as a principle of fairness by spreading out the adjustment costs beyond those most directly affected, and as a method for persuading those who are affected to buy into the changes by reallocating some of the gains from those who benefit to those who bare the greatest share of the adjustment costs. These adjustment costs likely will rise if the scope of trade agreements expand beyond single trading partner to incorporate large numbers of trading partners.

REFERENCES

[1] For additional information, see CRS Report RL33743, *Trade Promotion Authority (TPA): Issues, Options, and Prospects for Renewal*, by J. F. Hornbeck and William H. Cooper.

[2] For additional information and status of the current negotiations, see CRS Report RL3 3463, *Trade Negotiations During the 110th Congress*, by Ian F. Fergusson.

[3] CRS Report RL32060, *World Trade Organization Negotiations: The Doha Development Agenda*, by Ian F. Fergusson.

[4] CRS Report RS20864, *A Free Trade Area of the Americas: Major Policy Issues and Status of Negotiations*, by J. F. Hornbeck.

[5] CRS Report RS21387, United States-Southern African Customs Union (SACU) Free Trade Agreement Negotiations: Background and Potential Issues, by Danielle Langton.

[6] See http://www.whitehouse.gov/news/releases/2002/10/20021026-7.html

[7] CRS Report RL32770, *Andean-U.S. Free-Trade Agreement Negotiations*, by M. Angeles Villarreal.

[8] CRS Report RL3 1870, *The Dominican Republic-Central America-United States Free Trade Agreement (CAFTA-DR)*, by J. F. Hornbeck.

[9] CRS Report RS21 846, *U.S.-Bahrain Free Trade Agreement*, by Martin A. Weiss.

[10] CRS Report RL3 1144, *The U.S.-Chile Free Trade Agreement: Economic and Trade Policy Issues*, by J. F. Hornbeck.

[11] CRS Report RS2 1464, *Morocco-U.S. Free Trade Agreement*, by Raymond J. Ahearn.

[12] CRS Report RL34108, *U.S.-Peru Economic Relations and the U.S.-Peru Trade Promotion Agreement*, by M. Angeles Villarreal

[13] CRS Report RL3 1789, *The U.S.-Singapore Free Trade Agreement*, by Dick K. Nanto.

[14] CRS Report RL32540, *The Proposed U.S.-Panama Free Trade Agreement*, by J. F. Hornbeck, *The Proposed U.S.- Panama Free Trade Agreement*, by J.F. Hornbeck.

[15] CRS Report RL3 3445, *The Proposed U.S.-Malaysia Free Trade Agreement*, by Michael F. Martin.

[16] Economic trade theory argues that natural resources, which serve as the building blocks of production within an economy, are limited at any one point in time, whereas demands for those resources are unlimited, creating a scarcity of resources. This scarcity of resources means that nations strive to use their resources in the most efficient way possible in order to maximize the goods and services that are available to their citizens, a common definition of a nation's standard of living. Nations then specialize in the production of certain goods and then trade with other nations for the goods they do not produce. These concepts of specialization and trade lead to the conclusion that a nation will find that it is in its economic self-interest to engage in trade with other nations even if it can produce all goods and services at a lower cost than any other nation. By specializing in the production of those goods and services in which it is most efficient, or in which it has a comparative advantage, a nation maximizes its total productive capability and national income.

[17] Gottschalk, Peter, and Timothy M. Smeeding, Cross-National Comparisons of Earnings and Income Inequality. *Journal of Economic Literature*, June 1997. p. 645.

[18] Krugman, Paul R. *Rethinking International Trade*. Cambridge, The MIT Press, 1990; Romer, Paul M. Capital, Labor, and Productivity. *Brookings Papers on Economic Activity: Microeconomics 1990*. Washington, the Brookings Institution. p. 337-367; Romer, Paul M. Increasing Returns and Long-Run Growth. *Journal of Political Economy*, October 1986. p. 1002-1037; Grossman, Gene M., and Elhanan Helpman. *Endogenous Product Cycles*. Cambridge, National Bureau of Economic Research, March 1989. (Working Paper No. 2913).

[19] *The Dynamic Effects of Trade Liberalization: A Survey*. Washington, United States International Trade Commission. (USITC Publication 2608). February, 1993. p. 11

[20] A compilation of studies can be found in: Brown, Drusilla K., and Robert M. Stern, Measurement and Modeling of the Economic Effects of Trade and Investment Barriers in Services. The *Review of International Economics*, May 2001; Hoekman, Bernard, the Next Round of Services Negotiations: Identifying Priorities and Options. *Review*, Federal Reserve Bank of St. Louis, July/August 2000; and Dihel, Nora, *Quantification of the Costs to National Welfare of Barriers to Trade in Services: Scoping Paper*. Paris, Organization for Economic Cooperation and Development, November 21, 2000.

[21] Gravity models have been used for 40 years to estimate trade flows between countries. They are based on the conclusion that the volume of exports between any two trading partners is an increasing function of their national incomes, and a decreasing function of the distance between them. Although the models have been criticized for lacking a strong theoretical basis, recent work has demonstrated that the model is consistent with the Ricardian and HeckscherOhlin models. An important drawback of the model is that it can estimate only the aggregate flows of goods, but it does not provide any information about the effects on labor or on individual sectors in the economy. See Wall, Howard, J., Using the Gravity Model to Estimate the Costs of Protection. Review, Federal Reserve Bank of St. Louis, January/February, 1999. p. 39.

[22] Rivera, Sandra A., Key Methods for Quantifying the Effects of Trade Liberalization. *International Economic Review*, January/February 2003. p. 2-5.

[23] Zarazaga, Carlos, E.J.M., Measuring the Benefits of Unilateral Trade Liberalization Part 1: Static Models. *Economic and Financial Review*, Federal Reserve Bank of Dallas, Third Quarter 1999. p. 15; also see Zarazaga, Carlos, E.J.M., Measuring the Benefits of Unilateral Trade Liberalization Part 2: Dynamic Models. *Economic and Financial Review*, Federal Reserve Bank of Dallas, First Quarter 2000.

[24] Now known as the Michigan Brown-Deardorff-Stern Model, the Michigan Model of World Production and Trade includes data on 29 industrial sectors for 18 industrialized countries and 16 newly industrialized and developing countries.

[25] Brown, Drusilla K., Alan V. Deardorff, and Robert M. Stern, *Multilateral, Regional, and Bilateral Trade-Policy Options for the United States and Japan*. Research Seminar in International Economics, Discussion Paper No. 490, The University of Michigan, December 16, 2002. Table 1; and Brown, Drusilla K., Alan V. Deardorff, and Robert M. Stern, *Computational Analysis of Multilateral Trade Liberalization in the Uruguay Round and Doha Development Round*. Research Seminar in International Economics, Discussion Paper No. 489, The University of Michigan, December 8, 2002.

[26] Reducing agricultural import tariffs lowers import prices and spurs the substitution of imports for domestic production, causing the domestic industry to contract. The extent

of this contraction would depend on whether the tariff reduction in the U.S. sector was more or less than in other countries. Reducing export subsidies lowers world prices; similarly, reducing production subsidies raises prices. The net of these effects depends on the extent of tariffs and subsidies in the domestic economy prior to reduction and on reductions in domestic tariffs and subsidies relative to similar reductions abroad.

[27] According to authors of the study, the estimated economic effects of the FTAA should be considered as the most positive effects that are possible under the proposed terms of the agreement. These effects are expected to accrue over a considerable period of time and that the process of negotiations could be hampered by less than full compliance on the part of some of the members of the FTAA.

[28] Brown, Drusilla K., Kozo Kiyota, and Robert M. Stern, *Computational Analysis of the U.S. FTA With the Southern African Customs Union (SACU)*. Research Seminar in International Economics, Discussion Paper No. 545, May 31, 2006..

[29] The estimates for job losses in services is surprising and is a product of the particular estimating method used in the model. For a more complete explanation see page 13 of this chapter.

[30] Brown, and Stern, Measurement and Modeling of the Economic Effects of Trade and Investment Barriers in Services, p. 280.

[31] Hoekman, Bernard, The Next Round of Services Negotiations: Identifying Priorities and Options. *Review,* the Federal Reserve Bank of St. Louis, July/August 2000. p. 38.

[32] Nicoletti, Giuseppe, *The Economy-Wide Effects of Product Market Policies*. Paris, Organization for Economic Cooperation and Development, 4-5 March 2002.

[33] Hoekman, The Next Round of Services Negotiations: Identifying Priorities and Options, p. 37.

[34] *Ibid.*, p. 41.

[35] For instance, see the scope of the U.S. services offer at the Doha round: CRS Report RS2 1492, *Services Negotiations in the WTO: An Overview of the U.S. Offer*, by James K. Jackson.

In: Globalization
Editors: M. G. Massari and K. J. Lutz, pp. 25-32-

ISBN: 978-1-61470-327-3
© 2012 Nova Science Publishers, Inc.

Chapter 2

U.S. TRADE DEFICIT AND THE IMPACT OF CHANGING OIL PRICES

*James K. Jackson**

SUMMARY

Petroleum prices rose sharply in the first half of 2008, at one time reaching more than $140 per barrel of crude oil. Since July, however, petroleum prices and import volumes have fallen at a historically rapid pace; in January 2009, prices of crude oil fell below $40 per barrel. At the same time the average monthly volume of imports of energy-related petroleum products fell slightly. The sharp rise in the cost of energy imports added an estimated $28 billion to the nation's trade deficit in 2007 and $120 billion in 2008. The fall in the cost of energy imports combined with the drop in import volumes as a result of the slowdown in economic activity reversed the trend of rising energy import costs and sharply reduced the overall costs of U.S. energy imports for 2008 and for the first two months of 2009. Beginning in March 2009, the import price of petroleum products rose each month through September 2009, the most recent period for data. This report provides an estimate of the initial impact of the changing oil prices on the nation's merchandise trade deficit.

BACKGROUND

According to data published by the Census Bureau of the Department of Commerce,[1] the prices of petroleum products over the first half of 2008 rose sharply, generally rising considerably faster than the change in demand for those products, before falling at a historic rate. After falling each month between August 2008 and February 2009, average petroleum

---

* Email: jjackson@crs.loc.gov
[1] Census Bureau, Department of Commerce. Report FT900, *U.S. International Trade in Goods and Services,* November 13, 2009. Table 17. The report and supporting tables are available at http://www.census.gov/ foreign-trade/Press-Release/currentjress_release/ftdpress.pdf.

prices reversed course and rose by 65% between February and September 2009, climbing to nearly $80 per barrel at times. As a result of changing petroleum prices, the price changes in imported energy-related petroleum products worsened the U.S. trade deficit in 2006, 2007, and 2008. Energy-related petroleum products is a term used by the Census Bureau that includes crude oil, petroleum preparations, and liquefied propane and butane gas. Crude oil comprises the largest share by far within this broad category of energy-related imports. The slowdown in the rate of growth in the U.S. economy reduced the amount of energy the country imports and helped to push down world energy prices. As economic growth improves, energy imports will increase and energy prices are expected to rise. In isolation from other events, lower energy prices tend to aid the U.S. economy, which makes it a more attractive destination for foreign investment. Such capital inflows place upward pressure on the dollar against a broad range of other currencies. To the extent that the additions to the merchandise trade deficit are returned to the U.S. economy as payment for additional U.S. exports or to acquire such assets as securities or U.S. businesses, the U.S. trade deficit could be mitigated further.

Table 1. Summary Data of U.S. Imports of Energy-Related Petroleum Products, Including Oil (not seasonally adjusted)

| | January through September | | | | | |
| | 2008 | | 2009 | | | |
	Quantity (thousands of barrels)	Value ($ thousands)	Quantity (thousands of barrels)	% change 2008 to 2009	Value ($ thousands)	% change 2008 to 2009
Total energy-related Petroleum Products	3,114,482	$323,698,054	2,909,784	-6.6%	$149,641,187	-53.8%
Crude oil	2,437,398	$252,155,488	2,244,319	-7.9%	$113,457,896	-55.0%
	January through September					
	2008		2009			
	Quantity (thousands of barrels)	Value ($ thousands)	Quantity (thousands of barrels)	% change 2008 to 2009	Value ($ thousands)	% change 2008 to 2009
Total energy-related Petroleum Products	4,613,626	$438,745,954	4,310,397	-6.6%	$202,826,259	-53.8%
Crude oil	3,591,136	$341,978,528	3,306,663	-7.9%	$153,873,963	-55.0%

Source: Census Bureau, Department of Commerce. Report FT900, *U.S. International Trade in Goods and Services,* November 13, 2009. Table 17.

Note: Estimates for January through December 2009 were developed by CRS from data through September 2009 and data through 2008 published by the Census Bureau using a straight line extrapolation.

Summary data from the Census Bureau for the change in the volume, or quantity, of energy- related petroleum imports and the change in the price, or the value, of those imports for 2008 and for 2009 are presented in Table 1. The data indicate that during the first nine months of 2009, the United States imported 3,372 million barrels of energy-related petroleum products, valued at $174 billion. Energy-related imports for this nine-month period were down 5.2% in volume terms from the same period in 2008 and cost slightly less than half the value of such imports during the same period in 2008.

The data also indicate that the United States imported 4.6 billion barrels of total energy-related petroleum products in 2008, valued at $439 billion, compared with a total value of $319 billion in 2007. Also, in 2008, the quantity of energy-related petroleum imports fell by 4.0% compared with the comparable period in 2007; crude oil imports also fell by 2.7% from the same period in 2007. Year-over-year, the average value of energy-related petroleum products imports rose by 3 7.6%, while the average value of crude oil imports rose by 44.2%. As Figure 1 shows, imports of energy-related petroleum products can vary sharply on a monthly basis. In 2008, imports of energy-related petroleum products averaged about 384 million barrels a month, but through the first nine months of 2009, such imports have averaged 363 million barrels a month.

In value terms, energy-related imports rose from $319 billion in 2007 to $439 billion in 2008, or an increase of 38%, to account for about 22% of the value of total U.S. merchandise imports. The sharp rise experienced in energy prices in 2007 continued from January through July 2008 and did not follow previous trends of falling during the winter months. As Figure 2 shows, the cost of U.S. imports of energy-related petroleum products rose from about $17 billion per month in early 2007 to $53 billion a month in July 2008, but fell to $13.6 billion in February 2009, reflecting a drop in the price and in the volume of imported oil. The average price of imported oil in September 2009 was down 37% from the average price in July 2008, reflecting the sharp decrease in the price of imported oil in August 2008 through February 2009, as indicated in Table 2.

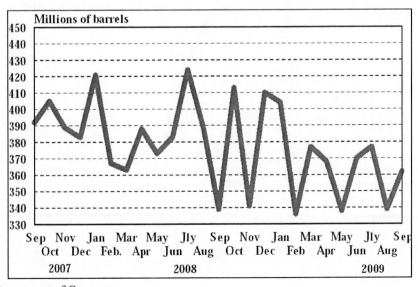

Source: Department of Commerce

Figure 1. Quantity of U.S. Imports of Energy-Related Petroleum Products.

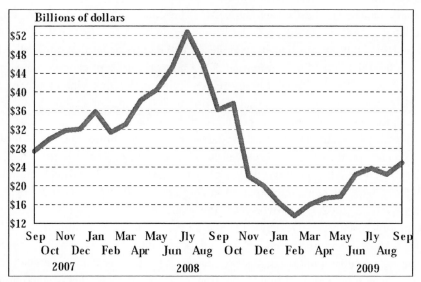

Source: Department of Commerce

Figure 2. Value of U.S. Imports of Energy-Related Petroleum Products.

As a result of the overall rise in the value of energy-related imports in 2008, the trade deficit in energy-related imports amounted to $386 billion, or 47% of the total U.S. trade deficit of $821 billion for the year. In the nine-month period of January-September 2009, the drop in oil prices, year over year, combined with reduced demand for energy imports pushed down the overall value of energy imports, which accounted for 43% of the total merchandise trade deficit. This share is up from the same period in 2008, primarily due to a relatively large drop in the non-petroleum trade deficit.

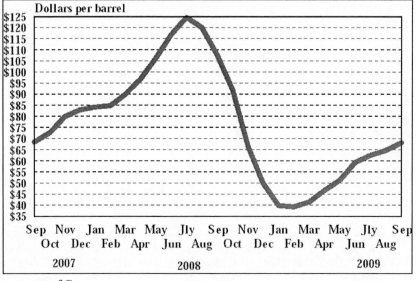

Source: Department of Commerce

Figure 3. U.S. Import Price of Crude Oil.

Crude oil comprises the largest share of energy-related petroleum products imports. According to Census Bureau data[2], imports of crude oil fell from an average of 10.11 million barrels of crude oil imports per day in 2007 to an average of 9.8 million barrels per day in 2008, or a decrease of 3%. In December 2008, such imports averaged 10.3 million barrels per day, or an increase of 7.4% over the volume of such imports recorded in December 2007. From June 2007 to June 2008, the average price of crude oil increased from $61 per barrel to $117 per barrel, or an increase of 92%, as shown in Figure 3. As a result, the value of U.S. crude oil imports rose from about $19 billion a month in June 2007 to $35 billion a month in June 2008.

Table 2. U.S. Imports of Energy-Related Petroleum Products, Including Crude Oil (not seasonally adjusted)

Period	Total energy-related petroleum products		Crude oil			
	Quantity (thousands of barrels)	Value ($ thousands)	Quantity (thousands of barrels)	Thousands of barrels per day (average)	Value ($ thousands)	Unit price (dollars)
2008						
Jan.-Dec.	4,613,444	$438,686,820	3,590,628	9,810	$341,912,489	$95.22
Jan.-Sept.	3,450,431	359,454,064	2,688,497	9,812	279,098,862	103.81
March	363,252	33,146,123	278,571	8,986	25,030,666	89.85
April	388,145	38,185,528	303,050	10,102	29,339,760	96.81
May	373,287	40,360,232	293,995	9,484	31,245,288	106.28
June	382,675	45,207,376	297,532	9,918	34,850,146	117.13
July	424,467	52,813,717	342,024	11,033	42,637,563	124.66
August	388,679	46,012,928	308,380	9,948	37,000,980	119.99
September	339,044	36,179,838	253,276	8,443	27,247,205	107.58
October	413,766	37,632,930	324,185	10,458	29,830,414	92.02
November	341,870	21,995,613	261,600	8,720	17,452,979	66.72
December	410,426	20,018,803	319,834	10,317	15,968,127	49.93
2009						
Jan.-Sept.	3,271,740	$174,513,474	2,530,537	9,269	$132,969,541	$52.55
January	404,658	16,342,408	300,137	9,682	11,949,605	39.81
February	335,912	13,618,145	254,874	9,103	9,996,300	39.22
March	377,470	16,047,403	289,693	9,345	11,983,004	41.36
April	367,943	17,403,719	292,601	9,753	13,633,848	46.60
May	338,081	17,703,718	261,888	8,448	13,410,641	51.21
June	369,963	22,415,123	280,424	9,347	16,592,370	59.17
July	377,218	23,720,887	296,274	9,557	18,510,434	62.48
August	338,539	22,389,783	268,429	8,659	17,381,693	64.75
September	361,956	24,872,287	286,217	9,541	19,511,645	68.17

Source: Census Bureau, Department of Commerce. Report FT900, *U.S. International Transactions in Goods and Services*. November 13, 2009. Table 17.

a. Energy-related petroleum products is a term used by the Census Bureau and includes crude oil, petroleum preparations, and liquefied propane and butane gas.

---

[2] Report FT900, U.S. International Trade in Goods and Services, November 13, 2009. Table 17.

Data for 2008 indicate that a number of factors combined to push oil prices to record levels in July 2008, before the prices tumbled quickly. The sharp rise in oil prices combined with a small decrease in the volumes of oil imports experienced during the period to post a large jump in the overall cost of imported energy. At times, crude oil traded for nearly $148 per barrel in July 2008, indicating that the cost of energy imports would have a significant impact on the overall costs of U.S. imports and on the value of the U.S. trade deficit. Since those record prices, the price per barrel of imported crude oil fell to under $40 per barrel at times in January and February 2009. For the year 2008, the imported volume of energy-related petroleum products fell by 4.0%, due in large part to a slowdown in economic activity. At an average price of $95 per barrel, compared with an average price of $64 per barrel in 2007, energy-related import prices added nearly $100 billion to the trade deficit on an annual basis in 2008, pushing the annual trade deficit to just over $820 billion. For 2009, the total cost of energy imports is projected to rise to just less than half the $438 billion experienced in 2008

ISSUES FOR CONGRESS

The sharp rise in prices of energy imports experienced since early 2007 through July 2008 was expected to affect the U.S. rate of inflation and have a slightly negative impact on the rate of economic growth in 2008. Various factors, dominated by the sharp slowdown in the rate of economic growth in the United States and most other areas of the world, are combining to push down the cost of energy imports. Typically, energy import prices have followed a cyclical pattern that has caused energy prices to decline in the winter. A slowdown in the rate of economic growth in the United States and elsewhere has reduced the demand for energy imports and caused oil prices to tumble from the heights they reached in July 2008. An important factor that often affects crude oil prices is the impact Atlantic hurricanes have on the production of crude oil in the Gulf of Mexico The drop in oil prices likely will lessen the nation's merchandise trade deficit, although the most important factor affecting the trade deficit throughout 2009 will be the rate of growth in the U.S. economy.

The return to a positive rate of economic growth has placed upward pressure on the prices of energy imports that is contributing to the nation's merchandise trade deficit. Some of the impact of this deficit could be offset if some of the dollars that accrue abroad are returned to the U.S. economy through increased purchases of U.S. goods and services or through purchases of such other assets as corporate securities or acquisitions of U.S. businesses. Some of the return in dollars likely will come through sovereign wealth funds (SWFs), or funds controlled and managed by foreign governments, as foreign exchange reserves boost the dollar holdings of such funds. Such investments likely will add to concerns about the national security implications of foreign acquisitions of U.S. firms, especially by foreign governments, and to concerns about the growing share of outstanding U.S. Treasury securities that are owned by foreigners.

It is likely that the economy will again face high and rising prices for imported energy products as national economies recover to a more robust rate of economic growth. It is possible for the economy to adjust to the higher prices of energy imports by improving its energy efficiency, finding alternative sources of energy, or searching out additional supplies of energy. There may well be increased pressure applied to Congress to assist in this process. For Congress, the increase in the nation's merchandise trade deficit could add to existing inflationary pressures and complicate efforts to stimulate the economy should the rate of economic growth slowdown. In particular, Congress, through its direct role in making economic policy and its oversight role over the Federal Reserve, could face the dilemma of rising inflation, which generally is treated by raising interest rates to tighten credit, and a slow rate of economic growth, which is usually addressed by lowering interest rates to stimulate investment. A sharp rise in the trade deficit may also add to pressures for Congress to examine the causes of the deficit and to address the underlying factors that are generating that deficit. In addition, the rise in prices of energy imports could add to concerns about the nation's reliance on foreign supplies for energy imports and add impetus to examining the nation's energy strategy.

In: Globalization
Editors: M. G. Massari and K. J. Lutz, pp. 33-47-
ISBN: 978-1-61470-327-3

Chapter 3

FREE TRADE AGREEMENTS: IMPACT ON U.S. TRADE AND IMPLICATIONS FOR U.S. TRADE POLICY

William H. Cooper[*]

SUMMARY

Free trade areas (FTAs) are arrangements among two or more countries under which they agree to eliminate tariffs and nontariff barriers on trade in goods among themselves. However, each country maintains its own policies, including tariffs, on trade outside the region.

In the last few years, the United States has engaged or has proposed to engage in negotiations to establish bilateral and regional free trade arrangements with a number of trading partners. Such arrangements are not new in U.S. trade policy. The United States has had a free trade arrangement with Israel since 1985 and with Canada since 1989, which was expanded to include Mexico and became the North American Free Trade Agreement (NAFTA) effective in January 1994.

U.S. interest in bilateral and regional free trade arrangements surged, and the Bush Administration accelerated the pace of negotiations after the enactment of the Trade Promotion Authority in August 2002. U.S. participation in free trade agreements can occur only with the concurrence of the Congress. In addition, FTAs affect the U.S. economy, with the impact varying across sectors.

The 111th Congress and the Obama Administration face the question of whether and when to act on three pending FTAs—with Colombia, Panama, and South Korea. Although the Bush Administration signed these agreements, it and the leaders of the 110th Congress could not reach agreement on proceeding to enact them. In addition, the Trade Promotion Authority (TPA) expired on July 1, 2007, meaning that any new FTAs agreed to would not likely receive expedited legislative consideration, unless the authority is renewed. While expressing some support for the agreements, President Obama and his Administration have indicated that outstanding issues remain for each of them which need to be addressed before

[*] Email: wcooper@crs.loc.gov

he would send implementing legislation to Congress. The Administration had not indicated a timeline for this process.

In the meantime, on November 14, 2009, President Obama committed to work with the current and prospective members the Trans-Pacific Strategic Economic Partnership Agreement (TPP). The TPP is a free trade agreement that includes nations on both sides of the Pacific. The TPP, which originally came into effect in 2006, currently includes Brunei, Chile, New Zealand, and Singapore. Besides the United States, Australia, Peru, and Vietnam have also expressed interest in joining.

FTAs could raise some important policy issues, if the 111th Congress considers implementing legislation and as it monitors ongoing negotiations as part of its oversight responsibilities: Do FTAs serve or impede U.S. long-term national interests and trade policy objectives? Which type of an FTA arrangement meets U.S. national interests? What should U.S. criteria be in choosing FTA partners? Are FTAs a substitute for or a complement to U.S. commitments and interests in promoting a multilateral trading system via the World Trade Organization (WTO)? What effect will the expiration of TPA have on the future of FTAs as a trade policy strategy?

In the last few years, the United States has considered bilateral and regional free trade areas (FTAs) with a number of trading partners. Such arrangements are not new in U.S. trade policy. The United States has had a free trade arrangement with Israel since 1985 and with Canada since 1989. The latter was suspended when the North American Free Trade Agreement (NAFTA) that included the United States, Canada, and Mexico, went into effect in January 1994.

U.S. interest in bilateral and regional free trade arrangements surged, and the Bush Administration accelerated the pace of negotiations after the enactment of the Trade Promotion Authority in August 2002. U.S. participation in free trade agreements can occur only with the concurrence of the Congress. In addition, FTAs affect the U.S. economy, with the impact varying across sectors.

The 111th Congress and the Obama Administration face the question of whether and when to act on three pending FTAs—with Colombia, Panama, and South Korea. Although the Bush Administration signed these agreements, it and the leaders of the 110th Congress could not reach agreement on proceeding to enact them. In addition, the Trade Promotion Authority (TPA) expired on July 1, 2007, meaning that any new FTAs agreed to would not likely receive expedited legislative consideration, unless the authority is renewed. While expressing some support for the agreements, President Obama and his Administration have indicated that outstanding issues remain for each of them which need to be addressed before he would send implementing legislation to Congress. The Administration had not indicated a timeline for this process.

In the meantime, on November 14, 2009, President Obama committed to work with the current and prospective members the Trans-Pacific Strategic Economic Partnership Agreement (TPP). The TPP is a free trade agreement that includes nations on both sides of the Pacific. The TPP, which originally came into effect in 2006, currently includes Brunei, Chile, New Zealand, and Singapore. Besides the United States, Australia, Peru, and Vietnam have also expressed interest in joining.

FTAs could raise some important policy issues if the 111th Congress considers implementing legislation and as it monitors ongoing negotiations as part of its oversight responsibilities: Do FTAs serve or impede U.S. long-term national interests and trade policy objectives? Which type of an FTA arrangement meets U.S. national interests? What should U.S. criteria be in choosing FTA partners? Are FTAs a substitute for or a complement to U.S. commitments and interests in promoting a multilateral trading system via the World Trade Organization (WTO)? What effect will the expiration of TPA have on the future of FTAs as a trade policy strategy?

This report will monitor pending and possible proposals for U.S. FTAs, relevant legislation and other congressional interest in U.S. FTAs.

WHAT ARE FREE TRADE AREAS?

Free trade areas are part of the broad category of trade arrangements under which member- countries grant one another preferential treatment in trade. Preferential trade arrangements include the following:

- *free trade areas* (FTAs) under which member countries agree to eliminate tariffs and nontariff barriers on trade in goods within the FTA, but each country maintains its own trade policies, including tariffs on trade outside the region;
- *customs unions* in which members conduct free trade among themselves and maintain common tariffs and other trade policies outside the arrangement;
- *common markets* in which member countries go beyond a customs union by eliminating barriers to labor and capital flows across national borders within the market; and
- *economic unions* where members merge their economies even further by establishing a common currency, and therefore a unified monetary policy, along with other common economic institutions. The European Union is the most significant example of a group of countries that has gone from a customs union to an economic union.[1]

The process of forming an FTA usually begins with discussions between trading partners to ascertain the feasibility of forming an FTA. If they agree to go forward, then the countries undertake negotiations on what the FTA would look like. At a minimum, participants in an FTA agree to eliminate tariffs and some other nontariff trade barriers and agree to do so over a specific time period. In addition, the partner countries usually agree on rules of origin, that is, a definition of what constitutes a product manufactured within the FTA and, therefore, one that is eligible to receive duty-free and other preferential trade treatment. Rules of origin prevent products from nonmembers entering an FTA market over the lowest tariff wall. Most FTAs also include procedures on the settlement of disputes arising among members and rules on the implementation of border controls, such as product safety certification and sanitary and phytosanitary requirements. Most recent FTAs contain rules on economic activities besides

---

[1] Besides the arrangements described above under which member countries extend *reciprocal* preferential treatment, there are trade arrangements under which one party agrees to extend nonreciprocal preferential treatment to the imports of a country or group of countries unilaterally. Such arrangements involve primarily developed countries extending nonreciprocal preferential treatment to the imports from developing countries. For example, the United States employs the Generalized System of Preferences (GSP), the Andean Trade Preferences Act (ATPA), the Caribbean Basin Initiative (CBI), and the Africa Growth and Opportunity Act (AGOA). The main objective of these nonreciprocal arrangements is to encourage economic development in developing countries.

trade in goods, including foreign investment, intellectual property rights protection, treatment of labor and environment, and trade in services. The size and complexity of the FTA will largely reflect the size and complexity of the economic relations among the participating countries. U.S. FTAs with Israel and Jordan are relatively basic, while the NAFTA (the United States, Canada, and Mexico) is very complex.

WHY COUNTRIES FORM FTAS

Countries form free trade areas for a number of economic and political reasons. Most basically, by eliminating tariffs and some nontariff barriers, FTAs permit the products of FTA partners easier access to one another's markets. The 1989 FTA between the United States and Canada was formed arguably for this purpose. Developed countries have also formed FTAs with developing countries to encourage them toward trade and investment liberalization.

FTAs may be used to protect local exporters from losing out to foreign companies that might receive preferential treatment under other FTAs. For example, some supporters of the U.S.-Chile FTA argued that U.S. firms were at a disadvantage vis-à-vis their Canadian competitors whose exports face no Chilean tariffs under the Canada-Chile FTA. Slow progress in multilateral negotiations has been another impetus for FTAs. For example, when the 1986-1994 Uruguay Round negotiations got bogged down, the impetus for the United States, Mexico, and Canada to form NAFTA seemed to increase. Arguably the surge in FTA formation worldwide in the past few years has been a result of the difficulties encountered in launching and implementing the Doha Development Agenda round of negotiations in the WTO.

Political considerations are also a motivation to form FTAs. The United States formed FTAs with Israel and with Jordan to reaffirm American support of those countries and to strengthen relations with them.

FTAS IN THE CONTEXT OF U.S. TRADE POLICY

Post-World War II trade policy under various presidential administrations has had several interrelated objectives. One has been to secure open markets for U.S. exports. A second has been to protect domestic producers from foreign unfair trade practices and from rapid surges in fairly traded imports. A third has been to control trade for foreign policy and national security reasons. A fourth objective has been to help foster global trade to promote world economic growth.

In fulfilling these objectives, U.S. political leaders have formed and conducted trade policy along three tracks. One track has been the use of multilateral negotiations to establish and develop a rules-based trading system. The United States was a major player in the development and signing of the General Agreement on Tariffs and Trade (GATT) in 1947. It was a leader in nine rounds of negotiations that have expanded the coverage of GATT and that led to the establishment in 1995 of the World Trade Organization (WTO), the body that administers the GATT and other multilateral trade agreements. The United States has continued this approach as a leader in the latest round–the Doha Development Agenda (DDA).

U.S. policymakers have used a second track which can be labeled the "unilateral" track. Under this approach, the United States threatens retaliation, usually in the form of restricting trade partners' access to the vast U.S. market, in order to get the partner to open its markets to U.S. exports or to cease other offensive commercial practices and policies. The United States has employed this approach primarily against foreign practices not covered by GATT/WTO rules or because the multilateral dispute settlement process proved too slow and ineffective to meet U.S. needs. For several decades, especially in the 1970s and 1 980s, the United States conducted its trade policy with Japan "unilaterally" to get Japan to amend domestic laws, regulations and practices that prevented U.S. exporters from securing what they considered to be a fair share of the Japanese market.

More and more, however, U.S. trade policy is becoming dominated by a third track—bilateral and regional negotiations to establish FTAs. The United States completed its first FTA with Israel in 1985 under President Reagan. It completed its second with Canada under President Bush in 1989, whose Administration was involved in the process of expanding it to Mexico, a process that was completed by the Clinton Administration in 1993. However, even after the completion of NAFTA, it was still unclear whether bilateral and regional FTAs had become a fixture in U.S. foreign trade policymaking or anomalies to cement already strong economic relationships.

By 1994 it seemed apparent that FTAs were indeed becoming a fixture when the United States, under the Clinton Administration, led a group of trade ministers from 33 other Western Hemispheric countries in agreeing to work toward establishing a Free Trade Area of the Americas (FTAA) by 2005. In the same year, political leaders from the United States and other member- countries of the Asian-Pacific Economic Cooperation (APEC) forum signed a declaration in Bogor, Indonesia, to work toward free trade and investment in the region by 2010 for developed countries and by 2020 for all member-countries. Both of those efforts have flagged.

The pursuit of FTAs continued when, on June 6, 2000, President Clinton and Jordanian King Abdullah announced that their two countries would begin negotiations on establishing a free trade area. An agreement was quickly reached and was signed on October 24, 2001. Similarly, President Clinton and Singapore Prime Minister Goh Chok Tong announced, somewhat unexpectedly, on November 16, 2000, that their two nations would launch negotiations to complete a free trade agreement. And on December 6, 2000, the United States and Chile had started negotiations to establish an FTA. Chile had long been mentioned as a potential addition to NAFTA or as a partner in a stand-alone FTA.

In the meantime, many countries, including the other major trading powers, were actively negotiating free trade agreements. The WTO has reported that more than 200 FTAs are in force. For example, Canada formed an FTA with Chile as did Mexico. The EU has formed FTAs with a number of countries. Japan, which had shunned the use of FTAs, formed an FTA with Singapore and is exploring the possibility of forming an FTA with Korea, although those negotiations have been suspended.

The Bush Administration had affirmed the strategy of pursuing U.S. trade policy goals through the multilateral trade system but gave strong emphasis to building bilateral and regional trade ties through free trade agreements through a policy called a *competition in liberalization*.

Table 1. U.S. Free Trade Agreements

	FTAs in Force
U.S.-Israel FTA	Implemented by P.L. 99-47 (June 11, 1985) Entered into force September 1, 1985.
U.S.-Canada FTA	Implemented by P.L. 100-449 (September 28, 1988). Entered into force January 1, 1989. Suspended with implementation of NAFTA.
North American Free Trade Agreement (NAFTA)	Implemented by P.L. 103-182 (December 8, 1993). Entered into force January 1, 1994.
U.S.-Jordan FTA	Implemented by P.L. 107-43 (September 28, 2001. Entered into force December 17, 2001.
U.S.-Singapore FTA	Implemented by P.L. 108-78 (September 3, 2003) Entered into force January 1, 2004.
U.S.-Chile FTA	Implemented by P.L. 108-77, (September 3, 2003). Entered into force January 1, 2004.
U.S.-Australia FTA	Implemented by P.L. 108-286 (August 3, 2004). Entered into force on January 1, 2005.
U.S.-Morocco FTA	Implemented by P.L. 108-302, August 17, 2004. Entered into force on January 1, 2006.
U.S.-Bahrain FTA	Implemented by P.L. 109-169, January 11, 2006. Entered into force on August 1, 2006.
U.S.-Dominican Republic- Central American FTA (DR-CAFTA)	President signed implementing bill (H.R. 3045) on August 2, 2005 (P.L. 109-53). Entered into force with El Salvador (March 1, 2006), Honduras and Nicaragua (April 1, 2006, Guatemala (July 1, 2006), the Dominican Republic (March 1, 2007) and Costa Rica (January 1, 2009).
U.S.-Oman FTA	President signed implementing bill on September 26, 2006 (P.L. 109-283). Entered into force on January 1, 2009.
U.S.-Peru FTA	Agreement with Peru signed April 12, 2006. President signed implementing bill (H.R. 3688) on December 14, 2007 (P.L. 110-138). Implemented on February 1, 2009.
	FTAs Under Negotiation or Completed
U.S.-Colombia FTA	Agreement signed November 22, 2006. President submitted implementing legislation(H.R. 5724, S. 2830, on April 8, 2008.
U.S.-Panama FTA	Agreement signed on June 28, 2007.
U.S.-South Korea FTA	Agreement signed on June 30, 2007.
Trans-Pacific Strategic Economic Partnership Agreement	Negotiations underway.
U.S. -Malaysia FTA	Negotiations underway.
U.S.-Thailand FTA	Negotiations dormant.
U.S.-Southern African Customs Union FTA	Negotiations dormant.
U.S.-United Arab Emirates FTA	Negotiations dormant.

The Bush Administration continued negotiations that the Clinton Administration initiated. At the end of 2002, the Bush Administration completed FTA negotiations with Chile and Singapore first begun by the Clinton Administration in 2000. The FTAs with Chile and Singapore entered into force on January 1, 2004.

Perhaps encouraged by the passage and enactment of legislation granting the President trade promotion authority (TPA), as contained in the Trade Act of 2002 (P.L. 107-210— signed into law on August 6, 2002), the Bush Administration moved ahead with a trade agenda that contained an unprecedented number of FTAs. In 2004, agreements with Australia and Morocco were signed, approved by the Congress. The agreement with Australia entered into force on January 1, 2005 and the one with Morocco on January 1, 2006. An agreement with Central American countries and one with the Dominican Republic were also signed and combined into one agreement, the DR-CAFTA. The President sent Congress draft implementing legislation on June 23, 2005. The House and Senate passed the legislation (H.R. 3045) on July 27 and 28, 2005, respectively, and President Bush signed it into law on August 2, 2005 (P.L. 109-53). The agreement with El Salvador entered into force on March 1, 2006, with Honduras and Nicaragua on April 1, 2006, with Guatemala on July 1, 2006 with the Dominican Republic on March 1, 2007 and with Costa Rica on January 1, 2009.

An agreement with Bahrain was signed on September 14, 2004, for which Congress passed and the President signed implementing legislation (H.R. 4340/P.L. 109-169, January 11, 2006). The agreement entered into force on August 1, 2006. The Congress passed and the President signed implementing legislation (P.L. 109-283) for an FTA with Oman, which entered into force on January 1, 2009. The United States has signed FTAs with Colombia, Peru, Panama, and South Korea (see Table 1).[2] The House passed (285-132) on November 8, 2007, and the Senate passed on December 4, 2007, implementing legislation (H.R. 3688) for the U.S.-Peru FTA. The President signed the bill into law (P.L. 110-138) on December 14, 2007. The FTA entered into force on February 1, 2009.

After several months of negotiations, on May 10, 2007, congressional leaders and the Bush Administration reached an agreement on new policy priorities that are to be included in pending FTAs. These priorities included the enforcement of five core labor standards that are part of the International Labor Organization's Declaration on Fundamental Principles and Rights of Work, commitment to enforce seven multilateral environmental agreements to which FTA partners are parties; the availability affordable generic pharmaceuticals, port security, and foreign investor rights in investor-state disputes.

OBAMA ADMINISTRATION POLICY AND RECENT DEVELOPMENTS

President Obama and his Administration have expressed support for the pending FTAs— with Colombia, Panama, and South Korea—but with the understanding that some outstanding issues needed to be addressed. Specifically, regarding Colombia, critics, particularly labor unions, remain concerned about the treatment of union leaders and other labor activists. While supporters have cited data showing that violence against union leaders has decreased, critics charge that the violence is still unacceptably high.[3] Regarding Panama, the primary

---

[2] The President submitted implementing legislation for the U.S.-Colombia Free Tree Agreement which was introduced in the 110th Congress (H.R. 5724/ S. 2830) on April 8, 2008. However, the House voted (H.Res. 1092) to make certain expedited procedures, including established deadlines under section 151 of the Trade Act of 1974, not applicable to the bill. The 110th Congress has taken no further action on the legislation.

[3] CRS Report RL34470, *The Proposed U.S.-Colombia Free Trade Agreement: Economic and Political Implications*, by M. Angeles Villarreal.

concerns raised pertain to Panamanian tax policy which, critics charge, allows Panama to be a haven for companies and individuals to avoid taxes.[4]

The South Korean agreement is perhaps the most challenging case. Some Detroit-based car manufacturers, especially Ford and Chrysler, oppose the agreement because, they assert, the agreement does not adequately address South Korean barriers to auto imports. (GM has taken a neutral position on the KORUS FTA.) U.S.-based steel manufacturers have also opposed the agreement because, they argue, it would weaken U.S. trade remedy (antidumping, countervailing duty) laws. Major labor unions also oppose the agreement.[5]

The Administration has indicated that it is working with the relevant groups to work out solutions to these issues . President Obama himself expressed support for the FTAs as part of a longer-term trade policy designed to expand U.S. exports and to enforce U.S. laws and rights. Nevertheless, the Administration provided no timeline for the completion of the process.[6]

In the meantime, on November 14, 2009, President Obama committed to work with the current and prospective members Trans-Pacific Strategic Economic Partnership Agreement (TPP). The TPP is a free trade agreement that includes nations on both sides of the Pacific. The TPP, which originally came into effect in 2006, currently includes Brunei, Chile, New Zealand, and Singapore. Besides the United States, Australia, Peru, and Vietnam have also expressed interest in joining.[7]

ECONOMIC IMPACT OF FTAS

The surge in U.S. interest in FTAs and in the formation of FTAs worldwide raises the question of their impact on the countries included in an FTA and on the rest of the world. It is an issue that economists have long studied and debated. Interest in the issue has peaked at various times in the post-World War II period. The first time was the formation of the European Common market. Interest has peaked again with the current trends in FTAs. The debate has relied largely on theory since empirical data are scarce save for the experience of the European Union. The debate has also divided economists between those who strongly oppose FTAs as an economically inefficient mechanism and those who support them as a means to build freer trade.

Economists usually base their analysis of the impact of FTAs on the concepts of *trade creation* and *trade diversion*. These concepts were first developed by economist Jacob Viner in 1950.[8] Viner focused his work on the economic effects of customs unions, but his conclusions have been largely applied to FTAs and other preferential trade arrangements. His analysis was also confined to static (one-time) effects of these arrangements.

Trade creation occurs when a member of an FTA replaces domestic production of a good with imports of the good from another member of the FTA, because the formation of the FTA

---

[4] CRS Report RL32540, *The Proposed U.S.-Panama Free Trade Agreement*, by J. F. Hornbeck.
[5] CRS Report RL34330, *The Proposed U.S.-South Korea Free Trade Agreement (KORUS FTA): Provisions and Implications*, coordinated by William H. Cooper.
[6] *Inside U.S. Trade*. February 12, 2010.
[7] CRS Report R40502, *The Trans-Pacific Strategic Economic Partnership Agreement*, by Ian F. Fergusson and Bruce Vaughn.
[8] Viner, Jacob. *The Customs Union Issue.* Carnegie Endowment for International Peace. 1950. New York.

has made it cheaper to import rather than produce domestically. The creation of the trade is said to improve economic welfare within the group because resources are being shifted to more efficient uses. Trade diversion occurs when a member of an FTA switches its import of a good from an efficient nonmember to a less efficient member because the removal of tariffs within the group and the continuation of tariffs on imports from nonmembers make it cheaper to do so. Trade diversion is said to reduce economic welfare because resources are being diverted from an efficient producer to a less efficient producer.

In most cases, it appears that FTAs lead to both trade diversion and trade creation with the net effects determined by the structure of the FTA. Therefore, even if two or more countries are moving toward freer trade among themselves in an FTA, the FTA could make those countries and the world as a whole worse off if the FTA diverts more trade than it creates, according to economic theory.[9] (See box below for illustrative examples of trade diversion and trade creation.)

TRADE CREATION OR TRADE DIVERSION?

Economist Robert Z. Lawrence has provided the following example to illustrate the difference between trade creation and trade diversion:

Assume that prior to implementing a free trade agreement with the United States, all television sets purchased in Mexico are subject to a tariff of 10 percent. Assume that Japan produces TVs under competitive conditions, which it sells at a cost of $100, but the United States could only produce such sets at $105. Initially, all TVs sold in Mexico and elsewhere would be Japanese. These would be imported at a price of $100 from Japan and sold to Mexican consumers for $110, with the additional $10 representing the tariff that would be paid by Mexican consumers to the Mexican government. Assume now that a free trade agreement is signed between Mexico and the United States which removes tariffs between Mexico and the United States but retains Mexican tariffs on other countries. Mexican consumers will now have a choice between buying American TVs, which will sell in Mexico at $105, or Japanese TVs, which will sell at $110. They will buy the U.S. TVs and be better off. However, the Mexican economy as a whole will be worse off. Before the agreement, Mexico bought TVs from Japan. Although consumers paid $110, $10 was just a transfer from Mexican consumers to the Mexican government. The economy as a whole, therefore, spent $100 per TV. After the agreement, however, Mexico is spending $105 per TV. TV prices in Mexico do not reflect their social opportunity costs. The impact of the agreement is to expand TV production in the United States, which is relatively less efficient, and to reduce it in Japan, which is relatively more efficient.

Of course, not all of the increased trade between partners will represent expansion from a less efficient source. Pure trade creation would also result. Assume in the example that initially Mexico could produce TV sets for $107. In this case, prior to the agreement Mexico would not have imported them from Japan, instead it would have supplied these

---

[9] This conclusion is called the General Theory of the Second Best and was developed by economists Richard Lipsey and Kelvin Lancaster. Lipsey, Richard and Kelvin Lancaster. The General Theory of the Second Best. *Review of Economic Studies.* vol 24. p. 11-32. Cited and discussed in Lawrence, Robert Z. *International National Economies: Regionalism, Multilateralism, and Deeper Integration.* Brookings Institution. Washington, DC. 1996. p. 22.

TV sets domestically. In this case, Mexico would benefit from the agreement, which would allow it [to] pay only $105 per TV, although of course it would have done better by liberalizing fully and buying the sets from Japan.

Source: Lawrence, Robert Z. *International National Economies: Regionalism, Multilateralism, and Deeper Integration.* Brookings Institution. Washington. 1996. pp. 24-25.

Trade policymakers encounter circumstances much more complicated than what are depicted in economic theory. Many functioning and proposed FTAs encompass more than two countries and involve a range of products, both goods and services, making it much more challenging to evaluate their economic impact. To provide an analytical framework, some economists have developed sets of conditions under which, they have concluded, an FTA would create more trade than its diverts. They state that trade creation is likely to exceed trade diversion—

- the larger the tariffs or other trade barriers among members before the FTA is formed;
- the lower the tariffs and other barriers in trade with nonmembers;
- the greater the number of countries included in the FTA;
- the more competitive or the less complementary the economies joining the FTA; and
- the closer the economic relationship among the members before the FTA was formed.[10]

Economists also have determined that, along with the immediate, static effects of trade diversion and creation, FTAs generate long-term dynamic effects that might include the following:

- increased efficiency of production as producers face increased competition with the removal of trade barriers;
- economies of scale, that is decreased unit costs of production as producers can have larger production runs since the markets for their goods have been enlarged; and
- increased foreign investment from outside the FTA as firms seek to locate operations within the borders of the FTA to take advantage of the preferential trade arrangements.[11]

Until recently not many FTAs were in operation; therefore, available data on their impact have been limited to the experience of the formation of the European Common Market and subsequently the European Union. Most studies have concluded that the European Community has resulted in more trade creation than trade diversion. However, in some sectors, such as agriculture, the net effect has been trade diversion because the EU's Common Agricultural Policy raised barriers to agricultural trade outside the EU.[12]

---

[10] Salvatore, Dominick. *International Economics.* Fifth Edition. Englewood Cliffs, NJ: Prentice-Hall, 1995, pp. 305- 306.

[11] Ibid, p.307.

[12] CRS Report 97-663. *Regional Trade Agreements: Implications for U.S. Trade Policy*, by George Holliday.

FTAS AND THE WTO

A basic principle of the General Agreement on Tariffs and Trade (GATT) that is administered by the WTO is the most-favored nation (MFN) principle. Article I of GATT requires that "any advantage, favor, privilege, or immunity granted by any contracting party to any product originating in or destined for any other country shall be accorded immediately and unconditionally to the like product originating in or destined for the territories of all other contracting parties." FTAs, by definition, violate the MFN principle, since products of FTA member countries are given preferential treatment over nonmember products. However, the original GATT signatories recognized that FTAs and customs unions, while violating the MFN principle, improve economic welfare of all members, if certain conditions are met to minimize trade diversion.

Article XXIV of the GATT requires that FTA members shall not erect higher or more restrictive tariff or nontariff barriers on trade with nonmembers than existed prior to the formation of the FTA. Furthermore, Article XXIV requires the elimination of tariffs and other trade restrictions be applied to "substantially all the trade between the constituent territories in products originating in such territories." In addition, Article XXIV stipulates that the elimination of duties and other trade restrictions on trade within the FTA to be accomplished "within a reasonable length of time," meaning a period of no longer than 10 years, according to the "Understanding of the Interpretation of Article XXIV of the General Agreement on Tariffs and Trade" reached during the Uruguay Round. Member countries are required to report to the WTO their intention to form FTAs. In addition to Article XXIV, the "Enabling Clause," agreed to by GATT signatories in 1979, allows developing countries to form preferential trading arrangements without the conditions under Article XXIV.

Article V of the General Agreement on Trade in Services (GATS), the agreement that governs trade in services under the WTO, provides for the preferential treatment of trade in services within FTAs or similar regional trading arrangements. Article V lays out requirements of substantial coverage of the elimination of trade restrictions and the prohibition on the *ex post facto* imposition of higher restrictions on services trade with nonmember countries.

The WTO formed the Committee on Regional Trade Agreements (CRTA) in 1996 to review pending and operating FTAs and customs unions to determine whether they conform to WTO rules under the GATT and the GATS. However, the rules are sufficiently ambiguous as to be subject to continuing debate within the CRTA. For example, the members have been unable to agree on what constitutes "substantially all trade" under Article XXIV (GATT) or "substantially all sectors" under Article V (GATS).[13] The number of FTAs and customs unions worldwide has increased at a rapid rate. As of July 2007, 380 FTAs and customs unions had been notified to the GATT/WTO. Some 205 FTAs and customs unions are in force. The remaining FTAs and customs unions were largely superseded by other agreements involving the same participants.[14]

---

[13] The CRTA meets several times during the year.

[14] WTO Secretariat. http://www.wto.org. Trade Agreements Section. Trade Policies Review Division. *The Changing Landscape of RTAs.* A paper prepared for a seminar on Regional Trade Agreements and the WTO. November 14, 2003. p. 2.

Yet, none of the reports of notifications has been completed because CRTA members have not been able to reach a consensus on any of them. Nevertheless, the vast majority of the FTAs have gone into operation. For example, the CRTA has not completed its report on NAFTA, which went into effect in January 1994. The proliferation of FTAs and disagreements on rules have crippled the WTO review process and led WTO members to place review of the rules on regional agreements on the agenda of the Doha Development Agenda round. The Doha Ministerial Declaration, which established the agenda for the new round, states that the negotiations will strive at "clarifying and improving disciplines and procedures under the existing WTO provisions applying to regional trade agreements."

THE DEBATE OVER FTAS

The surge in the number of FTAs worldwide has been driving a spirited debate among experts, policymakers, and other observers over whether they promote or damage U.S. economic interests and the economic interests of the world at large. The differing views can be categorized into three main groups. One group consists of those who oppose FTAs because, they assert, FTAs undermine the development of the multilateral trading system and act as a "stumbling block" to global trade liberalization. A second group supports FTAs because, they believe, FTAs act as a "building block" to multilateral trade liberalization. The third category are those individuals and groups that are opposed to trade liberalization in general because they believe its impact on workers in import-sensitive sectors or on the environment is unacceptable, or because, they assert, it undermines U.S. sovereignty.

Among representatives of the first group of experts are international economists Jagdish Bhagwati and Anne O. Krueger, who have strongly advocated that the United States and other national governments should not pursue FTAs at the expense of multilateral negotiations in the WTO. Bhagwati has concluded that FTAs are by definition discriminatory and therefore trade diverting. He argues that tariffs remain high on many goods imported into developing countries and even on some labor-intensive goods (such as wearing apparel and agricultural products) imported into developed countries. Consequently, he asserts, trade diversion will likely result when an FTA is formed.[15]

Both Bhagwati and Krueger cite the "rules of origin" and other conditions of an FTA's establishment for strong criticism. Bhagwati claims, for example, that the rules of origin in one FTA more than likely do not coincide with the rules of origin in many of the other FTAs. Furthermore, he argues, the schedule of implementation of the tariff reductions and other conditions for one FTA will not match the schedule of other FTAs. The incongruity of these regulations across FTAs has created what Bhagwati sees as a customs administration nightmare and calls the "spaghetti-bowl" phenomenon.[16]

In her criticism, Krueger claims that in order to meet the input thresholds of rules of origin requirements, producers in one FTA partner will be encouraged to purchase as many inputs as possible from other partner countries, even if a non-FTA member can produce and sell the inputs more cheaply and even if the tariff rate on inputs from non-FTA producers is

---

[15] Bhagwati, Jagdish. *The Wind of the Hundred Days: How Washington Mismanaged Globalization.* The MIT Press. Cambridge, MA. 2000. p. 240-245.

[16] Ibid.

zero. Importing inputs from within the FTA to meet the rules of origin threshold allows the producer to sell the final product within the FTA duty free. Under such circumstances imports of inputs are diverted from efficient producers outside the FTA to less efficient producers inside the FTA. A corollary to Krueger's conclusion is that the higher the threshold established in the rules of origin, the greater the chance that trade diversion will take place.[17]

A range of economists, policymakers, and other experts embrace a second view that FTAs can enhance trade and should be pursued. Economist Robert Z. Lawrence argues, for example, that recent FTAs involve much more economic integration than the elimination of tariffs. NAFTA, he points out, has led to the reduction in barriers on services trade, foreign investment, and other economic activities not covered by the GATT/WTO. In addition, under NAFTA, Mexico has affirmed its commitment to economic reform, making its economy more efficient. Lawrence asserts that the theory traditionally applied to FTAs (by Bhagwati, Krueger, and others) does not take into account these dynamic welfare enhancing characteristics of FTAs which he believes are likely to outweigh any trade diversion that results from the elimination of tariffs.[18]

A CATO Institute study by economist Edward L. Hudgins argues that while it may be preferable to liberalize trade multilaterally, countries should take any available avenue, including bilateral or regional FTAs, even if they lead to some trade diversion. Furthermore, Hudgins asserts that FTAs can be more efficient vehicles for addressing difficult trade barriers than the WTO, where the large membership requires compromise to the least common denominator to achieve consensus.

FTAs have also have provided momentum for GATT/WTO members to move ahead with new trade rounds, he claims.[19]

Economist C. Fred Bergsten holds a position similar to the one expressed in the CATO study, that in lieu of multilateral trade negotiations, FTAs are the next best thing and promote global trade liberalization. Bergsten has advocated establishing U.S. FTAs with New Zealand and with South Korea. Economist Jeffrey Schott argues that some U.S. firms are being discriminated against because FTAs are rapidly forming in which the United States is not a participant; therefore, in his review, the United States must negotiate FTAs.[20]

Bergsten and others have also advocated structuring FTAs in a manner that could serve as building blocks of a global free trade system. Using the APEC plan as a model, Bergsten argues for an FTA based on "open regionalism," that is establishing the road map for free trade and investment in the Asian-Pacific region for 2010/2020 among the members but allowing other countries to join if they agree to accede to the conditions. In order to minimize trade diversion, he suggests that trade and investment could be implemented on an MFN principle, perhaps conditional MFN in order to limit the "free rider" effects. Other countries, and other regional groupings, Bergsten presumes, would be willing to accept the conditions

---

[17] Krueger, Anne O. "Free Trade Agreements As Protectionist Devices: Rules of Origin," in Melvin, James R., James C. Moore, and Raymond Riezman (eds.). *Trade, Theory, and Econometrics: Essays in Honor of John C. Chipman.* Routledge Press. New York. 1999. pp. 91-101.

[18] Lawrence, Robert Z. *Regionalism, Multilateralism, and Deeper Integration: Changing Paradigms for Developing Countries.* in Mendoza, Miguel Rodriquez, Patrick Low, and Barbara Kotschwar (eds.). *Trade Rules in the Making.* Organization of American States/Brookings Institution Press. Washington, DC. 1999. p. 41-45.

[19] Hudgins, Edward. L. Regional and Multilateral Trade Agreements: Complementary Means to Open Markets. *Cato Journal.* Vol. 15. No. 23. Fall/Winter 1995/96.

[20] Schott, Jeffrey J. *Free Trade Agreements: The Cost of U.S. Nonparticipation.* Testimony before the Subcommittee on Trade. House Ways and Means Committee. March 29, 2001. http://www.iie.com.

having been enticed by the trade and investment opportunities until most of the membership of the WTO would be engaged in forming a free trade area.[21] A Heritage Foundation report draws up a similar proposal for a "Global Free Trade Association."[22]

A third group opposes FTAs but also trade liberalization or "globalization" in general. Included in this group are representatives of import-sensitive industries, for example labor unions, and representatives of social action groups such as some environmentalists, who question the wisdom of trade liberalization whether done through multilateral negotiations or through bilateral and regional trading arrangements. They assert that trade liberalization unfairly affects workers by exporting jobs to countries with lower wages and undermines the nation's ability to protect the environment by allowing companies to relocate to countries with less stringent environmental regulations.[23] For example, the United Auto Workers (UAW) union has stated the following position regarding the Free Trade Area of the Americas (FTAA):

> Such an agreement would provide broader protections for the rights of corporations, further undermine the ability of governments in the region to regulate their economies in the interests of their citizens and intensify the downward pressure on workers' incomes through competition for jobs and investments. All of this would take place in the absence of any counter-balancing protections for workers, consumers or the environment. This is why the UAW has consistently opposed the direction of these negotiations, the positions taken by the U.S. government, and worked closely with other organizations in the region to oppose the creation of an FTAA.[24]

CONCLUSIONS AND IMPLICATIONS FOR CONGRESS

Free trade agreements are viewed by many as a significant trade policy vehicle for the United States and for other major trading nations. Over the last 10-15 years, the debate in U.S. trade policy has shifted from, "Should the United States form FTAs?" to "Should the United States form any more FTAs and, if so, with whom, when, and under what conditions?" Congress has a direct role in addressing those questions. Before any FTA can go into effect, the Congress must review it as part of implementing legislation.

The 111th Congress and the Obama Administration face the question of whether and when to act on three pending FTAs—with Colombia, Panama, and South Korea. Although the Bush Administration signed these agreements, it and the leaders of the 110th Congress could not reach agreement on proceeding to enact them. In addition, the Trade Promotion Authority (TPA) expired on July 1, 2007, meaning that any new FTAs concluded would not likely receive expedited legislative consideration, unless that the authority is renewed.

A number of questions regarding FTAs could arise. One question pertains to the economic impact of an FTA. As with any trade liberalizing measure, an FTA can have positive effects on some sectors and adverse effects on others. An FTA may create trade for

---

[21] Bergsten, C. Fred. *Open Regionalism.* Working paper 97. Institute for International Economics. 1997.

[22] Hulsman, John C. and Aaron Schavey. *The Global Free Trade Association: A New Trade Agenda.* The Heritage Foundation Backgrounder No. 1441. May 16, 2001.

[23] For more information, see for example, the United Auto Workers positions on trade policy at http://www.uaw.com and the positions of Public Citizen's Global Trade Watch at http://www.citizen.org.

[24] http://www.uaw.com.

one sector of the U.S. economy but divert trade away from others. A Member of Congress is placed in the position of weighing the effects on his/her constituency versus the overall impact on the United States and other trading partners. Because conditions can differ radically from one FTA to another, the evaluation will likely differ in each case. Furthermore, Members might take into account not only the immediate static effects of FTAs but also the long-term, dynamic effects which could play an important role in evaluating their contribution to U.S. economy.

A second, broader question is whether bilateral and regional FTAs are the appropriate trade policy strategy to promote U.S. national interests. Economic specialists differ sharply on this question with some viewing the proliferation of FTAs as leading to confusion and serving as stumbling blocks to the development of a rules-based multilateral trading system. Other specialists consider FTAs as appropriate trade policy vehicles for promoting freer trade, as building blocks to a multilateral system and as necessary to protect U.S. interests against the FTAs that other countries are forming without the United States. Still others oppose trade liberalization in any form as counter to U.S. interests.

A third question is whether the Office of the United States Trade Representative and other trade policy agencies have sufficient time and human resources to negotiate a number of FTAs simultaneously while managing trade policy in the WTO and other fora. Others might find some U.S. interests being short-changed.

A fourth question is to what degree, if any, should non-trade concerns be included in FTAs? This issue has emerged in a number of completed and ongoing FTA negotiations.

A fifth overarching question is what criteria should the United States employ in determining which countries would make appropriate FTA partners. For example, to what degree should political factors be given weight over economic factors?

In: Globalization

Editors: M. G. Massari and K. J. Lutz, pp. 49-74-

ISBN: 978-1-61470-327-3

© 2012 Nova Science Publishers, Inc.

Chapter 4

CENTERS FOR DISEASE CONTROL AND PREVENTION GLOBAL HEALTH PROGRAMS: FY2001-FY2011[*]

Tiaji Salaam-Blyther

ABSTRACT

A number of U.S. agencies and departments implement U.S. government global health interventions. Overall, U.S. global health assistance is not always coordinated. Exceptions to this include U.S. international responses to key infectious diseases; for example, U.S. programs to address HIV/AIDS through the President's Emergency Plan for AIDS Relief (PEPFAR), malaria through the President's Malaria Initiative (PMI), and avian and pandemic influenza through the Avian Flu Task Force. Although several U.S. agencies and departments implement global health programs, this chapter focuses on funding for global health programs conducted by the U.S. Centers for Disease Control and Prevention (CDC), a key recipient of U.S. global health funding.

Congress appropriates funds to CDC for its global health efforts through five main budget lines: Global HIV/AIDS, Global Immunization, Global Disease Detection, Malaria, and Other Global Health. Although Congress provides funds for some of CDC's global health efforts through the above-mentioned budget lines, CDC does not, in practice, treat its domestic and global programs separately. Instead, the same experts are mostly used in domestic and global responses to health issues. As such, CDC often leverages its own resources in response to global requests for technical assistance in a number of areas that also have domestic components, such as outbreak response; the prevention and control of injuries and chronic diseases; emergency assistance and disaster response; environmental health; reproductive health; and safe water, hygiene, and sanitation.

President Barack Obama has indicated early in his Administration that global health is a priority and that his Administration would continue to focus global health efforts on addressing HIV/AIDS. When releasing his FY2010 budget request, President Obama indicated that his Administration would increase investments in global health programs and, through his Global Health Initiative, improve the coordination of all global health programs. The President requested that in FY2011, Congress appropriate $353 million to

---

[*] This is an edited, reformatted and augmeneted version of CRS Report R40239, dated April 7, 2010.

CDC for global health programs—an estimated 5% increase over FY2010 enacted levels. From FY2001 to FY2010, Congress made available more than $3 billion available to CDC for global health programs.

CDC also partners in programs for which it does not have specific appropriations, such as global efforts to address tuberculosis (TB) and respond to pandemic influenza. In addition, the State Department and the U.S. Agency for International Development (USAID) transfer funds to CDC for its role as an implementing partner in U.S. coordinated initiatives, including PEPFAR, PMI, and the Neglected Tropical Diseases (NTD) Initiative.

There is a growing consensus that U.S. global health assistance needs to become more efficient and effective. There is some debate, however, on the best strategies. This chapter explains the role CDC plays in U.S. global health assistance, highlights how much the agency has spent on global health efforts from FY2001 to FY2010, and discusses how funding to each of its programs has changed during this period. For more information on U.S. funding for other global health efforts, including those implemented by USAID, the Department of Defense (DOD), and the Global Fund to Fight AIDS, Tuberculosis, and Malaria (Global Fund) and debates about making U.S. global health assistance more efficient, see CRS Report R40740, *U.S. Global Health Assistance: Background, Priorities, and Issues for the 111th Congress*.

INTRODUCTION

Several U.S. agencies and departments implement global health interventions. With the exceptions of initiatives to fight HIV/AIDS through the President's Emergency Plan for AIDS Relief (PEPFAR), malaria through the President's Malaria Initiative (PMI), and pandemic flu through the Avian Flu Task Force, the funding and implementation of U.S. global health initiatives are not always coordinated among agencies and departments. There is a growing consensus that U.S. foreign assistance needs to become more efficient and effective. There is some debate, however, on the best strategies. As Congress considers how best to improve foreign assistance, some Members are attempting to identify the scope and breadth of U.S. global health assistance [1] This chapter highlights the global health efforts that the Centers for Disease Control and Prevention (CDC) undertakes, outlines how much CDC has spent on such efforts from FY2001 to FY2010, highlights FY2011 proposed and enacted funding levels, and discusses some issues the 111th Congress and the incoming director face.

Since 1958, CDC has been engaged in global health efforts. At first, CDC's global health engagement focused primarily on malaria control. CDC's global health mandate has grown considerably since then. In 1962, CDC played a key role in the international effort that led to smallpox eradication and in 1967 expanded its surveillance efforts overseas to include other diseases, when the Foreign Quarantine Service was transferred to CDC from the U.S. Treasury Department [2]. As CDC's mission expanded, so have the authorities under which it operates [3] Today, CDC is a partner in a number of global disease control and prevention efforts, including those related to HIV/AIDS, influenza, polio, measles, and tuberculosis (TB). In addition to its work in controlling the spread of infectious diseases, CDC's global health efforts aim to address other global health challenges, such as chronic disease, injury prevention, child and maternal health, and environmental health concerns.

CDC's Global Health Programs

Congress provides funds to CDC for global health efforts through Labor, Health and Human Services (HHS), and Education appropriations. The bulk of funds for CDC's global health programs are provided to the Center for Global Health through five main budget lines: Global HIV/AIDS, Global Malaria, Global Disease Detection, Global Immunization, and Other Global Health. CDC programs are implemented bilaterally and in cooperation with other U.S. agencies, international organizations, foreign governments, foundations, and nonprofit organizations [4].

CDC is engaged in a wider range of global-health activities than what Congress appropriates for global health initiatives. The HHS Office of Global Health Affairs, for example, transfers funds to the Center for Global Health in support of global health efforts. In addition, CDC receives support from other U.S. government agencies and departments, such as the Office of the Global AIDS Coordinator (OGAC) at the U.S. Department of State, for the implementation of PEPFAR programs, [5] and the U.S. Agency for International Development (USAID), for partnership in PMI and the Neglected Tropical Diseases (NTD) Initiative, among other programs [6]. The section below describes global health activities that Congress funds the Center for Global Health to implement.

Global HIV/AIDS

CDC launched its Global AIDS Program (GAP) in 2000 under the LIFE Initiative [7]. GAP supports HIV/AIDS interventions in 41 countries and offers technical assistance in an additional 29 others [8]. To combat HIV/AIDS, CDC sends clinicians, epidemiologists, and other health experts to assist foreign governments, health institutions, and other entities that work on a range of HIV/AIDS-related activities. The key objectives of GAP are to help resource-constrained countries prevent HIV infection; improve treatment, care, and support for people living with HIV; and build health care capacity and infrastructure. Specific activities within the projects include:

- developing and implementing integrated evidence-based prevention, care, and treatment programs;
- building sustainable public health capacity in laboratory services and systems;
- evaluating the scope and quality of global HIV/AIDS programs;
- strengthening in-country capacity to design and implement HIV/AIDS surveillance systems and surveys; and
- supporting host government capacity to monitor and evaluate the process, outcome, and impact of HIV prevention, care, and treatment programs [9]

President's Emergency Plan for AIDS Relief (PEPFAR)

CDC's spending on global HIV/AIDS programs increased significantly after the launching of PEPFAR. From FY2004 through FY2008, appropriations to GAP changed little and amounted to $753.2 million, representing about 40% of CDC's global health spending. Increased spending on global HIV/AIDS programs by CDC during this time period was caused primarily by transfers provided to the Center for the implementation of PEPFAR [10] From FY2004 to FY2008, OGAC transferred some $3.4 billion to CDC for global HIV/AIDS activities. When OGAC transfers are added, from FY2004 to FY2008, HIV/AIDS spending accounted for nearly 80% of all spending by CDC on global health. In FY2009, OGAC transferred about $1.3 billion to CDC for implementation of PEPFAR programs and has not yet released how much it transferred to CDC for FY2010 [11]

Global Immunization

According to the latest estimates, which were based on data collected in 2002, 1.4 million children under age five die annually from vaccine- preventable diseases (VPDs) [12] CDC has increasingly supported efforts to prevent the transmission of vaccine-preventable diseases, particularly polio and measles. CDC global immunization activities primarily focus on children younger than age five, who are at the highest risk of contracting polio, measles, and other VPDs. Appropriations in support of these efforts have grown from $3.1 million in FY199113 to $153.7 million in FY2010. Nearly all of the funds that Congress provides CDC for global immunizations are earmarked for polio and measles interventions. CDC leverages funds from other sources to prevent other VPDs and respond to global requests for technical assistance on immunization- related epidemiologic and laboratory science.

CDC implements immunization programs bilaterally and through international partnerships with groups such as WHO, UNICEF, PAHO, the World Bank, the American Red Cross, and Rotary International. CDC staff are seconded to these organizations and offer technical and operational support in improving global usage of immunizations. In addition, CDC officials serve on the Global Alliance for Vaccines and Immunization (GAVI Alliance) and act as implementing partners in a number of initiatives, including GAVI's Hib and Accelerated Vaccine Introduction Initiatives and the Meningitis Vaccine Project, all of which seek to accelerate introduction of new or underutilized vaccines in developing countries that can reduce child mortality [14].

In partnership with WHO and UNICEF, CDC developed the Global Immunization Vision and Strategy for 2006-2015 (GIVS), [15] which among other goals, outlines how the international community will collaborate to reduce vaccine-preventable deaths and sickness by at least two- thirds from 2000 levels. The strategy aims to sustain the gains made over the past decades in eradicating polio and eliminating measles (see below) by helping to ensure universal application of routine immunizations and using those efforts to strengthen health systems.

Polio

Polio is a highly contagious virus that mostly affects children under five years of age [16] There is no cure for polio; it can only be prevented through immunization. Less than 1% of those who contract polio (one in 200) become irreversibly paralyzed. Between 5% and 10% of those who become paralyzed die of respiratory failure—when the lungs become paralyzed. As a result of global eradication efforts, polio cases have declined by more than 99% from an estimated 350,000 cases in 1998 to 1,648 cases reported in 2008 [17].

The number of polio-endemic countries has decreased from 125 in 1988 to four in 2008: Afghanistan, India, Nigeria and Pakistan [18]. Polio was nearly eradicated but resurged in 2003, when some northern states in Nigeria suspended inoculations citing safety concerns. This action led to a national epidemic and many global outbreaks. Between 2003 and 2007, the wild poliovirus originating in Nigeria reached 20 countries and an Indian strain reached six additional countries. By May 2007, most of the resulting outbreaks were arrested. However, six of the 26 countries that reported polio reinfection had not yet stopped transmission (Angola, Bangladesh, Democratic Republic of the Congo, Ethiopia, Myanmar, Somalia); four additional countries that border endemic areas continued to experience sporadic importations (Cameroon, Chad, Nepal, Niger) [19]. Polio threatens not only countries bordering endemic countries, but all countries until its transmission has been stopped globally.

CDC provides technical expertise and support to national governments and international organizations in support of the global effort to eradicate polio [20] Its laboratory support is an important component of such efforts. Over more than 20 years, CDC has helped countries build laboratory capacity in polio, resulting in a global polio network that now involves 145 laboratories around the world, which processed almost 180,000 lab specimens in 2008. In its multilateral efforts, CDC works closely with the other founding partners of the Global Polio Eradication Initiative—WHO, UNICEF, and Rotary International—and houses the global reference laboratory for polio [21].

Measles

Measles is another highly contagious virus that mostly affects children younger than five years of age [22]. In 2007, measles killed about 197,000 people worldwide, most of whom were children. Healthy people usually recover from measles or suffer moderately from the disease. Measles severely affects those who are poorly nourished, particularly those suffering from Vitamin A deficiency or immune suppressing diseases, such as HIV/AIDS. Those who survive severe measles infection may become blind or suffer from encephalitis (an inflammation of the brain), diarrhea and related dehydration, ear infections, or respiratory infections such as pneumonia. Among populations with high levels of malnutrition and a lack of adequate health care, up to 10% of measles cases result in death.

From FY2001 through FY2009, CDC spent more than $342 million on global measles control activities in 42 sub-Saharan African countries and 6 Asia ones (Table 5) [23]. With the funds, CDC has purchased over 200 million measles vaccine doses and provided technical support to ministries of health in those countries. Key technical support activities include:

- planning, monitoring, and evaluating large-scale measles vaccination campaigns;
- conducting epidemiological investigations and laboratory surveillance of measles outbreaks; and
- conducting operations research [24]

Along with WHO, UNICEF, the United Nations Foundation, and the American Red Cross, CDC is a partner in the Measles Initiative, which has facilitated the precipitous decline in measles- related deaths from 2000 to 2007. During this period, about 576 million children who live in high risk countries were vaccinated against the disease [25]. As a result, measles-related deaths decreased globally by 74% during that time. The greatest improvements in measles death rates occurred in the Middle East and sub-Saharan Africa, where measles deaths declined by about 90%. Although measles was eliminated from the United States in 2000, travelers can carry the disease and cause sporadic cases annually. At the end of 2008, CDC's global measles campaign contributed to the decline in measles-related deaths from an estimated 733,000 deaths to about 164,000 in 2008 [26].

Global Malaria

Through its malaria programs, CDC conducts research and engages in prevention and control efforts [27]. CDC staff provide technical assistance that helps several malaria endemic countries strengthen their malaria control activities. Their work includes policy development, program guidance and support, scientific research, and monitoring and evaluation. CDC malaria programs are implemented bilaterally, in partnership with other multilateral organizations, and as part of the coordinated U.S. strategy—PMI. CDC combats malaria bilaterally with foreign Ministries of Health, through international initiatives such as Roll Back Malaria (RBM), and with multilateral partners, such as the World Health Organization (WHO), the United Nations Children's Fund (UNICEF), the Global Fund to Fight AIDS, Tuberculosis, and Malaria (Global Fund) and the World Bank. Through its multilateral partnerships, CDC has staff posted at the Global Fund, UNICEF, and the World Bank.

CDC's global malaria efforts focus on utilizing data and applying research to develop evidence- based strategies for malaria prevention and control, and monitoring and evaluating existing malaria projects [28]. Specific activities include:

- designing technical and programmatic strategies, which include training, supervision, laboratory, communications, monitoring and evaluation, and surveillance systems;
- developing plans to estimate the impact of malaria control and prevention efforts;
- evaluating impact of long-lasting insecticide-treated nets (LLINs) and monitoring the spread of insecticide resistance;
- improving surveillance with the use of hand-held computers equipped with global positioning systems to conduct household surveys in remote villages; and
- evaluating the performance of health workers.

President's Malaria Initiative

In addition to appropriations CDC receives for global malaria efforts, USAID transfers funds to CDC as an implementing partner of the President's Malaria Initiative. In June 2005, President Bush proposed the initiative and asserted that with $1.2 billion spent between FY2006 and FY2010, PMI would seek to halve malaria deaths in 15 target countries. PMI is led by USAID and jointly implemented by CDC and USAID. From FY2006 through FY2008, USAID transferred an estimated $25 million to CDC for global malaria programs. In FY2009, USAID transferred $15 million to CDC, of which some $13 million was for PMI and nearly $2 million for malaria efforts in the Mekong region.

Global Disease Detection

Established in 2004, CDC's Global Disease Detection (GDD) efforts aim to "protect the health of Americans and the global community by developing and strengthening public health capacity to rapidly detect and respond to emerging infectious diseases and bioterrorist threats." [29]. The GDD program draws upon existing international expertise across CDC programs to strengthen and support public health surveillance, training, and laboratory methods; build in-country capacity; and enhance rapid response capacity for emerging infectious diseases.

CDC has established seven GDD centers, which serve as regional resources to bolster laboratory capacity and epidemiology programs of the host countries and neighboring ones. Through the centers—which are in China, Egypt, Guatemala, India, Kazakhstan, Kenya, and Thailand—CDC focuses on five key activities: (1) outbreak response, (2) surveillance, (3) pathogen discovery, (4) training, and (5) networking. During health emergencies—such as the emergence of pandemic flu in 2009—CDC can use the centers for bilateral response or as part of the Global Outbreak Alert and Response Network (GOARN), which is coordinated by WHO [30]. Examples of GDD activities include CDC responses to severe acute respiratory syndrome (SARS) outbreaks in 2003; the Asian tsunami in 2004; ongoing avian influenza outbreaks, which began in 2004; and cholera outbreaks in Zimbabwe in 2008 [31] In FY2009, CDC provided emergency technical assistance in over 70 humanitarian assistance missions.

Other CDC Global Health Programs

Congress funds CDC's efforts to build public health capacity among country leaders, particularly health ministries, through the budget line entitled "Other Global Health." Two key components of these efforts are the Field Epidemiology (and Laboratory) Training Program (FE(L)TP) and the Sustainable Management Development Program (SMDP) [32] While these two programs received direct Congressional appropriations, they are also supported by funds from other sources, including USAID, DOD, and the private sector.

FE(L)TP, established in 1980, is a full-time, two-year postgraduate applied public health training program for public health leaders to help strengthen health systems, train health professionals, build capacity to assess disease surveillance, and improve health interventions [33]. The program is modeled after CDC's Epidemic Intelligence Service and is adapted to meet local needs. Participants spend about 25% of their time in the classroom and 75% in field placements, providing public health services to host countries' health ministries. CDC develops the FE(L)TP in conjunction with local health leaders to ensure sustainability and ultimately hand-off the trainings to local officials (typically after four to six years). From 1980 to 2008, CDC has consulted with and supported 30 FE(L)TPs and similar programs in 40 countries. CDC is currently supporting FETP programs in 13 countries, FE(L)TP operations in 23 countries, and is developing 10 new programs.

The Sustainable Management Development Program, established in 1992, also aims to strengthen public health systems by bolstering leadership and management capacity of health workers. SMDP participants take part in a six-week Management for International Public Health (MIPH) course that trains managers from developing countries in the basic management skills of planning, priority setting, problem solving, budgeting, and supervision. The program also works with its partners to analyze the quality of organizational leadership, assess management skills, and identify performance gaps in health systems. CDC helps the health leadership to create an action plan for capacity development that includes a budget, a timeline, and measurable outcomes. After concluding the program, CDC provides post-course technical assistance to support the development of sustainable management development programs and post-training incentives to stimulate lifelong learning. These incentives include website access, regional networking among alumni, conferences, fellowships, and career development opportunities [34]

Non-earmarked Global Health Activities

CDC's activities related to improving global health outcomes expand beyond those funded through the Center for Global Health. CDC also leverages other resources to respond to global requests for technical assistance related to disease outbreak response; prevention and control of injuries and chronic diseases; emergency assistance and disaster response; environmental health; reproductive health; and safe water, hygiene, and sanitation [35] Specifically, CDC supports global TB and pandemic flu programs, which are a key priority for the Administration and Congress. In addition, in FY2011 the Administration proposes that other programs previously funded through other sources be transferred to the Center for Global Health, such as the Afghan Health Initiative and the Health Diplomacy Initiative. The section below highlights those activities.

Global Tuberculosis

CDC collaborates with U.S. and multilateral partners to provide technical support in the global effort to eliminate tuberculosis (TB). [36] Bilateral partners include the National Institutes of Health (NIH) and USAID; multilateral partners include the Global Fund and WHO. Key activities in CDC's bilateral TB interventions include:

- operations research; [37]
- improvement of TB screening and diagnostics;
- surveillance of TB/HIV prevalence and multi-drug resistant TB (MDR-TB) prevalence;
- laboratory strengthening; and
- infection control.

CDC also provides technical assistance to multilateral efforts to contain TB, including the Directly Observed Therapy Short Course (DOTS) program and the Green Light Committee Initiative, which helps countries access high-quality second-line anti-TB drugs for those infected with MDR-TB and extensively drug resistant TB (XDR-TB). [38] Multilateral partnerships also include joint efforts with WHO to conduct surveillance of drug-resistant TB.

Pandemic and Avian Influenza

CDC works in over 35 high-risk countries around the world to prevent the spread of avian influenza to humans and to help countries prepare and respond to any pandemic influenza that might arise, including the 2009 H1N1 pandemic flu (discussed below). CDC influenza work is implemented bilaterally and in cooperation with WHO, CDC's GDD centers, Department of Defense (DOD) international field stations and other groups. In this capacity, CDC helps governments and WHO respond to and control avian influenza outbreaks, and to develop rapid response teams in high-risk countries. Additional related activities include:

- helping foreign governments detect novel influenza viruses by building laboratory capacity;
- strengthening epidemiology and avian influenza surveillance;
- enhancing laboratory safety;
- developing and training rapid response teams; and
- supporting the establishment of influenza treatment and vaccine stockpiles.

In FY2005, Congress provided emergency supplemental funds for U.S. efforts related to global pandemic influenza preparedness and response. In each appropriation year since, Congress has funded U.S. efforts to train health workers in foreign countries to prepare for and respond to a pandemic that might occur from any influenza virus, including H5N1 avian flu and H1N1. The U.S. Department of State announced in October 2008 that since FY2005, the United States has pledged about $949 million for global avian and pandemic influenza efforts, accounting for 30.9% of overall international donor pledges of $3.07 billion [39] The United States is the largest single donor to global avian and pandemic preparedness efforts [40]. The funds have been used to support international efforts in more than 100 nations and jurisdictions. The assistance focused on three areas: preparedness and communication, surveillance and detection, and response and containment. The $949 million was provided for the following efforts:

- $319 million for bilateral activities;
- $196 million for support to international organizations, including WHO, the U.N. Food and Agriculture Organization (FAO), the U.N. Development Program (UNDP), the International Federation of the Red Cross and Red Crescent Societies (IFRC), the U.N. System Influenza Coordinator (UNSIC), the World Organization for Animal Health (OIE), and the U.N. Children's Fund (UNICEF);
- $123 million for regional programs, including disease detection sites;
- $83 million for a global worldwide contingency, available to address the evolving nature of the threat;
- $77 million for international technical and humanitarian assistance and international coordination;
- $71 million for international influenza research (including vaccines and modeling of influenza outbreaks) and wild bird surveillance, including the U.S. launch of the Global Avian Influenza Network for Surveillance (GAINS) for wild birds, with a collection of tens of thousands of samples for H5N1 analysis; [41]

- $67 million for stockpiles of non-pharmaceutical supplies, including over 1.6 million PPE kits, approximately 250 laboratory specimen collection kits and 15,000 decontamination kits for use in surveillance, outbreak investigation and emergency response and containment efforts; and
- $13 million for global communications and outreach.

The cumulative pledge of $949 million consists of the following contributions, by agency:

- USAID: $542 million.
- HHS, including CDC, the National Institutes of Health (NIH), and the Food and Drug Administration (FDA): $353 million.
- U.S. Department of Agriculture (USDA): $37 million.
- Department of Defense (DOD): $10 million.
- Department of State (DOS): $7 million.

In April 2009, an influenza virus that had never circulated among humans before began to spread around the world. The virus is called Influenza A/HIN1; it is mostly treatable, and less than 1% of those who have contracted the virus have died. By June 2009, WHO declared that the virus had spread so pervasively that it had become a pandemic. The characterization was based on the reach of the virus, not its virulence. As of August 12, 2009, WHO has confirmed 177,457 human H1N1 cases, including 1,462 deaths. About 87% of those fatalities occurred in the Americas, though the WHO European region reported the highest number of cases—more than 32,000. WHO and HHS maintain that the laboratory-confirmed cases are far lower than the actual number of cases, given that countries are no longer required to test and report individual cases. Many countries use laboratory tests to confirm H1N1 only in patients who are severely ill or have other high-risk health conditions.

CDC has been engaged in international H1N1 pandemic responses since the virus was identified. As one of four WHO collaborating centers around the world, the CDC influenza laboratory in Atlanta routinely receives viral samples from many countries, including Mexico. [42] CDC creates or develops reagents that are used to detect subtypes of influenza that are sent to national influenza centers around the world [43]. Once the subtype of influenza is identified, CDC generates testing kits that are sent to public health laboratories worldwide at no cost. At the onset of the outbreak, CDC sent experts out to the field to help strengthen laboratory capacity and train health experts to control the spread of a virus.

CDC has deployed 16 staff to Mexico and one health expert to Guatemala, including experts in influenza epidemiology, laboratory, health communications, and emergency operations, including distribution of supplies and medications, information technology, and veterinary sciences. These teams work under the auspices of the WHO/Pan American Health Organization Global Outbreak Alert and Response Network and a trilateral team of Mexican, Canadian, and American experts. The teams aim to better understand the clinical illness severity and transmission patterns of H 1N 1 and improve laboratory capacity in Mexico. CDC's Emergency Operations Center also coordinates and collaborates with the European Centre for Disease Prevention and Control (ECDC) and the China CDC.

HHS Secretary Kathleen Sebelius announced on April 30, 2009, that the department "began moving 400,000 treatment courses—valued at $10 million—to Mexico, which represent less than 1% of the total American stockpile." [44] In July 2009, Secretary Sebelius announced at a high-level meeting held in Cancun, Mexico, with Mexican President Felipe Calderon, WHO Director- General Margaret Chan, Pan American Health Organization (PAHO) Director Mirta Roses, and other health ministers from throughout the Americas to discuss strategies to combat influenza that the United States would donate an additional 420,000 courses of Tamiflu to countries in Latin America and the Caribbean [45]. In total, the Administration aims to distribute 2 million courses in Latin America and the Caribbean.

As of May 18, 2009, the United States has provided more than $16 million to assist countries in Latin America and the Caribbean respond to the H1N1 pandemic (Table 1).

Table 1. U.S. Assistance for International H1N1 Responses, FY2009
(U.S. $ thousands)

Agency/Implementing Partner	Activity	Location	Amount
HHS/Government of Mexico	Health	Mexico	10,000.0
USAID/Government of Mexico	Emergency Relief Supplies	Mexico	875.0
USAID/Pan American Health Organization (PAHO)	Emergency Relief Supplies	Panama	262.0
USAID/PAHO	Health	Central America	2,500.0
USAID/World Health Organization	Health	Central America	2,500.0
USAID	Administrative Support	Mexico	100.0
USAID Total			6,237.0
DOD/Ministries of Health	Emergency Relief Supplies	Central America	234.7
Total U.S. Assistance		16,471.7	

Source: USAID, Global—Influenza A/H1N1, Fact Sheet # 3, May 18, 2009.

These funds are used for H1N1 responses specifically, and build on influenza pandemic preparedness efforts that began in earnest after the 2003 severe acute respiratory syndrome (SARS) outbreak and were expanded at the peak of H5N1 outbreaks. U.S. international responses to the H1N1 pandemic are conducted mostly by CDC and USAID, though the Department of Defense (DOD) also provides support.

In response to President Obama's request for supplemental funding for U.S. domestic and international pandemic preparedness and response activities, [46] Congress made available $50 million for USAID pandemic preparedness activities and $200 million to CDC for domestic and international H1N1 activities through the FY2009 Supplemental Appropriations (P.L. 111-32). Officials from CDC's Budget Office indicate that CDC spent $50.9 million on global pandemic flu preparedness efforts in FY2009 (Table 4) [47]

Afghan Health Initiative

According to the United Nations Children's Fund (UNICEF), Afghanistan has the highest child mortality rate in the world [48]. In 2008, an average of 65 children younger than five years died for every 1,000 born worldwide. In sub-Saharan Africa, the child mortality rate reached 144; in Afghanistan, it was 257. Similarly, in 2004, of every 1,000 children born in Afghanistan, 60 died within their first month.

In contrast, the average global neonatal rate was 28 and 38 for sub- Saharan Africa. Statistics for maternal health in Afghanistan are equally abysmal. In 2005, UNICEF estimated that 18 of every 1,000 Afghan mothers died from pregnancy-related causes, and that over an Afghan mother's lifetime, one of every eight is likely to die from pregnancy- related causes. Meanwhile, in that same year, the average global maternal mortality rate was 4.0 and 8.2 for sub-Saharan Africa. Similarly, one of every 92 women worldwide is likely to die from pregnancy-related causes, and one of every 22 in sub-Saharan Africa.

The Afghan Health Initiative aims to improve the skills of health workers in Afghanistan and improve health outcomes in the country. The FY2011 budget request includes a proposal to transfer the daily management of the Afghan Health Initiative from the HHS Office of Global Health Affairs to the Center for Global Health. Specifically, HHS sought to reduce by 20% the number of maternal and neonatal (the first month of life) deaths in targeted Afghan hospitals by the end of 2008. The FY2011 CBJ reported mixed results in key measures taken to reach this goal.

Health Diplomacy

CDC's health diplomacy activities aim to bolster ongoing efforts to control, eradicate, and eliminate diseases worldwide. In particular, the objective is to strengthen the public health capacity of partner organizations and governments globally and improve international responses to natural and manmade disasters. For example, CDC proposes for FY2011 that it conduct trainings in Latin American countries on adopting evidence-based approaches to health, including chronic diseases, and that it support national field epidemiology training programs in the region.

CDC GLOBAL HEALTH SPENDING: FY2001-FY2011

From FY2001 to FY2010, Congress provided CDC more than $3 billion for global health activities—increasing funding for global health activities by about 50% in that time period. Since PEPFAR was launched in 2004, the United States has apportioned the bulk of its global health spending on the plan. In light of the dominant role that PEPFAR has played in shaping U.S. global health assistance, analysis about funding for CDC's global health programs in this section is organized to reflect changes that occurred before and after PEPFAR authorization.

Table 2. CDC Global Health Spending: FY2001-FY2003 (current U.S. $ millions, actual)

Program	FY2001	FY2002	FY2003	FY2001-FY2003	% Change: FY2001-FY2003	% of Total Global Health
Global HIV/AIDS	104.5	168.7	182.6	455.8	74.7%	51.6%
PMTCT/Global AIDS Trust Fund	n/s	25.0	39.7	64.7	n/a	n/a
Global Immunization	106.6	133.7	147.8	388.1	38.6%	44.0%
Polio	91.2	102.3	105.7	299.2	15.9%	33.9
Other Global/Measles	15.4	31.4	42.1	88.9	173.4%	10.1
Global Malaria	13.0	13.0	12.6	38.6	-3.1%	4.4%
Global Disease Detection (GDD)	n/a	n/a	n/a	n/a	n/a	n/a
Other Global Health	n/a	n/a	n/a	n/a	n/a	n/a
Total Global Health	224.1	315.4	342.9	882.5	53.1%	100.0%
Global Tuberculosis	0.8	1.0	1.1	2.9	37.5%	

Source: Appropriations legislation and correspondence with Anstice Brand, CDC Washington, and Julie Racine-Parshall, CDC Atlanta.

Note: n/a means not applicable.

Table 3. CDC Global Health Spending: FY2004-FY2008 (Current U.S. $ millions, actual)

Program	FY2004	FY2005	FY2006	FY2007	FY2008	FY2004-FY2008 (Total)	Change: FY2004-FY2008	% of Global Health: FY2004-FY2008
Global HIV/AIDS PMTCTa	266.9	123.8	122.6 State	121.0	118.9	753.2a	-4.8%	40.5% n/a
Global Immunization	142.0 137.9	State 144.3	144.3	State 142.3	State 139.9	142.0 708.7	n/a 1.5%	47.0%
Poliob	96.8	101.2	101.1	99.8	98.0	496.9	1.2%	32.9%
Other Global/Measlesb	41.0 9.2	43.2 9.1	43.2 9.0	42.6 8.9	41.8 8.7	211.8 44.9	2.0% -5.4%	14.0% 3.0%
Global Malaria								
Global Disease Detection	11.6	21.4	32.4	32.0	31.4	128.8	170.7%	8.5%
Other Global Health	2.4	3.4	3.4	3.3	3.5	16.0	45.8%	1.1%
Total Global Health	428.0	302.0	311.7	307.5	302.4	1,509.6	5.73%	100.0%
Total Global Health w/out PMTCT	286.0	302.0	311.7	307.5	302.4	1,651.6	16.2%	n/a
Transfers for HIV/AIDS	184.5 n/a	436.3 n/a	603.1 2.8	916.9 9.6	1,262.7	3,403.6	584.2%	n/a n/a
Transfers for Malaria Total w/Transfers, including PMTCT	612.5 2.0	738.3 2.3	914.8 2.2	1,224.4	12.6	25.0	350.0%	n/a n/a
Global Tuberculosisc	0.0	15.0	132.0	1.9 22.0	1,565.1	4,913.2	155.5% 0.0%	
Pandemic/Avian Influenzac					2.0 67.8	10.4 236.8	353.3%	

Sources: Appropriations legislation and correspondence with Anstice Brand and Rebecca Miller, CDC Washington Office.

Notes: n/a means not applicable.

Spending levels on HIV/AIDS programs after FY2004 is lower because Congress began to include funds for the International Mother and Child HIV Prevention in appropriations to the Global HIV/AIDS Initiative (GHAI).

a. Although PMTCT funds are included in the totals, they are not included in the calculations for changes in fiscal years and proportions of global health budget as they are not a sustained part of CDC's global health budget.

b. The figures for polio, and "other global/measles" are italicized to indicate that they are included in the Global Immunization total.

c. Congress does not appropriate funds for global TB efforts and global pandemic/avian influenza activities to the Center for Global Health. As such, those figures are not included in the global health totals. They are included in this chart, however, because they are an important part of CDC's global health work.

Table 4. CDC Global Health Funding: FY2009-FY2011 (current $ U.S. millions and %)

Program	FY2009 Estimate	FY2010 Request	FY2010 Estimate	Change FY2009-FY2010	FY2011 Request	Change FY2010-FY2011
Global AIDS Program	118.9	119.0	119.0	0.0%	118.1	-0.8%
Global Immunizations	143.3	153.5	153.7	7.3%	152.8	-0.6%
Polio	101.5	101.6	101.8	0.3%	101.6	-0.2%
Other/Measles	41.8	51.9	51.9	24.2%	51.2	-1.3%
Global Malaria	9.4	9.4	9.4	0.0%	9.2	-2.1%
Global Disease Detection	33.7	33.8	37.8	12.2%	37.8	0.0%
Other Global Health	13.8	13.8	16.3	18.1%	35.1	115.3%
Afghanistan Health Initiative	5.8	5.8	5.8	0.0	5.8	0.0%
Health Diplomacy Initiative	4.5	4.5	2.0	-55.6%	2.0	0.0%
Total CDC Global Health	319.1	329.5	336.2	5.4%	353.0	5.0%
Global Tuberculosis	1.6	n/s	n/s	n/s	n/s	n/s
Global Pandemic/Avian Flu	50.9	n/s	49.9	-2.0%	n/s	n/s

Source: Congressional Budget Justifications, appropriations legislation, and CDC officials.

Notes: n/s means not specified. Transfers for the Afghanistan Health and Health Diplomacy programs will not occur until FY2011; the FY2009 and FY2010 budgets are adjusted for comparability purposes.

Table 5. CDC Global Health Spending: FY2001-FY2011 (current U.S. $ millions and %)

Program	FY 2001 Actual	FY 2002 Actual	FY 2003 Actual	FY 2004 Actual	FY 2005 Actual	FY 2006 Actual	FY 2007 Actual	FY 2008 Actual	FY 2009 Estimate	FY 2010 Estimate	Change FY2009-FY2010	FY 2001-FY2010 Total	Change FY2001-FY2010	FY 2011 Request	Change FY2010-FY2011
Global AIDS Program	104.5	168.7	182.6	266.9	123.8	122.6	121.0	118.9	118.9	119.0	0.1%	1,446.9	13.9%	118.1	-0.8%
PMTCT/Global AIDS Funda	n/s	25.0	39.7	142.0	State	State	State	State	State	State	n/a	n/a	n/a	n/a	n/a
Immunizations	106.6	133.7	147.8	137.9	144.3	144.3	142.3	139.9	143.3	153.7	7.3%	1,393.8	44.2%	152.8	-0.6%
Poliob	91.2	102.3	105.7	96.8	101.2	101.1	99.8	98.0	101.5	101.8	0.3%	999.4	11.6%	101.6	-0.2%
Other Global/Measlesb	15.4	31.4	42.1	41.0	43.2	43.2	42.6	41.8	41.8	51.9	24.2%	394.4	237.0%	51.2	-1.3%
Malaria	13.0	13.0	12.6	9.2	9.1	9.0	8.9	8.7	9.4	9.4	0.0%	102.3	-27.7%	9.2	-2.1%
Global Disease Detection	0.0	0.0	0.0	11.6	21.4	32.4	32.0	31.4	33.7	37.8	12.2%	200.3	n/a	37.8	0.0%
Other Global Health	0.0	0.0	0.0	2.4	3.4	3.4	3.3	3.5	13.8	16.3	18.1%	46.1	n/a	35.1	115.3%
Afghanistan Health Initiativec	n/a	n/a	n/a	n/a	n/a	n/a	n/a	n/a	5.8	5.8	0.0%	11.6	n/a	5.8	0.0%
Health Diplomacy Initiativec	n/a	n/a	n/a	n/a	n/a	n/a	n/a	n/a	4.5	2.0	-55.6%	6.5	n/a	2.0	0.0%
Total	224.1	315.4	343.0	428.0	302.0	311.7	307.5	302.4	308.9	328.4	5.4%	3,189.4	46.5%	353.0	5.0%
Tuberculosisd	0.0	1.0	1.1	2.0	2.3	2.2	1.9	2.0	1.6	TBD	n/a	n/a	n/a	n/a	n/a
Pandemic/Avian															

Program	FY 2001 Actual	FY 2002 Actual	FY 2003 Actual	FY 2004 Actual	FY 2005 Actual	FY 2006 Actual	FY 2007 Actual	FY 2008 Actual	FY 2009 Estimate	FY 2010 Estimate	Change FY2009-FY2010	FY 2001-FY2010 Total	Change FY2001-FY2010	FY 2011 Request	Change FY2010-FY2011
Flud	0.0	0.0	0.0	0.0	15.0	132.0	22.0	67.8	50.9	TBD	n/a	n/a	n/a	n/a	n/a
Transfers for PEPFAR	n/a	n/a	n/a	184.5	436,3	603.1	916.9	1,262.7	TBD	TBD	n/a	n/a	n/a	n/a	n/a
Transfers for PMI	n/a	n/a	n/a	n/a	n/a	2.8	9.6	12.6	13.2	TBD	n/a	n/a	n/a	n/a	n/a

Sources: Appropriations legislation and correspondence CDC officials.

Notes: Although FY2011 requested levels are lower than FY2010 enacted levels for all other categories, CDC officials indicate that this reduction reflects decreased spending on travel and contract investments rather than programming expenses.

PMTCT means Prevention of Mother-to-Child HIV Transmission; n/a means not applicable.

a. Global AIDS Fund refers to the appropriation that Congress provided for the Global Fund to Fight AIDS, Tuberculosis, and Malaria. The Global Fund had not yet been named. Congress began to direct funds to CDC for PMTCT activities in FY2003; the "n/s" in the FY2001 column indicates that Congress did not specify funds for that activity. After FY2004, Congress funded PMTCT activities through the State Department, which oversees all global HIV/AIDS funds, though CDC continues to implement PMTCT programs. "State" reflects this change.

b. Figures related to polio and "other global/measles" are italicized to indicate that they are included in the Global Immunization total.

c. Transfers for the Afghanistan and Health Diplomacy programs will not occur until FY2011; the FY2009 and FY2010 budgets have been adjusted for comparability purposes.

d. Congress does not appropriate funds to CDC for global TB and pandemic/avian influenza activities. CDC allots a portion of its TB and pandemic/avian Influenza appropriations to global programs. Spending on combating these diseases is included here, however, because the related interventions are critical parts of CDC's global health efforts.

CDC Global Health Spending: FY2001-FY2003

From FY001 to FY2003, Congress made available nearly $900 million to CDC for global health work (Table 2). During this time period, spending by CDC on global health increased by more than 50%. About half of that growth was targeted at HIV/AIDS interventions and about 40% at immunizations. At that time, there was vigorous debate about whether HIV/AIDS treatments could be safely and effectively used in low-resource settings, particularly in sub-Saharan Africa.

In FY2002, Congress began to fund the International Mother and Child HIV Prevention Initiative, which included the provision of HIV/AIDS medication that prevented mother-to-child HIV/AIDS transmission (PMTCT). During this period, GDD had not yet been created and Congress had not yet funded interventions against the reemergent H5N1 bird flu or the FE(L)TP programs. Global efforts to detect infectious diseases and strengthen health systems were underway, however.

CDC Global Health Spending: FY2004-FY2008

From FY2004 to FY2008, Congress made available about $1.7 billion to CDC for global health work and global health spending by CDC increased by about 6% (excluding funds provided for PMTCT efforts). During that time period, Congress became increasingly concerned about the spread of infectious diseases, such as SARS and H5N1 avian flu, and began funding GDD. Congress also appropriated funds for pandemic/avian flu preparedness and response efforts through Labor, HHS, and Education appropriations acts, though legislation did not specify how much CDC should spend on global efforts.

With mounting concerns about the global spread of infectious diseases, provisions for HIV/AIDS comprised a smaller proportion of CDC's global health budget. While Congress apportioned about 52% of CDC's global health appropriations on HIV/AIDS efforts from FY2001 to FY2003; from FY2004 to FY2008, spending on HIV/AIDS interventions amounted to about 46% of CDC's global health budget (excluding PMTCT efforts) and funding for GDD amounted to about comprised an estimated 8% of CDC's global health budget (Table 3).

Although funds for HIV/AIDS efforts comprised a smaller portion of CDC's global health budget through direct appropriations, due to transfers provided to CDC from OGAC for its role in PEPFAR, spending on programs to combat the virus internationally accounted for about 82% of CDC's global health spending from FY2004 through FY2008, while the transfers alone comprised about 69% of CDC's total global health budget during that five-year period. Transfers from OGAC also included funds for CDC to continue ongoing PMTCT activities. In FY2004, when PEPFAR was launched, Congress provided its last appropriation to CDC for PMTCT activities and directed the funds at OGAC to coordinate.

In FY2006, USAID began to transfer funds to CDC for its work as an implementing partner of PMI. When transfers for PEPFAR and PMI are included, CDC spent about $6.6 billion on global health activities from FY2004 through FY2008. Transfers for HIV/AIDS and malaria programs from FY2004 through FY2008 ($3.4 billion) exceeded congressional appropriations for all CDC global health activities ($1.5 billion) by nearly $2 billion.

CDC Global Health Funding: FY2009-FY2011

Global health has emerged as a key foreign policy goal early in the Obama Administration. When releasing his FY2010 budget request, President Obama indicated that his Administration would increase investments in global health programs [49]. On May 5, 2009, President Obama announced his new Global Health Initiative, a six-year plan to spend $63 billion using an integrated approach to fight the spread of infectious diseases while addressing other global health challenges [50] In announcing the initiative, the President stated,

> In the 21st century, disease flows freely across borders and oceans, and, in recent days, the 2009 H1N1 virus has reminded us of the urgent need for action. We cannot wall ourselves off from the world and hope for the best, nor ignore the public health challenges beyond our borders. An outbreak in Indonesia can reach Indiana within days, and public health crises abroad can cause widespread suffering, conflict, and economic contraction. We cannot simply confront individual preventable illnesses in isolation. The world is interconnected, and that demands an integrated approach to global health.

Publically available documents do not indicate to what extent CDC will contribute to GHI.

In FY2010, Congress made available $336.2 million for CDC's global health programs. The Administration requests that Congress provide about $350 million for CDC's global health programs in FY2011, some 5% more than FY2010 enacted levels (Table 4) [51] The bulk of the increase is attributed to the "other global health category," which is more than double the FY2010 enacted level. The President also requested a $49,000 increase for the Global Disease Detection (GDD) program. This is not evident in the table below, however, due to rounding. Although FY2011 requested levels are lower than FY2010 enacted levels for all other categories, CDC officials indicate that this reduction reflects decreased spending on travel and contract investments rather than programming expenses [52]. Suggested spending on travel and contracting services through global health programs declined by about $4.5 million from FY2010 enacted levels [53]

Priorities in the FY2011 Budget

In the FY2011 Congressional Budget Justification (CBJ) for CDC, the Administration highlighted key priorities for CDC's global health programs including the goal of eradicating polio in the remaining four polio-endemic countries through a partnership with the Organization of the Islamic Conference (OIC) [54]. Other areas of emphasis include increasing efforts to address and contain infectious disease. Key proposals include the following:

Other Global Health

The FY2011 budget includes $35.1 million for global health programs funded through the "other global health" line, some $19 million more than FY2010 enacted levels. According to the CBJ, the additional funds will be used to develop at least three new Field Epidemiology and Laboratory Training Programs (FELTP) and expand capacity at four existing programs. The Administration also proposes spending the additional resources on programs related to improving global water, sanitation, and hygiene ($10 million); and maternal, newborn, and child health ($2 million).

The HHS Office of Global Health Affairs (OGHA) also proposes transferring $5.8 million for implementation of the Afghanistan Health Initiative, which aims to improve the capacity of clinicians, particularly in the areas of logistics and health management. In addition, OGHA suggests transferring $2.0 million for the Health Diplomacy Initiative, which uses U.S. government and private sector resources to deliver direct patient care and train local health workers. This effort is being initiated in Central America.

Global Disease Detection and Humanitarian Health

The Administration proposes spending $37.8 million on GDD. Though not evident due to rounding, the FY2011 budget request is $49,000 higher than FY2010 enacted levels. The additional funds will be used to increase oversight activities in Atlanta [55] In addition, the FY2011 budget includes $6.3 million for global health efforts targeted at populations affected by humanitarian emergencies. These activities are funded through the International Emergency and Refugee Health Branch (IERHB). As part of ongoing reorganization efforts, IERHB will become part of the Center for Global Health.

RELATED POLICY ISSUES

On May 15, 2009, President Obama appointed Dr. Tom Frieden to be the new Director of CDC. Some health experts indicate that the recent appointment of Dr. Tom Frieden signals the Obama Administration's intention to raise the stature of CDC, expand its workforce, and address some of the world's most neglected health challenges, particularly those that CDC is most adept at confronting. The section below discusses some issues the 111th Congress, the Obama Administration and the incoming CDC Director might face.

CDC Reorganization

Dr. Julie Gerberding, over her seven-year term as the Director of CDC, conducted a comprehensive restructuring of CDC through the Futures Initiative [56]. One of the key changes that she made was to create coordinating centers that would "help CDC's scientists collaborate and innovate across organizational boundaries, improve efficiency so that more money can be redirected to science and programs in our divisions, and improve the internal services that support and develop CDC staff." [57] There was considerable debate, however, about this change.

Arguments centered on whether the restructuring was politically motivated and effective. Dr. Frieden has already begun to reorganize CDC. Although complete details about the reorganization are not yet available, some information has been made publically available. For example, Dr. Frieden has eliminated the coordinating centers that Dr. Gerberding established [58]

This decision was reportedly made following recommendations by an internal panel, which concluded, among other things, that CDC would function more efficiently if it had fewer bureaucratic levels [59]. The inclusion of key programs, such as the Afghanistan Health Initiative, in the FY2011 CBJ seem to indicate that activities funded through the Center for Global Health (formerly the Coordinating Office for Global Health under Dr. Gerberding) might be expanded. It remains to be seen what role, if any, the Center for Global Health will play in the implementation and coordination of other global health activities managed under other centers, such as safe water and sanitation programs overseen by the National Center for Environmental Health/Agency for Toxic Substances and Disease Registry.

What Role Should CDC Play in U.S. Global Health Assistance?

The Administration's emphasis on disease detection in the FY2011 global health budget request reflects CDC's goal of "protecting people worldwide from infectious, occupational, environmental, and terrorist threats." [60] The FY2011 proposal includes a $49,000 increase on activities that would strengthen the capacity of foreign health ministries to "to identify and mitigate emerging public health threats" [61] through the Global Disease Detection program. Nonetheless, some health experts would like more resources to be allotted to enhancing and expanding CDC's work in disease detection and surveillance. Despite the emergence and re-emergence of diseases such as severe acute respiratory syndrome (SARS), pandemic and avian flu, and MDR-TB and XDR-TB over the past decade, funding for GDD has consistently ranked third among the five global health areas—exceeding malaria and "other global health" but receiving less than HIV/AIDS and immunizations. Those expressing concern about GDD funding levels assert that higher funding levels for GDD would enable CDC to expand its global efforts to strengthen laboratory capacity, improve disease surveillance, prevent the spread of diseases, and identify and contain disease outbreaks before they become pandemics.

Some observers would like to see CDC's significant experience in monitoring and evaluating health programs more widely applied to U.S. global health programs. CDC's expertise in this area could be used to evaluate U.S. global health programs, as well as to identify data gaps. Evaluations could be used to determine the most efficient use of U.S. global health funds, particularly as it relates to identifying which health interventions would have the greatest impact on overall health outcomes, both within regions and within countries.

Global Health Initiative

On May 5, 2009, President Obama announced his new Global Health Initiative (GHI), a six-year, $63 billion from FY2009 to FY2014 to better coordinate the U.S. government's approach to global health programs [62]. For example, the GHI looks to accelerate the integration of services related to family planning, maternal health, and HIV/AID S [63]. In announcing the initiative, the President stated,

> In the 21st century, disease flows freely across borders and oceans, and, in recent days, the 2009 H1N1 virus has reminded us of the urgent need for action. We cannot wall ourselves off from the world and hope for the best, nor ignore the public health challenges beyond our borders. An outbreak in Indonesia can reach Indiana within days, and public health crises abroad can cause widespread suffering, conflict, and economic contraction. We cannot simply confront individual preventable illnesses in isolation. The world is interconnected, and that demands an integrated approach to global health.

ministration has indicated that it intends to apply the integrated approach of GHI to all global health programs. However, key documents published by the Administration on the Global Health Initiative focus primarily on global health programs implemented through USAID and the Department of State [64]. Little is known about the role other agencies, including CDC, might play in its implementation. CDC's FY2011 Congressional Budget Resolution indicates that CDC, along with other HHS agencies, will play a key role in GHI, but no further information is provided.

ACKNOWLEDGMENTS

Craig Moscetti, Intern, contributed to the January 29, 2010, update to this chapter.

REFERENCES

[1] For more information on debates about making U.S. global health assistance more efficient and U.S. funding for other global health efforts, including those implemented by USAID, the Department of Defense (DOD), and the Global Fund to Fight AIDS, Tuberculosis, and Malaria (Global Fund), see CRS Report R40740, U.S. *Global Health Assistance: Background, Priorities, and Issues for the 111th Congress.*

[2] In 1962, CDC established a smallpox surveillance unit, and a year later developed an innovative vaccination technique that the World Health Organization (WHO) later adopted in its smallpox eradication efforts. In 1977, smallpox was eradicated; the United States had invested $32 million on this effort. For more information, see CDC, "Historical Perspectives History of CDC," MMWR, vol. 45, no. 25 (June 28, 1996), pp. 526-530, http://www.cdc.gov/ mmwr/preview/mmwrhtml/00042732.htm. For more information on the Federal Quarantine Service, see CDC Website, History of Quarantine at http://www.cdc.gov/ncidod/dq/history.htm.

[3] CDC's global health work is authorized under a number of acts, including the Public Health Service Act; Foreign Assistance Act; Federal Employee International Organization Service Act; International Health Research Act; Agriculture Trade Development and Assistance Act; Economy Act; Foreign Employees Compensation Program; International Competition Requirement Exception; and relevant appropriations.

[4] For more information on CDC's partnerships, see http://www.cdc.gov/ cogh/ partnerships.htm.

[5] First authorized in 2003 through the U.S. Leadership Against HIV/AIDS, Tuberculosis, and Malaria Act (P.L. 108- 25), PEPFAR is a coordinated approach to combating HIV/AIDS globally. In 2008, Congress extended authorization of PEPFAR through the Tom Lantos and Henry J. Hyde United States Global Leadership Against HIV/AIDS, Tuberculosis, and Malaria Reauthorization Act (P.L. 110-293). For background information on PEPFAR, see http://www.pepfar.gov/ and CRS Report RL34569, *PEPFAR Reauthorization: Key Policy Debates and Changes to U.S. International HIV/AIDS, Tuberculosis, and Malaria Programs and Funding,* by Kellie Moss.

[6]   For background information on PMI, see http://www.pmi.gov/ and CRS Report R40494, *The President's Malaria Initiative and Other U.S. Global Efforts to Combat Malaria: Background, Issues for Congress, and Resources*, by Kellie Moss. For background information on the NTD Initiative, see CRS Report R40740, *U.S. Global Health Assistance: Background, Priorities, and Issues for the 111thCongress*, by Tiaji Salaam-Blyther and Kellie Moss.

[7]   For background information on the LIFE initiative and PEPFAR, see CRS Report RL33771, *Trends in U.S. Global AIDS Spending: FY2000-FY2008*, by Tiaji Salaam-Blyther.

[8]   For more information on GAP see http://www.cdc.gov/globalaids/about/. For more information on outcomes of GAP, see CDC, FY2009 Congressional Justification, pp. 317-322, http://www.cdc.gov/fmo/topic/Budget%20Information/ appropriations_budget_formjdf/FY09_CDC_CJ_Final.pdf.

[9]   These bullets were summarized by CRS from E-mail correspondence with Anstice Brand, Program Analyst, CDC Washington Office, February 2, 2009.

[10]   For background information on transfers made to CDC as an implementing partner of PEPFAR, see CRS Report RL33771, *Trends in U.S. Global AIDS Spending: FY2000-FY2008*, by Tiaji Salaam-Blyther.

[11]   E-mail from Elizabeth Crosby, Health Policy Analyst, March 26, 2010.

[12]   WHO Website, Vaccine-Preventable Diseases, http://www.who.int/ immunization_monitoring/diseases/en/.

[13]   CRS summarized information about CDC's global immunization efforts from CDC, Global Immunization Strategic Framework: 2006-2010, http://www.cdc. gov/vaccines/programs/global/downloads/gisf-2006-2010.pdf. For more information on outcomes of CDC immunization efforts, see CDC, FY2009 Congressional Justification, p. 327, http://www.cdc.gov/fmo/   topic/Budget%20Information/appropriations_budget_form_pdf/FY09_CDC_CJ_Final.pdf.

[14]   For more on GAVI, see http://www.gavialliance.org/; the Hib Initiative, see http://www.hibaction.org/; and the Accelerated Vaccine Introduction Initiative, see http://www.gavialliance.org/resources/6___Accelerated_Vaccine_Introduction.pdf; and the Meningitis Vaccine Project, see http://www.who.int/vaccines/en/ olddocs/meningACproject.shtml.

[15]   For more on the Global Immunization Vision and Strategy for 2006-2015, see http://www.who.int/vaccinesdocuments/DocsPDF05/GIVS_Final_EN.pdf.

[16]   Information about polio was summarized by CRS from WHO Website on polio at http://www.who.int/mediacentre/ factsheets/fs1 14/en/index.html.

[17]   Estimated polio cases for 2008 were taken from Global Polio Eradication Initiative, Wild Poliovirus Weekly Update, February 3, 2009, http://www.polioeradication.org/casecount.asp.

[18]   For a history of polio eradication efforts, see http://www.polioeradication.org/ history.asp.

[19]   Dr. Margaret Chan, WHO Director General, The Case for Completing Polio Eradication, WHO, May 10, 2007, p. 1, http://www.polioeradication.org/content/general/TheCase_FINAL.pdf.

[20]   Information on CDC's polio programs was summarized by CRS from U.S. Congress, Senate Committee on Appropriations, Subcommittee on Labor, Health and Human

Services, Education, and Related Agencies, *Global Health*, Prepared Statement by Michael Leavitt, Secretary of the U.S. Department of Health and Human Services, 110th Cong., 1st sess., May 2, 2007, S. Hrg. 110–443, pp. 9 and 10.

[21] For more information on the Global Polio Eradication Initiative, see http://www.polioeradication.org/.

[22] Information about measles was summarized by CRS from WHO, *Measles,* Fact Sheet, December 2008, http://www.who.int/mediacentre/factsheets/fs286/en/index.html.

[23] Senate Committee on Appropriations, Subcommittee on Labor, Health and Human Services, Education, and Related Agencies, *Hearing on the FY2008 Budget of HHS*, Hearing on H.R. 3043/S. 1710, 110th Cong., 1st sess., March 19, 2007, S. Hrg. 110–400, p. 650.

[24] CDC defines operations research as the application of scientific methods and models to improve decision-making, resource allocation, and processes to predict and improve program performance.

[25] WHO, Measles, Fact Sheet, December 2008, http://www.who.int/mediacentre/factsheets/fs286/en/index.html.

[26] FY2011 CBJ for CDC, p. 247.

[27] Information about CDC's global malaria activities was summarized by CRS from CDC's international malaria Website athttp://www.cdc.gov/malaria/cdcactivities/index.htm.

[28] For more on outcomes of CDC's malaria interventions, see CDC, FY2009 CBJ, p.333, http://www.cdc.gov/fmo/topic/Budget%20Information/appropriations_budget_form_pdf/FY09_CDC_CJ_Final.pdf

[29] Information about GDD was summarized by CRS from CDC, Global Disease Detection, Policy Paper, June 2008, http://www.cdc.gov/cogh/pdf/GDD_At_a_Glance_2008.pdf.

[30] For more information on GOARN, see http://www.who.int/csr/outbreaknetwork/en/.

[31] For more information on GDD outcomes see CDC, FY2009 CBJ, pp. 329-330, http://www.cdc.gov/fmo/topic/Budget%20Information/appropriations_budget_formjdf/FY09_CDC_CJ_Final.pdf. For more on CDC's response to cholera outbreaks in Zimbabwe, see CDC, "CDC Responds to Cholera Outbreak in Zimbabwe," CDC Global Health E-Brief, Fourth Quarter 2008, p. 6, http://www.cdc.gov/washington/EGlobalHealthEditions/pdf/4thQuarter2008Global
HealthE-Brief.pdf.

[32] The Field Epidemiology Training Program (FETP) and the Field Epidemiology and Laboratory Training Program (FETLP) are two different programs. FE(L)TP refers to both.

[33] This section on "Other Global Health Programs" was summarized by CRS from E-mail correspondence with Anstice Brand, Program Analyst, CDC Washington Office, February 2, 2009 and CDC, http://www.cdc.gov/smdp/about.htm.

[34] For information on outcomes of SMDP, see CDC, FY2009 CBJ, p. 338, http://www.cdc.gov/fmo/topic/Budget%20Information/appropriations_budget_formjdf/FY09_CDC_CJ_Final.pdf.

[35] For more information on other global health efforts, see http://www.cdc.gov/globalhealth/.

[36] For background information on CDC's efforts to address tuberculosis globally and on TB drug resistance, see CRS Report RL34246, *Tuberculosis: International Efforts and Issues for Congress*, by Tiaji Salaam-Blyther.

[37] CDC defines operations research as the application of scientific methods and models to improve decision-making, resource allocation, and processes to predict and improve program performance.

[38] For more information on DOTS, see http://www.who.int/tb/dots/en/ and for more information on the Green Light Committee Initiative, see http://www.who.int/tb/challenges/mdr/greenlightcommittee/en/.

[39] Correspondence with Jeffrey Lutz, Avian Influenza Action Group, U.S. Department of State, April 28, 2009 and U.S. Department of State press release, "U.S. International Avian and Pandemic Influenza Assistance Approaches $950 Million," October 25, 2008, http://2001-2009.state.gov/r/pa/prs/ps/2008/oct/111241.htm. Also see, State Department, *Avian and Pandemic Influenza*, October 2008. For information on domestic spending on pandemic preparedness, see CRS Report RS22576, *Pandemic Influenza: Appropriations for Public Health Preparedness and Response*, by Sarah Lister. For information on domestic spending on H1N1, see CRS Report R40554, *The 2009 Influenza Pandemic: An Overview*, by Sarah A. Lister and C. StephenRedhead.

[40] U.N. System Influenza Coordinator and World Bank, Responses to Avian Influenza and State of Pandemic Readiness, Fourth Global Progress Report, October 2008, p. 83, http://un-influenza.org/files/081006-Synopsis2008.pdf.

[41] For more information about GAINS, see http://www.gains.org/.

[42] The other collaborating centers are in Britain, Japan, and Australia. For more information on WHO Collaborating Centers, see http://www.who.int/csr/disease/influenza/collabcentres/en/.

[43] Taken from CDC, "Press Briefing: CDC Media Availability on Human Swine Influenza Cases," press release, April 27, 2009, http://www.cdc.gov/media/transcripts/2009/t090427.htm.

[44] HHS, "Secretary Sebelius Takes Two Key Actions On Strategic National Stockpile ," press release, April 30, 2009, http://www.hhs.gov/news/press/2009pres/04/20090430a.html. For information about the value of the 400,000 treatment courses, see USAID, Global—Influenza A/H1N1, Fact Sheet # 3, May 18, 2009, p. 2, http://www.usaid.gov/our_work/humanitarian_assistance/disaster_assistance/countries/pandemic_influenza/template/fs_sr/pandemic_influenza_fs03_05-1 8-2009.pdf.

[45] PAHO, press release, "PAHO Recognizes Important US Contribution of Antivirals for Latin America and Caribbean," July 3, 2009.

[46] The White House, "Letter from the President to the Speaker of the House," press release, April 30, 2009, http://www.whitehouse.gov/the_press_office/Letter-from-the-President-to-the-Speaker-of-the-House-ofRepresentatives/. Also see CRS Report R40531, *FY2009 Spring Supplemental Appropriations for Overseas Contingency Operations*, coordinated by Stephen Daggett and Susan B. Epstein.

[47] E-mail from Elizabeth Crosby, Program Analyst, CDC Atlanta, January 2010.

[48] Statistics taken from UNICEF, State of the World's Children, Special Edition, Statistical Tables, November 2009, http://www.unicef.org/rightsite/sowc/pdfs/statistics/SOWC_Spec_Ed_CRC_Statistical_Tables_EN_111809.pdf.

[49] The White House, A New Era of Responsibility: Renewing America's Promise, FY20
      10 Budget, February 26, 2009, p. 32, http://www.whitehouse.gov/omb/ assets/fy
      2010_new_era/A_New_Era_of_Responsibility2.pdf.

[50] The White House, "Statement by the President on Global Health Initiative," press
      release, May 5, 2009, http://www.whitehouse.gov/the_press_office/Statement-by-the-
      President-on-Global-Health-Initiative/.

[51] For background on CDC's global health programs, see CRS Report R40239, Centers
      for Disease Control and Prevention Global Health Programs: FY2001-FY2010, by Tiaji
      Salaam-Blyther.

[52] E-mail from Elizabeth Crosby, Health Policy Analyst, CDC, March 5, 2010.

[53] See the FY2011 CBJ for CDC, p.18.

[54] See the White House, "Remarks by the President on a New Beginning," press release,
      June 4, 2009, http://www.whitehouse.gov/the-press-office/remarks-president-cairo-
      university-6-04-09, and United Nations Children's Fund, "United States and
      Organization of the Islamic Conference Join Forces Against Polio," press release,
      December 3, 2009, http://www.unicef.org/immunization/index_51990.html.

[55] E-mail from Elizabeth Crosby, Health Policy Analyst, March 26, 2010.

[56] See the CDC webpage on the Futures Initiative at http://www.cdc.gov/futures/ and
      CRS Report RL34098, Public Health Service (PHS) Agencies: Background and
      Funding, coordinated by Pamela W. Smith.

[57] CDC, "Letter from Dr. Gerberding," press release, April 21, 2005, http://www.
      cdc.gov/futures/g_letter_04-21- 05.htm.

[58] See HHS, "Statement of Organization, Functions, and Delegations of Authority," 74
      Federal Register 68630-68631, December 28, 2009.

[59] Robert Koenig, "New Chief Orders CDC to Cut Management Layers," Science, August
      7, 2009, http://news.sciencemag.org/scienceinsider/2009/08/new-chief-order.html. Also
      see, Sheila Poole, "Science, efficiency to drive CDC changes ," Atlanta Journal-
      Constitution, January 1, 2010, http://www.ajc.com/health/science-efficiencyto-drive-
      264238.html.

[60] For more on CDC's health protection goals, see http://www.cdc.gov/osi/goals/index
      .html, and CDC, State of CDC, 2008, http://www.cdc.gov/about/ stateofcdc/pdf/S
      OCDC2008.pdf.

[61] HHS, FY2011 CBJ for CDC, p. 242.

[62] The White House, "Statement by the President on Global Health Initiative," press
      release, May 5, 2009, http://www.whitehouse.gov/the_press_office/Statement-by-the-
      President-on-Global-Health-Initiative/.

[63] Hillary Rodham Clinton, U.S. Department of State Secretary, "Remarks on the 15th
      Anniversary of the International Conference on Population and Development," January
      9, 2010, http://www.state.gov/secretary/rm/2010/01/135001.htm

[64] For more information on the GHI, see http://www.pepfar.gov/ghi/.

In: Globalization

Editors: M. G. Massari and K. J. Lutz, pp. 75-116

ISBN: 978-1-61470-327-3

© 2012 Nova Science Publishers, Inc

Chapter 5

THE 2009 INFLUENZA PANDEMIC: AN OVERVIEW

Sarah A. Lister[1]* and C. Stephen Redhead[2]

SUMMARY

On June 11, 2009, in response to the global spread of a new strain of H1N1 influenza ("flu"), the World Health Organization (WHO) declared the outbreak to be an influenza pandemic, the first since 1968. The novel "H1N1 swine flu" was first identified in California in late April. Since then, cases have been reported around the world.

When the outbreak began, U.S. officials adopted a response posture under the overall coordination of the Secretary of Homeland Security. Among other things, officials established a government-wide informational website (http://www.flu.gov), released antiviral drugs from the national stockpile, developed new diagnostic tests for the H1N1 virus, and published guidance for the clinical management of patients and the management of community and school outbreaks.

Several federal emergency management authorities have been invoked for the response to the pandemic, including a presidential declaration of a national emergency, and a declaration by the Secretary of Health and Human Services (HHS) of a public health emergency. Among other things, these authorities have allowed federal officials to make certain unapproved drugs available to patients with severe cases of influenza, and to ease certain requirements on hospitals to aid them in caring for surges in the volume of patients.

Federal health officials have purchased millions of doses of H1N1 pandemic flu vaccine, approved through the routine licensing process used for seasonal flu vaccines. A voluntary nationwide vaccination program is underway, largely coordinated by state and local health officials and carried out through public clinics, private health care providers, schools, and others. The Secretary of HHS has implemented waivers of liability and an injury compensation program in the event of unforeseen vaccine safety problems. Allocation schemes were developed to give priority for limited vaccine doses to those in high-risk groups. However, there have been a number of problems associated with shortfalls of actual (versus predicted) vaccine availability, and charges that vaccine would not be available for

* Email: slister@crs.loc.gov

most of the individuals in designated priority groups until after the peak of pandemic virus transmission had passed. Some Members of Congress and others have questioned the adequacy of federal activities to improve the capacity for and timeliness of flu vaccine production.

To address the outbreak, the Obama Administration requested $2 billion in FY2009 emergency supplemental appropriations, and transfer authority for an additional amount of almost $7 billion from existing HHS accounts. On June 26, the President signed P.L. 111-32, the Supplemental Appropriations Act, 2009, which provided $1.9 billion immediately and an additional $5.8 billion contingent upon a presidential request documenting the need for, and proposed use of, additional funds. The President has subsequently asked for most of the contingent amount. A balance of almost $1.3 billion remains available.

This report provides a synopsis of key events in the H1N1 pandemic response, followed by information about selected federal emergency management authorities and actions taken by DHS, HHS, and state and local authorities. It then lists congressional hearings held to date; discusses appropriations and funding for pandemic flu preparedness and response activities; summarizes U.S. government pandemic flu planning documents; and lists sources for additional information. An Appendix describes the WHO process to determine the phase of an emerging flu pandemic.

SYNOPSIS

On June 11, 2009, in response to the global spread of a new strain of H1N1 influenza ("flu"), the World Health Organization (WHO) declared the outbreak to be a flu pandemic, the first since 1968. Officials believe the outbreak began in Mexico in March, or perhaps earlier. The novel "H1N1 swine flu" virus was first identified in California in late April. Since then, cases have been reported around the world. The H1N1 pandemic virus is a reassortment of several existing strains of influenza A, subtype H1N1 virus, including strains typically found in pigs, birds, and humans.

Since the H1N1 pandemic virus emerged in the spring, the U.S. Centers for Disease Control and Prevention (CDC) has continued the operation of U.S. seasonal (routine) flu surveillance systems, which are normally suspended during the summer. These systems track trends in rates of illness and hospitalization but are imprecise in their accounting for the total numbers of deaths and hospitalizations due to the pandemic. CDC has published an estimate of these counts, stating that between April and October 17, there were between 14 million and 34 million cases of H1N1 infection, between 63,000 and 153,000 H1N1-related hospitalizations, and between 2,500 and 6,000 H1N1-related deaths in the United States. (See "CDC: Disease Surveillance, and Estimates of Illnesses and Deaths.")

The CDC reports that the symptoms and transmission of the novel H1N1 flu from person to person are generally similar to seasonal flu. Laboratory testing of the new strain indicates that the antiviral drugs oseltamivir (Tamiflu) and zanamivir (Relenza) are generally effective in treating illnesses caused by the pandemic strain. In contrast to seasonal flu, the pandemic strain appears to cause serious illness more often among children, and less often among the elderly. However, like seasonal flu, pregnant women and individuals with serious chronic diseases appear to be at greater risk of serious illness from the pandemic strain.

2009 H1N1 INFLUENZA PANDEMIC STATUS
AS OF NOVEMBER 16, 2009

International: World Health Organization (WHO):
(http://www.who.int/csr/disease/swineflu/en/index.html)

- WHO declared an influenza pandemic (Phase 6) on June 11. On July 11, WHO asked nations to suspend routine reporting of cases, and stopped publishing case counts, saying they did not accurately reflect pandemic status.
- WHO advises no restriction of regular travel or closure of borders; however, sick individuals are advised to delay travel. Officials report no infection risk from consumption of well-cooked pork products.

United States Government:
(http://www.flu.gov/;   http://www.cdc.gov/h1n1flu;   http://www.fda.gov/ NewsEvents/ PublicHealthFocus/ucm150305.htm)

- A Public Health Emergency is in effect under Section 319 of the Public Health Service Act.
- CDC has released to states treatment courses of antiviral drugs, including Tamiflu, Relenza, and the intravenous drug peramivir.
- FDA has issued Emergency Use Authorizations for unapproved uses of Tamiflu and Relenza, use of the unapproved antiviral drug peramivir and unapproved diagnostic tests, and certain uses of protective equipment.
- CDC has issued guidances for the general public; for clinicians and laboratories; regarding pregnant women and other groups; regarding travel; regarding affected schools and communities; and others.
- Congress provided up to $7.7 billion in emergency supplemental appropriations for FY2009 (P.L. 111-32).
- FDA has approved five vaccines against H 1N 1 flu, through the routine flu vaccine licensing process.
- Health officials have launched a vaccination campaign. HHS Secretary Sebelius has waived liability associated with the use of pandemic vaccine, and enabled an injury compensation program. Priority groups have been identified.
- The President has declared the pandemic to be a national emergency, allowing waivers of some requirements under Medicare and Medicaid law to help health care facilities manage increased numbers of patients.
- CDC estimates that as of October 17, the pandemic had caused between 14 million and 34 million cases of H 1N 1 infection, between 63,000 and 153,000 H 1N 1-related hospitalizations, and between 2,500 and 6,000 H 1N 1-related deaths in the United States.

In response to the outbreak in April, Janet Napolitano, Secretary of the Department of Homeland Security (DHS), assumed the role of Principal Federal Official, coordinating federal response efforts. Charles E. Johnson, then the Acting Secretary of Health and Human

Services (HHS), declared a public health emergency, which remains in effect. Among other things, this has allowed the Food and Drug Administration (FDA) to issue Emergency Use Authorizations (EUAs), permitting certain unapproved uses of antiviral drugs (such as in very young children) and some types of protective facemasks, the use of unapproved diagnostic tests for the new flu strain, and the use of the unapproved antiviral drug peramivir. HHS has established a government-wide informational website (www.flu.gov) with information for planners, health care providers, and the public. On October 24, President Obama declared the pandemic to be a national emergency, which allowed waivers of some requirements under Medicare and Medicaid law to help health care facilities manage increased numbers of patients. To date, there has not been a presidential declaration regarding the pandemic under the Robert T. Stafford Disaster Relief and Emergency Assistance Act (the Stafford Act). The applicability of this Act to infectious disease incidents is unclear. (See "Key Federal Government Authorities and Actions" and Figure 1, "Selected Federal Emergency Management Authorities Applicable to the H1N1 Influenza Pandemic.")

Many U.S. communities closed schools when students were found to be infected with the new flu strain. School closure decisions, made by local officials, were based on initial CDC guidance, which was revised as it became clear that the virus was in wide circulation, and that the illnesses it caused were generally mild. CDC now recommends against routine school closures when small numbers of students are infected, arguing that such closures may do little to reduce the spread of the virus, while placing a considerable burden on the affected community. (See "Pandemic Preparedness and Response in Schools.")

The U.S. response to the pandemic triggered a slate of plans that were developed, beginning around 2004, to address concerns about the global spread of another novel flu strain, the H5N1 avian flu. (See box below for definitions.) In FY2006 supplemental appropriations, Congress provided $6.1 billion for pandemic planning across several departments and agencies. These earlier efforts, and others aimed at preparedness for bioterrorism and emerging infections in general, have generally streamlined the response to the H1N1 pandemic. To address the H1N1 outbreak, the Obama Administration requested $2 billion in FY2009 emergency supplemental appropriations, and transfer authority for an additional amount of almost $7 billion from existing HHS accounts. On June 26, the President signed P.L. 111-32, which provided $1.9 billion in FY2009 supplemental appropriations immediately, and an additional $5.8 billion contingent upon a presidential request documenting the need for additional funds. The President has twice requested portions of the contingent funding. (See "Appropriations and Funding.")

A voluntary national pandemic vaccination campaign is underway. In June, HHS Secretary Kathleen Sebelius issued a declaration waiving liability and enabling a compensation program in the event that injuries result from use of pandemic vaccine. CDC has developed recommendations for groups of individuals who should be given priority for vaccine when it is available in limited amounts. Costs associated with the vaccination program are being funded through both public and private sources. Vaccine is being provided to states as it becomes available, according to states' populations. Vaccine delivery is carried out by a CDC contractor. Decisions regarding vaccine distribution to health care providers, clinics, schools, and other vaccination sites are the responsibility of state and local governments. There have been a number of problems associated with shortfalls of actual (versus predicted) vaccine availability, and charges that vaccine would not be available for most of the individuals in designated priority groups until after the peak of pandemic virus transmission had passed. (See "Vaccines and Pandemic Influenza.")

INFLUENZA DEFINED

Influenza ("flu") is a respiratory illness that can be transmitted from person to person. Flu viruses are of two main genetic types: Influenza A and B. Influenza A strains are further identified by two important surface proteins that are responsible for virulence: hemagglutinin (H) and neuraminidase (N).

Seasonal flu circulates each year in the winter in each hemisphere. The dominant flu strains in global circulation change from year to year, but most people have some immunity. Infection can be fatal, however. CDC estimates that there are about 36,000 deaths from seasonal flu each year, on average. Vaccines are made each year based on predictions of the strains that are most likely to circulate in the upcoming flu season.

Avian flu ("bird flu") is caused by viruses that occur naturally among wild birds, and that may also affect domestic poultry. In 1997, a new H5N 1 strain of avian flu emerged in Asia, and has since caused millions of deaths among domestic poultry, and hundreds of deaths in humans. Health officials have been concerned that this strain could cause a human pandemic, and governments around the world have carried out a number of preparedness activities, including vaccine development and stockpiling, and planning for continuity of services.

Swine flu occurs naturally among wild and domestic swine. People do not normally get swine flu, but each year CDC identifies a few isolated cases of human flu that are caused by flu strains typically associated with swine.

Pandemic flu is caused when a novel strain of human flu (i.e., one that spreads from person to person) emerges and causes a global outbreak, or pandemic, of serious illness. Because there is little natural immunity, the disease is often more severe than is typical of seasonal flu.

(Adapted from HHS, "Flu Terms Defined," http://www.pandemicflu.gov. For more information about pandemic flu, see "Understanding Pandemic Influenza" in CRS Report RL33 145, *Pandemic Influenza: Domestic Preparedness Efforts.*)

This report provides information about selected federal emergency management authorities and actions taken by DHS and HHS, and actions taken by state and local authorities, in response to the pandemic. It then lists congressional hearings held to date; provides information about appropriations and funding for pandemic flu preparedness and response activities; summarizes U.S. government pandemic flu planning documents; and lists sources for additional information about the pandemic. An Appendix describes the WHO process to determine the phase of a threatened or emerging flu pandemic, and touches on several related issues. All dates in this report refer to 2009 unless otherwise specified. This report will be continually updated to reflect unfolding events.

KEY FEDERAL GOVERNMENT AUTHORITIES AND ACTIONS

Government-wide Pandemic Preparedness and Response

Leadership and Coordination

Under current law, the Secretary of Homeland Security leads all federal incident response activities, while the Secretary of HHS leads all federal public health and medical incident response activities under the overall leadership of the Secretary of Homeland Security.[1] The Government Accountability Office (GAO) has noted, in the context of pandemic flu planning, that "these federal leadership roles involve shared responsibilities between [HHS] and [DHS], and it is not clear how these would work in practice." GAO recommended that HHS and DHS conduct training and exercises to ensure that federal leadership roles are clearly defined and understood. As recently as July 2009, GAO testified that although some recommended exercises had been undertaken, it was unclear whether they rigorously tested federal leadership roles in a pandemic. GAO also recommended, among other things, that federal pandemic plans published in 2006 be updated.[2] In July, DHS Deputy Secretary Jane Holl Lute testified that an implementation plan for response to the current pandemic was being finalized under the leadership of the National Security Council.[3]

In August, the President's Council of Advisors on Science and Technology (PCAST) released a report assessing preparations for a possible resurgence of H1N1 flu and recommending additional actions.[4] PCAST also noted the potential ambiguity in the leadership roles of DHS and HHS, and recommended that the Homeland Security Advisor[5] be given primary responsibility for decision making during the pandemic response, saying:

> The Working Group has some concerns, based on conversations with representatives of the various agencies involved, that decision-making authorities and processes may not be completely clear in all cases. Primary Federal responsibilities for response to an epidemic are lodged in two departments ([HHS] and DHS), with significant involvement of others (Education, Defense, State, Agriculture, Labor), and coordination by White House staff. While the National Strategy for Pandemic Influenza Implementation Plan provides a comprehensive list of assignments for a multitude of offices, agencies, and departments involved in the Federal planning process, the large number of tasks and responsible units tends to obscure the primary seat of responsibility.... The Working Group believes it would be

---

[1] See CRS Report RL33579, *The Public Health and Medical Response to Disasters: Federal Authority and Funding*, by Sarah A. Lister.

[2] See, for example, U.S. Government Accountability Office, *Influenza Pandemic: Gaps in Pandemic Planning and Preparedness Need to Be Addressed*, GAO-09-909T, July 29, 2009, pp. 6-7, http://www.gao.gov.

[3] Comments of DHS Deputy Secretary Jane Holl Lute, U.S. Congress, House Committee on Homeland Security, *Beyond Readiness: An Examination of the Current Status and Future Outlook of the National Response to Pandemic Influenza*, 111th Cong., 1st sess., July 29, 2009.

[4] Executive Office of the President, President's Council of Advisors on Science and Technology, *Report to the President on U.S. Preparations for 2009-H1N1 Influenza*, August 7, 2009, press release and link to full report at http://www.whitehouse.gov/the_press_office/Presidents-Council-of-Advisors-on-Science-and-Technology-PCASTreleases-report-assessing-H1N1-preparations/ (hereafter referred to as PCAST report).

[5] This designation presumably refers to John Brennan, who serves as Assistant to the President for Homeland Security and Counterterrorism. For more information on the organization of the Homeland Security Council and its staff under the Obama Administration, see The White House, Office of the Press Secretary, "Statement by the President on the White House Organization for Homeland Security and Counterterrorism," press release, May 26, 2009, http://www.whitehouse.gov/briefing_room/ PressReleases/.

valuable to clarify these matters before events accelerate in September and assign to the Homeland Security Advisor the responsibility for ensuring that all of the important decisions are made in a timely fashion and with appropriate consultation with the President.[6]

Declaration of a National Emergency

On October 23, President Obama declared an emergency, pursuant to the National Emergencies Act, with respect to the H1N1 pandemic. Specifically, the President proclaimed that because "the rapid increase in illness across the nation may overburden health care resources and ... the temporary waiver of certain standard Federal requirements may be warranted in order to enable U.S. health care facilities to implement emergency operations plans, the 2009 H1N1 influenza pandemic in the United States constitutes a national emergency."[7]

The National Emergencies Act provides the President with broad authority to waive statutory requirements, or to invoke other authorities, limited to those he specifies in an emergency declaration. In this case, the declaration was limited to a set of requirements under the Social Security Act, enumerated in Section 1135 of that Act, that may be waived if there are in effect *concurrently* a declaration of public health emergency *and* a presidential declaration under *either* the National Emergencies Act *or* the Robert T. Stafford Disaster Relief and Emergency Assistance Act (the Stafford Act). The National Emergencies Act, the "Section 1135" waiver authority, and other federal emergency management authorities that have been invoked or could be invoked for the response to the flu pandemic are depicted in Figure 1. Because a public health emergency declaration was already in effect, the declaration under the National Emergencies Act provided the authority for the Secretary of HHS to waive the Social Security Act requirements in order to make it easier for health care facilities to manage surges in patient volume during the pandemic. The Stafford Act has not been invoked for the response to the H1N1 pandemic. It's possible applicability to this incident is discussed in a subsequent section of this report, "Applicability of the Stafford Act." Also, the "Section 1135" waivers are discussed in more detail in a subsequent section, "Waivers or Modifications Under Section 1135 of the Social Security Act."

Department of Homeland Security (DHS)

Leadership Designation

On April 27, Janet Napolitano, Secretary of the Department of Homeland Security (DHS), stated in a press briefing that she was serving as the coordinator of the federal response to the flu outbreak, having assumed the role of Principal Federal Official (PFO).[8] According to the National Response Framework (NRF), which guides a coordinated federal

---

[6] PCAST report, p. 32.

[7] The text of the President's Proclamation, "Declaration of a National Emergency with Respect to the 2009 H1N1 Influenza Pandemic," October 23, 2009, and related information are available at http://www.flu.gov/professional/federal/h1n1emergency10242009.html. See also CRS Report 98-505, *National Emergency Powers*, by L. Elaine Halchin.

[8] Department of Homeland Security, *Remarks by Secretary Napolitano at Media Briefing on H1N1 Flu Outbreak*, April 27, 2009, http://www.dhs.gov/ynews/.

response to disasters and emergencies in general, the Secretary of Homeland Security leads federal incident response.[9]

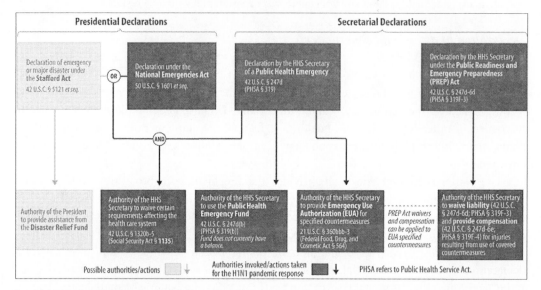

Source: Developed by Congressional Research Service.

Notes: (1) This figure depicts selected authorities that were invoked or could be invoked for the response to the H 1N 1 flu pandemic, and does not necessarily reflect all available authorities or actions. For example, the National Emergencies Act confers broad authority to the President to waive statutory requirements, or to invoke other authorities, as specified in the declaration of emergency. In this case the declaration was limited to authorities in Section 1135 of the Social Security Act. Similarly, presidential declarations under the Stafford Act may enable authorities, such as certain administrative waivers, in addition to the authority to use the Disaster Relief Fund.

(2) The authority for Emergency Use Authorization of specified countermeasures, which was triggered for the H 1N 1 pandemic by the HHS Secretary's declaration of a public health emergency, can alternatively be triggered by a declaration of a domestic emergency by the Secretary of Homeland Security, or a declaration of a military emergency by the Secretary of Defense. [21 U.S.C. § 360bbb-3(b)]

Figure 1. Selected Federal Emergency Management Authorities Applicable to the H1N1 Influenza Pandemic.

Applicability of the Stafford Act

As of November 16, the Stafford Act has not been invoked for the response to the H1N1 pandemic. The Act authorizes federal assistance to public and private not-for-profit entities affected by catastrophes, upon a presidential declaration. Two levels of declaration may be made, based on the scope and severity of an incident: a declaration of *emergency*, which provides a lower level of assistance, and a declaration of *major disaster*, which provides a higher level. The Stafford Act is administered by the Federal Emergency Management

---

[9] CRS Report RL34758, *The National Response Framework: Overview and Possible Issues for Congress*, by Bruce R. Lindsay. The PFO position has been controversial, however, because it may conflict with the role of the Federal Coordinating Officer (FCO), a leadership position established in the Robert T. Stafford Disaster Relief and Emergency Assistance Act (the Stafford Act).

Agency (FEMA), which can draw from a Disaster Relief Fund to provide assistance for activities that are eligible under the Act.[10]

Major disaster declarations under the Stafford Act have historically involved common meteorological or geological disasters, wildfires, and terrorist acts such as bombings. The applicability of major disaster assistance to infectious disease threats—whether natural (e.g., a flu pandemic) or intentional (bioterrorism)—has been a matter of debate. Historically, major disaster assistance has been tailored to address disaster consequences such as the destruction of infrastructure or the displacement of victims, neither of which is a likely consequence of infectious disease outbreaks.

A legal analysis by CRS concluded that emergency assistance under the Stafford Act could be provided by the President in the event of a flu pandemic, but also noted that whether major disaster assistance would be authorized is not clear. There is no precedent for a major disaster declaration in response to an infectious disease threat. Furthermore, the legislative history of the Stafford Act suggests that this issue was not addressed by Congress when it drafted the current definition of a major disaster, and neither inclusion nor exclusion of flu pandemics from major disaster assistance is required as a matter of statutory construction.[11]

In the *National Strategy for Pandemic Influenza: Implementation Plan*, the George W. Bush Administration assumed that the President's authority to declare a major disaster pursuant to the Stafford Act could be applied to a flu pandemic.[12] In 2007, FEMA issued a Disaster Assistance Policy regarding Stafford Act assistance that may be provided during a flu pandemic, which includes costs associated with emergency medical care when provided by an eligible entity (generally, a public or non-profit private entity).[13]

In July, DHS Secretary Janet Napolitano suggested that she did not plan to invoke the Stafford Act for the pandemic response.[14] However, DHS Deputy Secretary Jane Holl Lute has testified that the Stafford Act may be invoked for the pandemic response under certain circumstances, and that DHS has planned accordingly.[15] In information provided by HHS regarding the effects of the presidential declaration of national emergency on October 23, it is suggested that state governors may request that the President make a declaration under the Stafford Act in order to provide assistance if state and local resources become insufficient for the pandemic response.[16] A FEMA fact sheet was referenced in order to assist states in

---

[10] CRS Report RL33053, *Federal Stafford Act Disaster Assistance: Presidential Declarations, Eligible Activities, and Funding*, by Keith Bea; and CRS Report RL33579, *The Public Health and Medical Response to Disasters: Federal Authority and Funding*, by Sarah A. Lister.

[11] CRS Report RL34724, *Would an Influenza Pandemic Qualify as a Major Disaster Under the Stafford Act?*, by Edward C. Liu.

[12] Homeland Security Council, *National Strategy for Pandemic Influenza: Implementation Plan*, May 2006, Appendix C, "Authorities and References," p. 212.

[13] FEMA, "Emergency Assistance for Human Influenza Pandemic," Disaster Assistance Policy 9523.17, March 31, 2007, at http://www.fema.gov/pdf/government/grant/pa/policy.pdf.

[14] Kevin Robillard, "Officials Say Swine Flu Vaccine is Coming," *CQ Homeland Security*, July 9, 2009.

[15] Comments of DHS Deputy Secretary Jane Holl Lute, U.S. Congress, House Committee on Homeland Security, *Beyond Readiness: An Examination of the Current Status and Future Outlook of the National Response to Pandemic Influenza*, 111th Cong., 1st sess., July 29, 2009.

[16] HHS, "October 24, 2009–President Obama Signs Emergency Declaration for H1N1 Flu," in particular the answer to the questions " ... How does the President's National Emergency declaration under the National Emergencies Act differ from a Stafford Act declaration? How does the request process for assistance under the Stafford Act differ from the request process for 1135 waivers?," http://www.flu.gov/professional/federal/h1n1emergency10242009.html.

assessing impacts and evaluating the need for federal assistance under the Stafford Act.[17] The Stafford Act and other federal emergency management authorities that have been invoked or could be invoked for the response to the H1N1 flu pandemic are depicted in Figure 1.

Customs and Border Protection (CBP) Activities

When the H1N1 flu outbreak began in the United States, Customs and Border Protection (CBP), in DHS, reported monitoring incoming travelers at ports of entry (typically a visual inspection for possible symptoms), providing information about disease control measures, and referring symptomatic persons to a CDC quarantine station[18] or a local public health official for evaluation. According to DHS, "There are no border restrictions in effect. U.S. Customs and Border Protection continues to monitor the health status of incoming visitors at our land, sea and air ports watching out for illness as part of their standard operating procedure."[19]

Administration officials resisted calls for more aggressive measures such as closing the U.S.- Mexico border. WHO and CDC officials commented that scientific evidence does not support closure of a border to travelers as an effective means of controlling the spread of influenza.[20] Also, as a matter of law, U.S. citizens cannot be barred from entering the United States, so any border closure could only exclude aliens.[21] Finally, any such measures would likely be resource- intensive, involving considerable disruption of trade and other economic interests.[22]

Department of Health and Human Services (HHS)

Determination of a Public Health Emergency

On April 26, Charles E. Johnson, then the Acting HHS Secretary, declared a public health emergency pursuant to Section 319 of the Public Health Service Act (PHSA).[23] This enabled FDA to implement an authority in the Federal Food, Drug, and Cosmetic Act (FFDCA) allowing for the emergency use of unapproved medical treatments and tests, under specified conditions, if needed during an incident. (See the subsequent section "FDA: Emergency Use Authorizations.") In addition, while a public health emergency declaration is in effect, the HHS Secretary (or Acting Secretary) is authorized to draw funds for response to the situation

---

[17] FEMA, "Disaster Assistance Fact Sheet 9580.106: Pandemic Influenza," October 22, 2009, http://www.fema.gov/ pdf/emergency/pandemic_influenza_fact_sheet.pdf.

[18] CDC, "Quarantine Stations," http://www.cdc.gov/ncidod/dq/quarantine_stations.htm.

[19] DHS, "Department Response to H1N1 (Swine) Flu," July 24, 2009, http://www.dhs.gov/files/programs/swine-flu.shtm.

[20] Donald G. McNeil, "Containing Flu Is Not Feasible, Specialists Say," *The New York Times*, April 29, 2009. See also WHO, *No Rationale for Travel Restrictions*, May 1, 2009, http://www.who.int/csr/disease/swineflu/guidance/ public_health/travel_advice/en/index.html.

[21] See "Closing the Border" in CRS Report R40560, *The 2009 Influenza Pandemic: Selected Legal Issues*, coordinated by Kathleen S. Swendiman and Nancy Lee Jones.

[22] See "Port of Entry Policies and Procedures" in CRS Report R40570, *Immigration Policies and Issues on Health-Related Grounds for Exclusion*, by Chad C. Haddal and Ruth Ellen Wasem.

[23] 42 U.S.C. § 247d. See HHS, "HHS Declares Public Health Emergency for Swine Flu," press release, April 26, 2009, http://www.hhs.gov/news. More information about this authority is available in CRS Report R40560, *The 2009 Influenza Pandemic: Selected Legal Issues*, coordinated by Kathleen S. Swendiman and Nancy Lee Jones; and CRS Report RL33579, *The Public Health and Medical Response to Disasters: Federal Authority and Funding*, by Sarah A. Lister.

from a Public Health Emergency Fund. However, this fund has not had a balance since the 1990s, and hence the declaration did not provide access to this (or any other) emergency funding mechanism. (For more information, see the "Public Health Emergency Funding Mechanisms" section of this report.) The public health emergency determination, which would have expired after 90 days, was renewed by HHS Secretary Kathleen Sebelius on July 24 and again on October 1.[24]

The public health emergency authority and other federal emergency management authorities that have been invoked or could be invoked for the response to the H1N1 flu pandemic are depicted in Figure 1.

Waivers or Modifications under Section 1135 of the Social Security Act

When there are in effect *concurrently* a declaration of public health emergency *and* a presidential declaration under *either* the National Emergencies Act *or* the Stafford Act, the Secretary of HHS may waive or modify a number of administrative requirements of the Social Security Act and certain health information privacy provisions (as enumerated in Section 1135 of that Act) to streamline the delivery of health care services by facilities facing surges in patient volume.[25] These "1135 waivers" principally involve requirements for reimbursement through the Medicare and Medicaid programs, requirements that most health care facilities in the United States choose to meet.

As noted earlier, on October 23, President Obama declared a national emergency pursuant to the National Emergencies Act. (See the "Declaration of a National Emergency" section of this report.) Specifically, the President proclaimed that because "the rapid increase in illness across the nation may overburden health care resources and ... the temporary waiver of certain standard Federal requirements may be warranted in order to enable U.S. health care facilities to implement emergency operations plans, the 2009 H1N1 influenza pandemic in the United States constitutes a national emergency." The President further authorized the Secretary of HHS to "exercise the authority under section 1135 of the Social Security Act to temporarily waive or modify certain requirements of the Medicare, Medicaid, and State Children's Health Insurance programs and of the Health Insurance Portability and Accountability Act [HIPAA] Privacy Rule throughout the duration of the public health emergency declared in response to the 2009 H1N1 influenza pandemic." As noted earlier, a declaration of public health emergency, pursuant to Section 319 of the PHSA, was already in effect.

Section 1135 of the Social Security Act was enacted in the Public Health Security and Bioterrorism Preparedness and Response Act of 2002 (P.L. 107-188). Under this provision, the Secretary may, among other things, waive sanctions under the Emergency Medical Treatment and Active Labor Act (EMTALA) for certain transfers or redirections of patients away from hospital emergency rooms, allowing hospitals to perform triage and direct patients with flu symptoms to alternate facilities set up for that purpose.[26] The Secretary may also

---

[24] HHS, "Renewal of Determination that a Public Health Emergency Exists," July 24, 2009, http://www.flu.gov/professional/federal/h1n1emergency072409.html; and October 1, 2009, http://www.flu.gov/professional/federal/h1n1emergency100109.html.

[25] See "Section 1135 Waivers or Modifications" in CRS Report R40560, *The 2009 Influenza Pandemic: Selected Legal Issues*, coordinated by Kathleen S. Swendiman and Nancy Lee Jones.

[26] 42 U.S.C. § 1320b-5(b)(3). During a flu pandemic, patients can be relocated pursuant to a state's pandemic preparedness plan, if one exists. 42 U.S.C. § 1320b-5(b)(3)(B)(ii). For more information on EMTALA's requirements, see CRS Report RS22738, *EMTALA: Access to Emergency Medical Care*, by Edward C. Liu.

waive sanctions and penalties for violations of the HIPAA Privacy Rule in order to facilitate medical recordkeeping when such alternate facilities are used.[27] On October 27, the Secretary of HHS implemented the 1135 waivers, which are administered by the HHS Centers for Medicare and Medicaid Services (CMS).[28]

Waivers under Section 1135 may be applied by the Secretary to any geographic emergency area subject to the concurrent declarations.[29] Waivers have been implemented several times in recent years, beginning with the response to Hurricane Katrina in 2005, pursuant to concurrent public health emergency and Stafford Act declarations. The H 1N1 pandemic is the first instance in which the National Emergencies Act, rather than the Stafford Act, was used to enable the 1135 waivers. The "Section 1135" waiver authority and other federal emergency management authorities that have been invoked or could be invoked for the response to the H1N1 flu pandemic are depicted in Figure 1.

FDA: Emergency Use Authorizations

If an emerging defense, national security, or public health threat is identified for which no licensed or approved medical product exists, the FFDCA authorizes the FDA Commissioner, under certain conditions, to issue an Emergency Use Authorization (EUA) so that unapproved but potentially helpful countermeasures can be used to protect the public health.[30] Pursuant to authority provided by the public health emergency determination under Section 319 of the PHSA, FDA has issued EUAs to allow emergency use of (1) the antiviral drugs oseltamivir (Tamiflu), zanamivir (Relenza), and peramivir for the treatment or prophylaxis of influenza; (2) disposable respirators for use by the general public; and (3) unapproved diagnostic tests for the new flu strain.[31] Although Tamiflu and Relenza are already approved for use in the United States, the EUAs support federal recommendations to use them in ways not explicitly approved on the product label, such as the use of a product in young children, or beyond a certain duration of a patient's symptoms. Peramivir is an unapproved antiviral drug that can be given intravenously to seriously ill patients (such as patients on ventilators) who are unable to take the oral Tamiflu or inhaled Relenza preparations.

The EUA authority could have been invoked for a pandemic flu vaccine if one had been developed using approaches that are not used in currently licensed products, such as the addition to the vaccine of additives called adjuvants to enhance the immune response. At this time, however, the U.S. government has not purchased H1N1 pandemic vaccines containing adjuvants. All of the government-purchased vaccines have been approved through the routine licensing process used for seasonal flu vaccines. (See the "Pandemic Vaccine Development,

---

[27] 42 U.S.C. § 1320b-5(b)(7).

[28] The waivers and related information are available at CMS "H1N1 Overview," http://www.cms.hhs.gov/H1N1/.

[29] 42 U.S.C. § 1320b-5(b). When the 1135 waivers are available pursuant to a Stafford Act declaration, that declaration typically specifies the counties or other geographic areas in which emergency authorities are in effect. The determinations of both public health emergency and national emergency for the H1N1 pandemic apply nationwide.

[30] See CRS Report R40560, *The 2009 Influenza Pandemic: Selected Legal Issues*, coordinated by Kathleen S. Swendiman and Nancy Lee Jones. See also FDA, *Guidance: Emergency Use Authorization of Medical Products*, July 2007, http://www.fda.gov/RegulatoryInformation/Guidances/ucm125127.htm; and FDA/CDC, online course on Emergency Use Authorization, 2009, http://www.bt.cdc.gov/ training/eua/index.html.

[31] Information is available at FDA, "Emergency Use Authorizations Questions and Answers," http://www.fda.gov/ NewsEvents/PublicHealthFocus/ucm153297.htm; and "Influenza (Flu) Antiviral Drugs and Related Information," http://www.fda.gov/Drugs/DrugSafety/Informationby DrugClass/ucm100228.htm.

Procurement, Production, and Licensing" section of this report.) The Emergency Use Authorization and other federal emergency management authorities that have been invoked or could be invoked for the response to the H1N1 flu pandemic are depicted in Figure 1.

CDC: Disease Surveillance, and Estimates of Illnesses and Deaths

Because illnesses with the novel H1N1 flu have generally been mild, health officials note that the disease may be substantially underreported. Also, health officials in many U.S. states and cities have stopped running confirmatory tests on suspected cases of H1N1 flu, feeling that better use of epidemiology and laboratory resources can be made by monitoring disease spread to new areas, rather than repeatedly confirming its presence in an affected area.[32]

To get a clearer picture of the spread of H1N1 influenza in the United States, CDC has continued using its multi-layered surveillance system for seasonal flu (which is normally suspended each year in the spring), to which it has added an additional surveillance component to better track the pandemic. (See box below.) On August 30, CDC began accepting reports from states of all influenza- and pneumonia-associated hospitalizations and deaths for the 2009-2010 season. This component tracks both laboratory-confirmed cases of influenza and "syndromic" reports (i.e., cases coded as having pneumonia or influenza whether or not they were laboratory-confirmed as having influenza). Reporting only laboratory-confirmed cases underestimates the burden of illness due to influenza. (Even when testing is done, the test methods have a significant false- negative rate, meaning that the test is negative even though the patient is infected.) In contrast, syndromic reporting captures some cases of pneumonia that are due to causes other than influenza. As CDC notes, although each measure is imperfect, tracking each one nonetheless provides useful information about trends in the spread of the pandemic, and the burdens experienced by the health care system in responding to it.

According to CDC, "Routine seasonal surveillance does not count individual flu cases, hospitalizations or deaths (except for pediatric influenza deaths) but instead monitors activity levels and trends and virus characteristics through a nationwide surveillance system."[33] Except for pediatric deaths, the surveillance mechanisms currently available do not provide health officials with an accurate count of deaths attributable to the pandemic. Instead, officials derive estimates from a number of available sources of information, and these estimates are generally considered to reflect mortality more accurately than do "case counts." On November 12, CDC published a comprehensive estimate of the burden of illness caused by the H1N1 pandemic in the United States, stating that between April, when the novel flu strain was first identified, and October 17, there were between 14 million and 34 million cases of H1N1 infection; between 63,000 and 153,000 H1N1 -related hospitalizations; and between 2,500 and 6,000 H1N1 -related deaths in the United States.[34] CDC says it plans to update these estimates every three to four weeks.

---

[32] This approach should not affect medical care. Clinicians are advised to provide care, including treatment with antiviral drugs, based on the severity of a patient's symptoms, the presence of conditions that would place a patient at greater risk of severe infection, and other clinical considerations. It is not necessary that H1N1 flu be confirmed in order for appropriate treatment to be provided.

[33] CDC, "Reporting of Influenza and Pneumonia-Associated Hospitalizations and Deaths for the 2009-20 10 Season," September 11, 2009, http://www.cdc.gov/h1n1flu/reportingqa.htm#surveillancesystems.

[34] CDC, "CDC Estimates of 2009 H1N1 Influenza Cases, Hospitalizations and Deaths in the United States, April – October 17, 2009," November 12, 2009, http://www.cdc.gov/h1n1flu/estimates_2009_h1n1.htm.

CDC's Influenza Surveillance Activities

Regular surveillance components used during each annual flu season:

- Viral surveillance, which monitors the percentage of specimens tested for flu that are positive; the types and subtypes of flu viruses circulating; resistance to antiviral medications; and the emergence of new flu strains.
- Selected physician surveillance for influenza-like illness (ILI), which monitors the percentage of visits for symptoms that could be the flu.
- Hospitalization surveillance, which tracks numbers of hospitalizations with laboratory-confirmed flu infections among adults and children.
- Summary of the geographic spread of flu, which tracks the number of states affected by flu, and the degree to which they are affected.
- Deaths from 122 cities that report the total number of deaths and the percentage of those that are coded as influenza or pneumonia.
- The number of laboratory-confirmed deaths from flu among children.

Added surveillance component for the H1N1 flu pandemic:

- Reports by states of either laboratory-confirmed hospitalizations and deaths from flu, or syndromic cases, i.e. cases of presumed influenza and/or pneumonia based on ICD-9 coded hospitalizations or death reports.

Source: Adapted from CDC, "Reporting of Influenza and Pneumonia-Associated Hospitalizations and Deaths for the 2009-2010 Season," September 11, 2009, http://www.cdc.gov/h1n1flu/ reportingqa.htm# surveillance systems.

CDC's surveillance systems showed that during the week ending November 7, 2009, all of the typed flu viruses reported nationwide were the H1N1 pandemic strain. Thirty-five influenza- associated pediatric deaths were reported, the highest weekly total since the pandemic began. Almost all of the flu viruses tested were sensitive to the antiviral drug Tamiflu. Forty-six states reported widespread influenza activity. Indicators in some regions of the country showed evidence of increasing transmission of the virus, while indicators in some other regions showed declines from previous weeks.[35]

VACCINES AND PANDEMIC INFLUENZA

The 2009 H1N1 Pandemic Vaccine Program

In September, the FDA licensed four vaccines against the H1N1 pandemic flu strain. (A fifth vaccine was licensed in November.) As vaccine became available in early October, federal, state, and local health officials began a voluntary nationwide vaccination campaign, which some have said is the most extensive such effort ever undertaken in the United States.

---

[35] Information in this section is drawn from CDC, "FluView," http://www.cdc.gov/flu/weekly/.

This section discusses the production of the H1N1 pandemic vaccines, various activities involved in conducting the pandemic vaccination program, and associated issues.

Overview

Vaccination is considered the best preventive measure against influenza. But, because of continuous changes in the genes of flu viruses, vaccines must be "matched" to strains in circulation to provoke good immunity, and new vaccines must be developed for each year's flu season.

In the United States, all currently licensed seasonal flu vaccines are produced using a time-consuming process involving specially raised, fertilized hen's eggs. First, the virus is adapted for mass production and suitability for use in a vaccine. (The adapted virus is called a "seed" virus.) Next, the seed virus is grown in the eggs in large amounts. Next, small amounts of finished vaccine are produced for use in clinical trials. Finally, if trials demonstrate that the vaccine is safe and effective, then finished vaccine is mass produced.[36] Production capacity is finite, so vaccine becomes available in batches. To develop vaccine for a typical Northern Hemisphere flu season, three flu strains are selected in January or February of each year (based on strains circulating in the Southern Hemisphere). Vaccine is produced and becomes available over the next six to nine months, typically from September through December of each year, before the peak of each flu season. Adapting and growing the virus can take variable amounts of time, and different flu strains "behave" differently during this process. In the best case, all of the steps described above take at least four months. More typically, at least six months is required.

Because flu vaccines cannot be produced until the strains they would protect against are in circulation, it was essential, when the H1N1 pandemic was first recognized in late April, to begin development of a vaccine immediately. Although the new flu strain caused illnesses and deaths across the United States from the time it first emerged, it would be months before any vaccine made using current production methods would be available to protect against it.

Recent U.S. pandemic planning efforts have focused on (1) expanding domestic capacity to mass- produce flu vaccine in the near term; (2) developing approaches to speed up and "stretch" existing production capacity, such as through the use of *adjuvants,* vaccine additives that boost the immune response so that a lower virus dose is effective;[37] and (3) developing better approaches for flu vaccine production in the future. Although recent progress has been made to improve domestic production capacity, the vaccines developed for use in the United States against the H1N1 pandemic strain use the egg-based process, with its significant lag time.

---

[36] See, for example, the figure by Sanofi Pasteur (a flu vaccine manufacturer), "A(H1N1) Vaccine Production Process," May 2009, http://www.vaccineplace.com/docs/H1N1productionprocess.pdf. A comparable figure showing the process for production of seasonal flu vaccine is at http://www.vaccineplace.com/docs/Seasonalfluproductionprocess.pdf. For additional information about flu vaccine development and manufacturing, see Congressional Budget Office, *U.S. Policy Regarding Pandemic-Influenza Vaccines*, September 2008, https://www.cbo.gov/ftpdocs/95xx/doc9573/09-15- PandemicFlu.pdf.

[37] For more information about the use of adjuvants, including safety concerns and possible effects on the global supply of pandemic flu vaccine, see Declan Butler, "Regulators Face Tough Flu-jab Choices," *Nature News*, July 21, 2009, http://www.nature.com/news/2009/090721/full/460446a.html.

Pandemic Vaccine Development, Procurement, Production, and Licensing

This section discusses influenza vaccine development, procurement, production, and licensing for the H1N1 pandemic. Issues related to improving future influenza vaccine production capacity are discussed in a later section of this report, "Ways to Improve Influenza Vaccine Production in the Future."

Federal officials have said that there are three key decision points in developing and using pandemic flu vaccines: (1) to develop adapted "seed" viruses and a prototype vaccine(s), and to conduct clinical trials; (2) to purchase and mass-produce large amounts of a promising vaccine; and (3) to administer the vaccine widely, that is, to conduct a mass-vaccination campaign. These decision points are presented in a timeline of the U.S. pandemic flu vaccine strategy in Figure 2. The figure also shows that a second wave of heightened transmission of H 1N1 flu in the United States in the fall could precede the peak of seasonal flu activity and the initial availability of pandemic vaccine. Finally, the figure shows the overlap between the production of seasonal flu vaccine for the Northern Hemisphere and production of H1N1 pandemic vaccine.

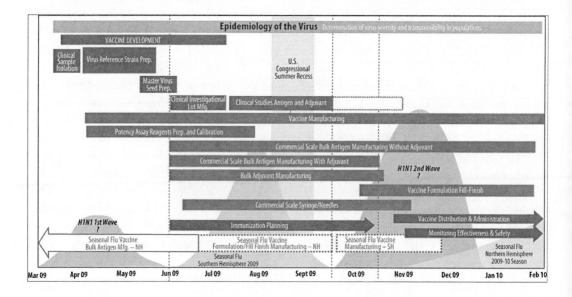

Source: Adapted by CRS from background material provided for a meeting of the National Biodefense Science Board (administered by HHS) regarding the U.S. 2009 H 1N 1 vaccine strategy, May 22, 2009, http://www.hhs.gov/aspr/conferences/nbsb/090522-nbsb-meeting.html.

Figure 2. Timeline for H1N1 Pandemic Vaccine Development, Manufacturing, and Possible Distribution and Administration.

Over the spring and summer, HHS issued purchase orders for H1N1 pandemic vaccine, based on existing contracts with producers of seasonal flu vaccines that are currently licensed in the United States.[38] Development and procurement efforts are led by the HHS Biomedical Advanced Research and Development Authority (BARDA), in coordination with the National Institutes of Health (NIH), FDA, CDC, and other HHS agencies.

The NIH National Institute of Allergy and Infectious Diseases (NIAID) is responsible for coordinating clinical trials to determine safety, effectiveness, and optimum dosing for the H1N1 pandemic vaccine.[39] Trials conducted in late summer on healthy adults yielded favorable results. First, the same dose of virus that is used in seasonal flu vaccines was protective when used for the pandemic vaccine. Second, one pandemic vaccine provided protection in adults; a "booster" would not be needed. Third, no serious safety concerns were noted. As a result, large numbers of pandemic vaccines could be produced with existing capacity. Also, adjuvants would not be used, which meant that pandemic vaccines could be evaluated for licensing through the usual process for seasonal flu vaccines; namely, as amendments to the existing product licenses. Emergency Use Authorizations would not be necessary. (See the prior section, "FDA: Emergency Use Authorizations," for more information about this authority.) H1N1 vaccine clinical trials on children, pregnant women, and individuals with HIV are also underway or have been completed. Finally, NIAID has begun clinical trials on H1N1 vaccines containing adjuvant. Officials have said that although they do not think that adjuvanted vaccine will be needed for the domestic pandemic vaccination program, it could be useful to have the option to use adjuvanted vaccine if the virus mutates to a different form (potentially rendering the non-adjuvanted vaccines less effective). They have also said that research on adjuvants contributes to the knowledge base to improve influenza vaccine production in general.

On September 16, FDA announced that it had approved H1N1 pandemic flu vaccines made by four companies: Sanofi Pasteur Inc., CSL Limited, Novartis Vaccines and Diagnostics Limited, and MedImmune LLC.[40] On November 10, FDA approved a fifth pandemic vaccine made by ID Biomedical Corporation of Quebec, a subsidiary of GlaxoSmithKline. The Medimmune product is an intranasal vaccine. The other four products are injectable vaccines. The approved uses of each product vary somewhat. In general, for the injectable vaccines, healthy adults should receive one dose, and children aged six months to nine years of age should receive two, in order to raise protective immunity. None of the products is approved for use in infants under six months of age. The approved uses for the intranasal vaccine are more narrow than for the injectable products. In general, the intranasal vaccine is approved for use in healthy individuals aged 2 to 49 years. None of the products

---

[38] See HHS, "HHS Takes Additional Steps Toward Development of Vaccine for the Novel Influenza A (H1N1)," press release, May 22, 2009; and HHS, "HHS Purchases Additional H1N1 Vaccine Ingredients," press release, July 13, 2009, (each at http://www.hhs.gov/news/). See, also, HHS, Biomedical Advanced Research and Development Authority (BARDA), "H1N1 Vaccines," http://www.hhs.gov/aspr/barda/index.html.

[39] Information in this paragraph is drawn from NIH, National Institute of Allergy and Infectious Diseases (NIAID): "H1N1 Clinical Studies" at http://www3.niaid.nih.gov/topics/Flu/; and news releases at http://www3.niaid.nih.gov/ news/newsreleases/.

[40] FDA, "Vaccines Approved for H1N1 Influenza Virus," press release, September 15, 2009, http://www.fda.gov/ NewsEvents/Newsroom. See also FDA, "Influenza A (H1N1) 2009 Monovalent," which includes questions and answers and other information about all of the licensed pandemic vaccines, http://www.fda.gov/ BiologicsBloodVaccines/Vaccines/ApprovedProducts/ucm1 8 1950.htm.

contains an adjuvant. The injectable products are available in both multi-dose vials containing a preservative, and in single-dose syringes without a preservative.[41]

Vaccine Financing[42]

Congress provided up to $7.65 billion in FY2009 supplemental appropriations to HHS for the pandemic response, part of which has been used to support the purchase of vaccine and associated costs of planning and carrying out a nationwide vaccination campaign. (See the subsequent section "Emergency Supplemental Appropriations for FY2009.") There are two types of costs associated with furnishing vaccinations to individuals: the costs of the vaccine and associated supplies, and the costs for administration of the vaccine, which typically include the value of a provider's time, costs for refrigerated storage and recordkeeping, and related costs.

According to CDC, all pandemic flu vaccines and necessary supplies—syringes, needles, sharps containers, and alcohol swabs—have been purchased by the federal government and are being made available to vaccinators across the country at no cost. In no case may a provider or insurer charge individuals for these costs. Plans for payment of administration costs vary. Medicare, the Department of Veterans Affairs, and many private insurers have said they will cover the costs of administration for seasonal flu vaccine and one or more pandemic vaccines. Private providers (including physicians and chain pharmacies) may charge appropriate fees for the costs of administration if public or private insurance is not available, or they may waive these fees. States are expected to use a portion of the federal funds they received for pandemic planning to support clinics at which individuals who are uninsured can be vaccinated without charge. Also, Federally Qualified Health Centers are expected to provide services, including vaccination for pandemic flu, regardless of ability to pay.

Vaccine Distribution[43]

Federal officials are working with state and local health officials to implement a "blended" public- and private-sector distribution approach to provide pandemic vaccines to any individuals who want to be vaccinated. During each flu season, much of the vaccine is purchased and delivered through private-sector distributors and providers. For the response to unanticipated threats such as bioterrorism, CDC maintains the Strategic National Stockpile (SNS) of drugs and medical supplies, and provides training and technical assistance to state and local health officials, who are responsible for distribution of stockpile materiel within their jurisdictions. Under the Vaccines for Children program, CDC distributes recommended pediatric vaccines (financed by the Medicaid program) to private providers for administration to eligible low-income children. The blended approach being used for the pandemic

---

[41] In the United States, seasonal flu vaccine is produced in multi-dose vials containing the preservative thimerosal, and in preservative-free single dose syringes. Thimerosal contains mercury. According to CDC, there is no convincing scientific evidence of harm caused by thimerosal in vaccines, but in 1999, the CDC, other federal agencies, the American Academy of Pediatrics, and vaccine manufacturers agreed that thimerosal should be reduced or eliminated in vaccines as a precautionary measure. As is the case for seasonal flu vaccine, a portion of the pandemic vaccine is being produced without preservatives for use in children and pregnant women. See CDC, "Mercury and Vaccines (Thimerosal)," http://www.cdc.gov/vaccinesafety/updates/thimerosal.htm.

[42] Information in this paragraph is drawn from CDC, "Questions and Answers on 2009 H1N1 Vaccine Financing," October 7, 2009, http://www.cdc.gov/H1N1flu/vaccination/statelocal/vaccinefinancing.htm.

[43] Unless otherwise noted, information in this paragraph is drawn from CDC, "H1N1 Flu Vaccination Resources," http://www.cdc.gov/h1n1flu/vaccination/.

vaccination campaign uses portions of each of these mechanisms to make vaccine available to a variety of public- and private-sector providers and clinics. To distribute vaccine as it becomes available, CDC has contracted with McKesson Corporation, the agency's contractor for distribution under the Vaccines for Children program.[44]

In early October, limited amounts of the approved intranasal H1N1 pandemic vaccine became available and were provided to states according to their populations. Available amounts were less than expected, posing problems for many states and localities, which had planned to conduct or coordinate vaccination clinics based on projected vaccine availability.[45] In August, CDC reported expecting "... somewhere between 45 million and 52 million doses of vaccine to be available by mid-October. This will be followed by weekly availability of vaccine up to about 195 million doses by the end of the year."[46] In mid-October, CDC reported that only 11.4 million doses of the injectable H1N1 vaccine were available.[47] CDC said that manufacturers were experiencing several problems that affected production volume, including slower than expected growth of the virus in eggs.

Despite high demand for the vaccine, some states appear to have had difficulty getting available vaccine into distribution in their jurisdictions. The distribution plan calls on states to "order" vaccine from their allotments when they are ready to direct how it is to be distributed within the state. HHS publishes daily updates of the total (national) amounts of vaccine *allocated* (i.e., available to states), *ordered* by states, and actually *shipped*, as well as daily updates of the number of vaccines shipped to each state.[48] Because vaccine is allocated to states according to population, calculating the number of vaccines shipped to each state according to its population should yield similar ratios if the states are similar in their efficiency at ordering and directing the distribution of vaccine within their jurisdictions. However, a news organization has published such an analysis and found considerable variation among the states.[49]

Despite some statements to the contrary, the civilian vaccination program for the H1N1 pandemic is voluntary. There have been no plans at the federal, state, or local level to require that members of the general public be vaccinated. However, requirements have been established by the Department of Defense, and by some states and private health systems, for the vaccination of health care workers. Public health officials recommend that health care workers be vaccinated against influenza (including pandemic flu) not only for their own protection, but also in order to protect patients from infection by their providers, and to

---

[44] Robert Roos, "States to Designate Providers to Give H1N1 Vaccines," *CIDRAP News* (Center for Infectious Disease Research and Policy), August 10, 2009, http://www.cidrap.umn.edu/cidrap/content/influenza/swineflu/news/index.html.

[45] See for example testimony of Dr. Donald Williamson, Alabama Department of Public Health, and Mr. Rob Fulton, St. Paul Ramsey County, Minnesota, Department of Public Health, at a briefing of the House Appropriations Subcommittee on Labor, Health and Human Services, Education, and Related Agencies, November 4, 2009, http://appropriations.house.gov/Subcommittees/sub_lhhse.shtml.

[46] Comments of Dr. Jay Butler, Director of CDC's H1N1 Vaccine Task Force, transcript of CDC/FDA media briefing, August 21, 2009, http://www.cdc.gov/media/.

[47] Comments of Dr. Anne Schuchat, Director of CDC's National Center for Immunization and Respiratory Diseases, transcript of CDC media briefing, October 16, 2009, http://www.cdc.gov/media/. Although doses of the FluMist intranasal product were also available, that product could not be used in some of the prioritized high-risk groups such as pregnant women and those with chronic diseases.

[48] HHS, "2009 H1N1 Influenza Vaccine Supply Status," http://www.flu.gov/individualfamily/vaccination/supply.html.

[49] Rebecca Ruiz, "Behind The H1N1 Vaccine Shortage," *Forbes*, October 30, 2009, and accompanying chart, "States With the Most and Least H1N1 Vaccine per 1,000 Residents," updated periodically.

prevent levels of absenteeism among providers that could threaten the quality of patient care.[50]

Allocation to Priority Groups[51]

CDC advises that anyone who wishes to be vaccinated for seasonal and/or pandemic influenza should seek the vaccine(s) when adequate supplies are available. Certain groups are especially advised to be vaccinated due to their risk of more serious complications from influenza, the risk that they would transmit influenza to others, or both. These groups, identified by the Advisory Committee on Immunization Practices (ACIP, which advises the CDC Director), are

- pregnant women;
- persons who live with or provide care for infants aged less than 6 months (e.g., parents, siblings, and daycare providers), because these infants cannot receive the vaccine;
- health-care and emergency medical services personnel;
- persons aged 6 months-24 years; and
- persons aged 25-64 years who have medical conditions that put them at higher risk for influenza-related complications.[52]

ACIP estimated that the five groups above comprise about 159 million persons in the United States.

Because the H1N1 pandemic vaccine is becoming available in phases, initial demand has exceeded supply. Anticipating this, ACIP also identified a subset of these groups that should be given priority when vaccine supplies are limited. These priority groups are

- pregnant women (as above);
- persons who live with or provide care for infants aged less than 6 months (as above);
- health-care and emergency medical services personnel who have direct contact with patients or infectious material (a subset of the recommended group above);
- children aged 6 months-4 years (only the youngest children); and
- children and adolescents aged 5-18 years who have medical conditions that put them at higher risk for influenza-related complications (only children with medical conditions, versus all persons under age 65 with medical conditions).[53]

ACIP estimated that this subset of priority groups comprises about 42 million persons in the United States.

---

[50] For information about public health recommendations for flu vaccination among health care workers, see CDC, "2009 H1N1 Vaccination Recommendations," http://www.cdc.gov/h1n1flu/vaccination/acip.htm. For information about the legal basis for mandatory vaccines, see CRS Report R40560, *The 2009 Influenza Pandemic: Selected Legal Issues*, coordinated by Kathleen S. Swendiman and Nancy Lee Jones; and CRS Report RS2 1414, *Mandatory Vaccinations: Precedent and Current Laws*, by Kathleen S. Swendiman.

[51] Unless otherwise noted, information in this paragraph is drawn from CDC, "H1N1 Flu Vaccination Resources," http://www.cdc.gov/h1n1flu/vaccination/.

[52] CDC, "Use of Influenza A (H1N1) 2009 Monovalent Vaccine: Recommendations of the Advisory Committee on Immunization Practices (ACIP), 2009," *MMWR,* vol. 58, August 21, 2009, http://www.cdc.gov/mmwr.

[53] Ibid.

Available vaccine may be either the injectable or intranasal formulation. In general, injectable H1N1 vaccine may be given to anyone in one of the priority groups who does not have a specific contraindication (such as an allergy to eggs). However, the intranasal vaccine is not licensed for use in some individuals within the pandemic priority groups. Prioritized individuals who should not receive the intranasal vaccine include pregnant women, children younger than two years of age, individuals of any age who have chronic illnesses, and health care workers who care for severely immune ocompromised patients, such as those who have recently undergone bone marrow transplantation. Although federal authorities provide guidance on vaccine allocation, final allocation decisions, and any enforcement of them, is made at the state and local levels.[54]

Adverse Event Monitoring[55]

Although clinical trials were conducted on the approved H1N1 pandemic vaccines and did not show any serious adverse events (i.e., side effects), rare adverse events would not necessarily manifest until a product was widely used. Health officials plan to monitor for any possible adverse events among persons who receive the H1N1 pandemic vaccine, using, among other approaches, the existing Vaccine Adverse Event Reporting System (VAERS), a national vaccine safety surveillance program co-sponsored by CDC and FDA. VAERS accepts reports from patients, providers, public health officials, and others through a website and toll-free number.[56]

In 1976, a U.S. vaccination campaign was carried out for a pandemic flu threat that did not materialize (also called "Swine Flu"). However, evidence suggested that among those vaccinated, there may have been an increased risk of a serious and sometimes fatal neurologic side effect, a form of paralysis called Guillain-Barre Syndrome (GBS). The vaccination campaign was called off, and the credibility of public health officials was significantly compromised by the incident.[57]

Liability and Compensation

On June 25, HHS Secretary Kathleen Sebelius issued a declaration under the Public Readiness and Emergency Preparedness Act (PREP Act, Division C of P.L. 109-148) regarding the H1N1 pandemic vaccine.[58] The PREP Act waives liability and establishes an injury compensation program for the use of certain "covered countermeasures." The June 25 declaration eliminates liability (with the exception of willful misconduct) for the United States, and for manufacturers, distributors, program planners, persons who prescribe, and employees of any of the above, who administer or dispense an H1N1 pandemic vaccine that qualifies as a "covered countermeasure" under conditions specified by the Secretary in the

---

[54] For a discussion of applicable state activities during the seasonal flu vaccine shortage of 2004-2005, see "Vaccine Rationing" in CRS Report RL32655, *Influenza Vaccine Shortages and Implications*, by Sarah A. Lister and Erin D. Williams.

[55] Unless otherwise noted, information in this section is drawn from CDC, "Vaccine Safety," http://www.cdc.gov/h1n1 flu/vaccination/vaccine _safety.htm.

[56] See http://vaers.hhs.gov/index.

[57] For more information, see Richard Neustadt and Harvey Fineberg, *The Swine Flu Affair: Decision-Making on a Slippery Disease* (U.S. Department of Health, Education, and Welfare, 1978), reprinted electronic edition at http://www.iom.edu/?id=65926.

[58] Department of Health and Human Services, Office of the Secretary, "Pandemic Influenza Vaccines–Amendment," 74 *Federal Register* 30294-3 0297, June 25, 2009.

declaration.[59] Under the law, claims under state law are preempted. As noted in Figure 1, authorities under the PREP Act are independent from other emergency authorities that have been invoked for the response to the H1N1 pandemic.[60]

In addition to the limitation of liability, the PREP Act declaration also establishes a federal program to compensate individuals who are vaccinated for any serious injuries or death that occurs as a result of the H1N1 vaccine, and authority for a fund to pay claims. The compensation program is administered by the HHS Health Resources and Services Administration (HRSA), using the Smallpox Vaccine Injury Compensation Program as an administrative model.[61] The fund, called the Covered Countermeasure Process Fund (CCPF), did not have a balance of funds when the H1N1 pandemic began. However, in providing emergency supplemental funding for pandemic preparedness (P.L. 111-32), Congress authorized the use of an unspecified amount of the appropriation for the CCPF.[62] On July 16, President Obama requested additional contingent funding under the new law, to be used for several activities, including funding for the CCPF.[63]

Ways to Improve Influenza Vaccine Production in the Future

Strengths and Limitations of Egg-Based Technology

In its 2005 strategy for influenza pandemic preparedness, the George W. Bush Administration set a goal to "establish domestic production capacity to ensure ... [s]ufficient vaccine to vaccinate the entire U.S. population within six months of the emergence of a virus with pandemic potential."[64] Because a flu pandemic could emerge at any time, federal officials saw this as a multi-pronged strategy, requiring concurrent investments in the expansion of production capacity using current approaches, and in the development of new approaches.

In January 2009, when announcing federal funding for a new private facility to manufacture cell- based influenza vaccine, an HHS official said that the strategic goal above " ... could not be accomplished using the traditional egg-based method of producing flu vaccine."[65] Nonetheless, significant federal investments were made to expand production

---

[59] For more information, see CRS Report RS22327, *Pandemic Flu and Medical Biodefense Countermeasure Liability Limitation*, by Henry Cohen and Vanessa K. Burrows, and "The Public Readiness and Emergency Preparedness Act (PREP Act)" in CRS Report R40560, *The 2009 Influenza Pandemic: Selected Legal Issues*, coordinated by Kathleen S. Swendiman and Nancy Lee Jones.

[60] In addition to liability waivers and compensation available for injuries related to the use of H1N1 pandemic vaccine, the PREP Act has also been invoked for the use of pandemic antiviral drugs, diagnostic tests, and protective equipment, as well as for the use of countermeasures for other threats such as anthrax and smallpox. See HRSA, "Countermeasures Injury Compensation Program: Covered Countermeasures," http://www.hrsa.gov/countermeasurescomp/ countermeasures.htm.

[61] Health Resources and Services Administration, "Preparedness Countermeasures Injury Compensation," http://www.hrsa.gov/countermeasurescomp/default.htm.

[62] H.Rept. 111-151, to accompany H.R. 2346, making supplemental appropriations for FY2009, June 12, 2009, pp. 114-115.

[63] The White House, Text of a Letter from the President to the Speaker of the House of Representatives, July 16, 2009, http://www.whitehouse.gov/the_press_office/Letter-from-the-President-regarding-H1N1/.

[64] Homeland Security Council, "National Strategy for Pandemic Influenza," November, 2005, p. 5, http://www.flu.gov/ professional/federal/index.html#national.

[65] HHS, "HHS Awards $487 Million Contract to Build First U.S. Manufacturing Facility for Cell-Based Influenza Vaccine," comments of Dr. Robin Robinson, Director of BARDA, press release, January 15, 2009, http://www.hhs.gov/news/.

capacity for egg-based vaccine in the event that a flu pandemic arose in the near term. Although concerns were largely driven at the time by the spread of H5N1 avian flu, it was the surprising emergence of H1N1 pandemic flu that proved to be the test of the federal strategy.

Investments to date have had mixed results. The United States has ordered H1N1 pandemic vaccine sufficient to provide 250 million doses, representing substantially greater total capacity than was available only several years ago. Yet the lag time inherent in egg-based vaccine technology is unavoidable, and its effects are stark as the H1N1 pandemic unfolds in a largely unimmunized population. Several observers have suggested that peak nationwide transmission of the virus will have occurred before substantial amounts of vaccine are available.[66]

Some have suggested that even though the lag time to first vaccine availability was unavoidable, there could have been more investment or better planning for the use of egg-based vaccine to avoid the shortage that persists more than a month into the vaccination campaign. For example, some assert that the decision to forgo the use of adjuvants in the pandemic vaccine was made when officials were more optimistic about a timely roll-out of the product, and that more vaccine doses would now be available if adjuvant had been used. However, there are no adjuvant- containing seasonal flu vaccines currently licensed in the United States, so the use of this approach for the pandemic would have required Emergency Use Authorization of the vaccine, which could well have delayed its availability. The use of adjuvants and an emergency licensing process could also have contributed to apprehensions among the public about the vaccine's safety.

Strengths and Limitations of Cell-Based Technology

Other observers assert that greater investment in cell-based (rather than egg-based) vaccine technology could potentially have made that approach viable for the response to the H1N1 pandemic, and that the current vaccination program could have been farther along in that case. In the cell-based approach, the influenza virus is grown in one of a number of types of cells, which are generally easier to manage on the industrial scale than is growth in eggs. The European Medicines Agency (EMEA) licensed a cell-based seasonal influenza vaccine, Optaflu, in 2007, and has also licensed a cell-based H1N1 pandemic vaccine, Celvapan.[67]

However, an HHS official, among others, has noted that cell-based approaches to the production of influenza vaccine are not likely to substantially shorten the time to first vaccine availability, compared with egg-based production, because the process still requires growing whole influenza virus in the cells.[68] Rather, the advantage of cell-based over egg-based production in the near term is one of scalability, or "throughput" (i.e., once virus is grown, vaccines can be finished in large quantities quickly, making hundreds of millions of doses available within weeks rather than months from the time the first batches become available). With egg-based approaches, the dependence on specially produced fertilized eggs limits this scalability. If cell-based approaches had been available for the response to the H1N1 pandemic, it is possible that more vaccine could have been finished by this point, although it

---

[66] See for example PCAST Report, p. viii.

[67] The EMEA is responsible for the scientific evaluation of applications for authorization for medical products. Authorized products can be marketed in all European Union (EU) and EEA-EFTA states (Iceland, Liechtenstein and Norway). Product information is available at http://www.emea.europa.eu/.

[68] See comments of Anthony Fauci, Director, NIH National Institute of Allergy and Infectious Diseases (NIAID), House Appropriations Subcommittee on Labor, Health and Human Services, Education, and Related Agencies, "Briefing on Federal-State-Local H1N1 Flu Response," Nov. 4, 2009.

still might not have first become available until several months into the pandemic, as was the case with the egg-based vaccines in use.

Recombinant, DNA-Based, and Other Advanced Technologies

Alternative approaches under development for the production of flu vaccine involve technologies that do not require the use of whole viruses (therefore eliminating the need to grow them), but rather focus on producing only those portions (subunits) of the virus that are needed to produce immunity, such as a particular protein in the virus coat. For example, using *recombinant* technology, the genes for the desired virus subunit may be inserted into another microorganism that grows well, such as yeast. The subunit is then replicated by the host microorganism, harvested, purified, and made into a vaccine containing only the subunit, not whole virus. Another recombinant approach places the genes for the desired virus subunit into another virus (called a vector) that introduces the subunit into the body, but does not itself cause disease. More sophisticated approaches to vaccine production involve making *DNA-based* vaccines consisting solely of the viral genes.[69] The "Holy Grail" for the prevention of influenza is the so-called *universal* influenza vaccine, one that could be administered in childhood to protect against whatever variations of seasonal or pandemic flu arise throughout one's lifetime.

Federal Efforts to Improve Influenza Vaccine Technology

All U.S.-licensed seasonal and pandemic flu vaccines are made using the whole virus, egg-based approach. As noted earlier, cell-based whole virus influenza vaccines have been licensed in Europe. Recombinant vaccines that have been licensed for use in the United States include those against hepatitis B and human papillomavirus. There has not yet been a DNA-based vaccine licensed for use in humans in the United States or Europe. Each of these approaches to vaccine production, including the production of influenza vaccine, is also applied in licensed or investigational products for veterinary uses in animals.

The NIH provides federal leadership for basic biomedical research on promising vaccine technologies. A search of the NIH ClinicalTrials.gov database yielded a number of clinical trials—in progress or completed—on influenza vaccine prototypes developed using recombinant techniques. The trials range from Phase I—the earliest stage of investigation involving small numbers of human subjects—to Phase III trials involving large numbers of subjects.[70] In addition, several Phase I trials of DNA-based influenza vaccines were found. In FY2008, NIH reported spending $204 million on influenza research, including a number of projects specifically involving advanced approaches to influenza vaccine production, and research on other aspects of influenza immunology that are applicable to vaccine development.[71] NIH has also sponsored many clinical trials of vaccines against H1N1 pandemic flu, as well as H5N1 avian and other flu strains, for the purposes of licensing and/or

---

[69] Each of the approaches discussed here involve growing or replicating virus subunits in cells of one kind or another at some point in the process. These approaches are "cell-based" in that sense. However, when discussing technologies that are currently available for making flu vaccine, the term "cell-based" usually refers to the process for growing whole influenza virus, to distinguish it from the egg-based process.

[70] For more information on clinical trials, see NIH, "Understanding Clinical Trials," http://clinicaltrials.gov/ct2/info/ understand. FDA generally requires that Phase I through III clinical trials be conducted on medical products to demonstrate safety and effectiveness, in order for a product to be licensed.

[71] NIH, "Estimates of Funding for Various Research, Condition, and Disease Categories," http://report.nih.gov/rcdc/ categories/. The listing for influenza spending for FY2008 links to more than 300 funded projects.

stockpiling these vaccines.[72] Federal leadership for advanced development of emergency medical countermeasures, including pandemic products, is provided by the Biomedical Advanced Research and Development Authority (BARDA), in HHS. Federal investments in the advanced development of flu vaccine technology came principally from FY2006 emergency supplemental funds for pandemic preparedness,[73] and were administered by BARDA. (See the subsequent section "Prior Funding for Pandemic Flu Preparedness.") HHS has published several reports, as required by Congress, detailing the use of these funds. Table 1 presents funding amounts for pandemic vaccine development activities, as reported by HHS in January 2009. The focus of this spending has been on expanding egg-based and cell-based vaccine production capacity, as these approaches were clearly viable to make products that could be licensed for use in the United States.

Along with contracts to purchase vaccine from companies developing these products, HHS funds have also been used to construct or retrofit domestic vaccine production facilities. As noted earlier, the national strategic goal for pandemic preparedness was the establishment of sufficient *domestic* flu vaccine production capacity. To this end, HHS funds were provided to Sanofi Pasteur and Medimmune to expand their domestic facilities for egg-based vaccine production.[74]

Table 1. FY2006 Supplemental Funding for Pandemic Influenza Vaccine Activities Obligations, dollars in millions, as of December 31, 2008

Activity	Amount
Egg-based vaccine capacity and purchases[a]	875.7
Retrofit existing facilities for emergency production[b]	121.0
Accelerate cell-based vaccine[c]	1,707.3
Advanced development of antigen-sparing techniques[d]	155.6
FDA activities[e]	20
SUBTOTAL, obligations for vaccine activities	2879.5
Unobligated funds for vaccine activities	316.5
TOTAL, allocations for vaccine activities	**3,196.0**

Source: Prepared by Congressional Research Service from HHS, Assistant Secretary for Resources and Technology, "Report to Congress: Pandemic Influenza Preparedness Spending," Table, pp. 16-17, January 2009, http://www.hhs.gov/aspr/barda/mcm/panflu/spending.html.

Notes: Numbers do not add due to rounding.

a. Includes funds for contracts with Chiron, GlaxoSmithKline, Novartis, and Sanofi Pasteur for purchase and maintenance of vaccine against H5N 1 avian flu.

b. Includes funds for contracts with Medimmune and Sanofi Pasteur.

c. Includes funds for contracts with Dynport, GlaxoSmithKline, Medimmune, Novartis, and Solvay.

d. Includes funds for several contracts to study use of adjuvants.

e. Includes funds to expand regulatory capacity, including laboratory expansion and supplies, information technology support, program management, and other activities.

---

[72] For more information about NIH research on influenza, see http://www3.niaid.nih.gov/topics/Flu/; and "NIAID Influenza Research: 2009 Progress Report," http://www3.niaid.nih.gov/topics/Flu/PDF/flu Research09.pdf.

[73] FY2009 emergency supplemental appropriations have been used for the immediate response to the H1N1 pandemic, including the development and procurement of H1N1 vaccine produced using eggs.

[74] The Sanofi Pasteur product is an injectable vaccine, produced in Swiftwater, PA. The Medimmune product is the intranasal vaccine, produced in Gaithersburg, MD.

In addition, HHS has awarded a $487 million contract to Novartis Vaccines and Diagnostics, Inc., to build a facility in North Carolina to make cell-based seasonal and pandemic flu vaccine.[75]

In April 2009, before the emergence of the H1N1 pandemic flu strain, BARDA announced an upcoming Request for Proposals (RFP) for advanced development of recombinant influenza vaccine products for both seasonal and pandemic use, which would provide federal funding to advance the commercial development of this technology. In its presolicitation notice, HHS said

> The timeline for the availability of egg- and cell-based inactivated [i.e., whole virus] pandemic influenza vaccines in the U.S. is estimated at 20-23 weeks post-pandemic onset, which may be towards the end of a first pandemic wave. Recombinant influenza vaccines, on the other hand, may benefit from manufacturing efficiencies, may not be dependent on pandemic influenza virus reference strain availability and/or the production and calibration of potency assay reagents needed for inactivated influenza vaccines. As a result, recombinant influenza vaccines may be available in a shorter time frame of 8 to 12 weeks post-pandemic onset. The effect of vaccination combined with influenza antiviral drugs and community mitigation measures may delay the peak incidence of pandemic influenza disease and reduce mortality and morbidity during a severe pandemic.[76]

In response to questions about the RFP above, HHS commented that it intends that successful applicants would pursue approaches applicable to both seasonal and pandemic flu vaccine production. There are obvious advantages to using a tried-and-true approach in an emergency (i.e., basing pandemic flu vaccine production on the approach used to make seasonal flu vaccine). Egg-based seasonal flu vaccine is a safe, inexpensive, and widely accepted product. A possible disadvantage of changing to a different approach is that seasonal flu vaccine could become more costly, at least initially. An HHS official, when asked whether use of cell-based and newer production methods could make seasonal flu vaccine more costly, replied that new technologies were likely to be more expensive initially.[77] Although there has been little public debate about this, an increase in the cost of seasonal flu vaccine could have consequences for public health efforts to expand the utilization of this product.

KEY STATE AND LOCAL PANDEMIC RESPONSE ACTIVITIES

State Pandemic Preparedness and Response

Since FY2002, all states have received HHS funds to prepare their public health and health care systems for public health threats and emergencies.[78] Beginning with FY2004,

---

[75] HHS, "HHS Awards $487 Million Contract to Build First U.S. Manufacturing Facility for Cell-Based Influenza Vaccine," press release, January 15, 2009, http://www.hhs.gov/news.

[76] HHS, BARDA, "Advanced Development of Recombinant Influenza Vaccine Products and Manufacturing Capabilities for Pandemic Preparedness," Solicitation Number HHS-BARDA-09-32, synopsis of presolicitation notice, April 17, 2009, http://www.fbo.gov. The solicitation was issued on July 10, 2009.

[77] See comments of Anthony Fauci, Director, NIH National Institute of Allergy and Infectious Diseases (NIAID), House Appropriations Subcommittee on Labor, Health and Human Services, Education, and Related Agencies, "Briefing on Federal-State-Local H1N1 Flu Response," Nov. 4, 2009.

[78] Funds are provided to the 50 states, DC, the territories, New York City, Chicago, and Los Angeles County.

states were required, as a condition of these funds, to develop plans specifically for the response to a flu pandemic. Subsequently, Congress provided $600 million in FY2006 emergency supplemental appropriations for states to continue their pandemic planning efforts.[79] When the H1N1 flu outbreak emerged, Congress provided an additional $350 million in FY2009 emergency supplemental appropriations for state pandemic response.[80] (See the subsequent section "Emergency Supplemental Appropriations for FY2009.")

Based on an analysis of state pandemic flu plans available as of July 2006, CRS found the plans to be more robust in their discussion of core public health activities such as disease surveillance and laboratory activities, and less robust in aspects of multi-sector preparedness, such as leadership designation, incident management, certain aspects of health care surge planning, and continuity planning for essential services such as food distribution.[81]

In January 2009, HHS and DHS published *Assessment of States' Operating Plans to Combat Pandemic Influenza: Report to Homeland Security Council* (state assessment report), the findings of their comprehensive joint assessment of state pandemic planning through 2008.[82] This assessment echoed the findings of CRS, saying that preparedness was most advanced with respect to objectives that are exclusively or primarily the responsibility of state public health agencies, namely infectious disease surveillance and clinical laboratory operations; distribution of antiviral drugs and vaccines; mass vaccination; and public communications. In contrast, the assessment found that states were having difficulty planning for surges in health care and emergency medical services, and were especially having difficulty planning for continuity of non-health services, such as continuity of state agency operations; coordination of military support to civil authorities; law enforcement continuity; and ensuring the safety of the food supply.

Thus far, dedicated federal funding to state and local governments for pandemic preparedness has been provided only through HHS grants. Noting the challenges states face in assuring preparedness in non-health sectors, the state assessment report comments, "The [U.S. Government] has provided guidance and technical assistance for many of these activities but generally has not been in a position to award funds to help States develop them in the context of pandemic influenza preparedness."[83]

If the pandemic continues to unfold as it has, producing generally mild to moderate illness, the pandemic's effects on non-health sectors such as transportation and public utilities could be minimal. However, despite the high marks for mass vaccination planning received by most states in the state assessment report, considerable public attention has focused on

---

[79] For more information, see the Appendix in CRS Report RL34 190, *Pandemic Influenza: An Analysis of State Preparedness and Response Plans*, by Sarah A. Lister and Holly Stockdale; and CRS Report RS22576, *Pandemic Influenza: Appropriations for Public Health Preparedness and Response*, by Sarah A. Lister.

[80] Award amounts are available at HHS, "States Eligible to Receive $350 Million for H1N1, Seasonal Flu Preparedness Efforts," press release, July 10, 2009, http://www.hhs.gov/news/.

[81] CRS Report RL34 190, *Pandemic Influenza: An Analysis of State Preparedness and Response Plans*, by Sarah A. Lister and Holly Stockdale.

[82] HHS and DHS, *Assessment of States' Operating Plans to Combat Pandemic Influenza: Report to Homeland Security Council,* January, 2009, http://www.pandemicflu.gov/plan/states/index.html. (Hereafter state assessment report).

[83] State assessment report, p. 43.

apparent delays by some states in ordering available vaccine from CDC and promptly distributing it.[84]

Pandemic Preparedness and Response in Schools[85]

When the H1N1 outbreak first began in the United States, some affected communities closed schools when students were found to be infected. Legal authority to close schools rests with state or local officials and is highly variable among the states. A CDC-requested study found that school closure is legally possible in most jurisdictions during both routine and emergency situations.[86] The study also indicated that state authority for closure may be vested at various levels of government and in different departments, generally the state or local education agencies or state or local departments of health.

When the H1N1 pandemic first emerged in the spring, CDC, in consultation with the U.S. Department of Education, issued guidance with respect to school closures (based on earlier guidance from 2007), recommending that "affected communities with laboratory-confirmed cases of influenza A H1N1 consider adopting school dismissal and childcare closure measures, including closing for up to 14 days depending on the extent and severity of illness."[87] School closures are challenging for all parties involved. Among other things, parents must find alternate arrangements for care of their children, educators must adopt alternate means of delivering their services, and children's education may be compromised. On May 5, CDC officials reissued their guidance regarding school closures, recommending against closures based on individual cases of H1N1 flu. It recommended instead that emphasis be placed on keeping sick students and employees home, and that closings be considered if absenteeism was substantial.[88]

As with CDC guidance in general, recommendations regarding school closure are intended to be weighed by local officials in light of local circumstances. In addition to uncertainty about the outbreak's initial severity, there may also have been uncertainty among state and local officials about decision-making protocols. In an assessment of state pandemic flu preparedness conducted by HHS and DHS in 2007 through 2008, planning for student dismissal and school closure was found to be a weakness among the states. More than half of

---

[84] See for example Rebecca Ruiz, "Behind The H1N1 Vaccine Shortage," *Forbes*, October 30, 2009, and accompanying chart, "States With the Most and Least H1N1 Vaccine per 1,000 Residents," updated periodically.

[85] For more information, see "School Closures" in CRS Report R40560, *The 2009 Influenza Pandemic: Selected Legal Issues*, coordinated by Kathleen S. Swendiman and Nancy Lee Jones, and CDC, "Guidance for Child Care Programs, Schools, Colleges and Universities," http://www.cdc.gov/h1n1 flu/guidance/.

[86] James G. Hodge, Jr., Dhrubajyoti Bhattacharya, and Jennifer Gray, "Legal Preparedness for School Closures in Response to Pandemic Influenza and Other Emergencies," http://www.pandemicflu. gov/plan/school/ schoolclosures.pdf.

[87] CDC, "Change in CDC's School and Childcare Closure Guidance," press release, May 5, 2009, http://www.cdc.gov/ media/. See, also, U.S. Department of Education, "H1N1 Flu Information," http://www.ed.gov/admins/lead/safety/ emergencyplan/pandemic/index.html.

[88] CDC, "Update on School (K–12) and Child Care Programs: Interim CDC Guidance in Response to Human Infections with the Novel Influenza A (H1N1) Virus," May 5, 2009 (continually updated), http://www.cdc.gov/h1n1flu/ K12_dismissal.htm.

them were graded as having either "many major gaps" or "inadequate preparedness" for this planning task.[89]

Outbreaks in schools largely subsided over the summer. Transmission of the H1N1 virus reemerged in a number of elementary and secondary schools and in colleges and universities as students returned for the fall. The American College Health Association (ACHA) began tracking voluntary reports of pandemic flu activity at colleges and universities.[90] For the week ending November 6, ACHA saw sustained high levels of nationwide reporting of influenza-like illnesses. Reporting was on the decline in many states, however.

CONGRESSIONAL HEARINGS

Congressional committees in both chambers have convened hearings to assess the emergenc

APPROPRIATIONS AND FUNDING

Public Health Emergency Funding Mechanisms

The Secretary of HHS does not have a dedicated source of funds to support the response to public health emergencies such as the current flu pandemic. Funds available to HHS from prior-year appropriations for pandemic flu could have supported vaccine development and modest procurements, but would not have been adequate for procurements and related activities sufficient to support a mass-vaccination campaign. GAO has noted that the *National Strategy for Pandemic Influenza: Implementation Plan* (2006), which lays out 324 action items for federal agencies to prepare for and respond to a flu pandemic, contains no discussion of the possible costs of these actions, or how they would be financed.[91]

Upon the determination of a public health emergency pursuant to Section 319 of the Public Health Service Act, the Secretary of HHS may access a no-year Public Health Emergency Fund. Such a determination was made with respect to the H1N1 flu outbreak on April 26. (See the earlier section "Determination of a Public Health Emergency.")[92] The fund has not received a recent appropriation and does not have a balance, however, so the Secretary is not currently able to use this funding mechanism for the pandemic response.

---

[89] HHS and DHS, *Assessment of States' Operating Plans to Combat Pandemic Influenza: Report to Homeland Security Council*, "Operating Objective B.4–Enhance State Plans to Enable Community Mitigation through Student Dismissal and School Closure," January 2009, pp. 25-26, http://www.pandemicflu.gov/plan/states/state_assessment.html.

[90] American College Health Association, "Pandemic Influenza Surveillance: Influenza Like Illness (ILI) in Colleges and Universities," http://www.acha.org/ILI_Surveillance.cfm.

[91] U.S. Government Accountability Office, *Influenza Pandemic: Continued Focus on the Nation's Planning and Preparedness Efforts Remains Essential*, GAO-09-760T, June 3, 2009, pp. 10-11, http://www.gao.gov. See also Homeland Security Council, *National Strategy for Pandemic Influenza: Implementation Plan*, May 2006, http://www.pandemicflu.gov/plan/federal/pandemic-influenza-implementation.pdf.

[92] For more information, see "Federal Funding to Support an ESF-8 Response," in CRS Report RL33579, *The Public Health and Medical Response to Disasters: Federal Authority and Funding*, by Sarah A. Lister.

Table 2. Congressional Hearings on the 2009 Influenza Pandemic

Date	Committee (/ Subcommittee)	Topic
SENATE		
Apr. 28, 2009	Appropriations / Labor, HHS, Education, and Related Agencies	The Public Health Response to the Swine Flu Epidemic
Apr. 29, 2009	Health, Education, Labor, and Pensions (HELP)	The Swine Flu Epidemic: The Public Health and Medical Response
Apr. 29, 2009	Homeland Security and Governmental Affairs Committee (HSGAC)	Swine Flu: Coordinating the Federal Response
May 7, 2009	Appropriations / Agriculture, Rural Development, and FDA	Hearing to Discuss the 2009 H1N1 Virus
June 3, 2009	HSGAC / State, Local and Private Sector Preparedness and Integration	Pandemic Flu: Closing the Gaps
June 16, 2009	HSGAC/Oversight of Government Management, the Federal Workforce and District of Columbia	Pandemic Flu Preparedness and the Federal Workforce
Sept. 21, 2009	HSGAC	H1N1 Flu: Protecting Our Community[a]
Oct. 21, 2009	HSGAC	H1N1 Flu: Monitoring the Nation's Response
Nov. 10, 2009	HELP / Children and Families	The Cost of Being Sick: H1N1 and Paid Sick Days
Nov. 17, 2009	HSGAC	H1N1 Flu: Getting the Vaccine to Where It Is Needed Most
HOUSE		
Apr. 30, 2009	Energy and Commerce / Health	Swine Flu Outbreak and the U.S. Federal Response
May 6, 2009	Foreign Affairs / Africa and Global Health	Global Health Emergencies Hit Home: The Swine Flu Outbreak
May 7, 2009	Education and Labor	Ensuring Preparedness Against the Flu Virus at School and Work
May 14, 2009	Oversight and Government Reform / Federal Workforce, Postal Service, and the District of Columbia	Protecting the Protectors: An Assessment of Front-Line Federal Workers in Response to the H1N1 Flu
May 20, 2009	Oversight and Government Reform	State and Local Pandemic Preparedness
July 29, 2009	Homeland Security	Beyond Readiness: An Examination of the Current Status and Future Outlook of the National Response to Pandemic Influenza
Sept. 9, 2009	Small Business	The Challenges of the 2009-H1N1 Influenza and its Potential Impact on Small Businesses and Healthcare Providers
Sept. 15, 2009	Energy and Commerce	Preparing for the 2009 Pandemic Flu

Date	Committee (/ Subcommittee)	Topic
Sept. 29, 2009	Oversight and Government Reform	The Administration's Flu Vaccine Program: Health, Safety, and Distribution
Oct. 27, 2009	Homeland Security / Subcommittee on Emerging Threats, Cybersecurity and Science, and Technology	Real-Time Assessment of the Federal Response to Pandemic Influenza
Nov. 17, 2009	Education and Labor	Protecting Employees, Employers and the Public: H1N1 and Sick Leave Policies
Nov. 18, 2009	Energy and Commerce / joint Health, Oversight and Investigations	H1N1 Preparedness: An Overview of Vaccine Production and Distribution

Source: Compiled by Congressional Research Service.

Notes: Hearings were held in Washington, DC unless otherwise noted. A Member briefing was held by the House Appropriations Subcommittee on Labor, Health and Human Services, Education, and Related Agencies on November 4, 2009, with panelists from HHS, and from state and local health agencies.

a. Field hearing in Hartford, CT.

There has not been a Stafford Act declaration for the current flu pandemic, so disaster relief funds administered by the Federal Emergency Management Agency (FEMA) are not available for response efforts. Many relevant activities may not be eligible for Stafford funds, even if they were available.[93] (See the earlier section, "Applicability of the Stafford Act.")

The Secretary has authority to use a Covered Countermeasure Process Fund to compensate individuals for harm that results from their use of medical countermeasures, as identified in a declaration issued by the HHS Secretary.[94] A declaration was issued for the use of the antiviral drugs Tamiflu and Relenza for a possible pandemic flu virus in October 2008.[95] As noted earlier, a declaration was issued for the use of H1N1 pandemic vaccines in June, 2009.[96] Compensation could be provided for serious physical injuries or deaths resulting from the use of these products in this situation, including for unapproved uses pursuant to an Emergency Use Authorization. (See "FDA: Emergency Use Authorizations.") In FY2009 emergency supplemental funding for pandemic preparedness (P.L. 111-32), Congress authorized the use of an unspecified amount of the appropriation for the Covered Countermeasure Process Fund, and President Obama has sought to use contingent funds provided under the law for this purpose.[97]

---

[93] See "Federal Statutory Authorities for Disaster Response" and "Federal Funding to Support an ESF-8 Response," in CRS Report RL33579, *The Public Health and Medical Response to Disasters: Federal Authority and Funding*, by Sarah A. Lister. See also CRS Report RL34724, *Would an Influenza Pandemic Qualify as a Major Disaster Under the Stafford Act?*, by Edward C. Liu.

[94] CRS Report RS22327, *Pandemic Flu and Medical Biodefense Countermeasure Liability Limitation*, by Henry Cohen and Vanessa K. Burrows. The compensation program is administered by the Health Resources and Services Administration (HRSA) in HHS.

[95] HHS, "Declaration Under the Public Readiness and Emergency Preparedness Act" (notice regarding use of Tamiflu and Relenza), 73 *Federal Register* 61861-61864, October 17, 2008.

[96] HHS, Office of the Secretary, "Pandemic Influenza Vaccines–Amendment," 74 *Federal Register* 30294-30297, June 25, 2009.

[97] H.Rept. 111-151, to accompany H.R. 2346, making supplemental appropriations for FY2009, June 12, 2009, pp. 114-115.

Emergency Supplemental Appropriations for FY2009[98]

In June, the Obama Administration requested $2 billion in FY2009 emergency supplemental appropriations for response to the H1N1 threat, and authority to transfer additional amounts, totaling almost $7 billion, from existing HHS accounts. The Supplemental Appropriations Act, FY2009 (P.L. 111-32), signed on June 24, 2009, provided $1.9 billion in supplemental appropriations immediately,[99] and an additional $5.8 billion contingent upon a presidential request documenting the need for additional funds. Amounts provided are as follows:[100]

- $1.85 billion to the HHS Public Health and Social Services Emergency Fund (PHSSEF), available until expended, including not less than $200 million to CDC for several specified activities, and not less than $350 million for state and local public health response capacity.
- Of the $1.3 billion to HHS not specifically designated, the Secretary may transfer funds to other HHS accounts and to other federal agencies. Also, these funds may be used for purchases for the Strategic National Stockpile (SNS), for construction or renovation of privately owned vaccine production facilities, and for the Covered Countermeasure Process Fund (CCPF).
- An additional contingent emergency appropriation of $5.8 billion to the HHS PHSSEF would become available for obligation 15 days after the President provided a detailed written request to Congress to obligate specific amounts for specific purposes, and only if needed to address the emergency. If such requirements were met, funds could generally be made available and transferred as above, including for purchases for the SNS and the CCPF. However, contingent funds could not be used for construction or renovation of privately owned vaccine production facilities.
- $50 million to the President for the Global Health and Child Survival account to support global efforts to control the spread of the outbreak.
- The conference report provided that if WHO were to announce that the current outbreak had progressed to a flu pandemic (i.e., Phase 6),[101] and upon the President's determination and notification to Congress, available funds in four accounts from prior appropriations acts for the Department of State, Foreign Operations, and Related Programs—Global Health and Child Survival; Development Assistance; Economic Support Fund; and Millennium Challenge Corporation—may be used for pandemic response activities.

President Obama has twice requested portions of the contingent funding, totaling $4.54 1 billion, leaving a balance of $1 .259 billion that the President may request at a later date. On July 16, the President requested $1 .825 billion of the contingent appropriation, to be used for procurement of vaccine adjuvant, immunization campaign planning, FDA regulatory

---

[98] Information in this section is tracked in greater detail in CRS Report R4053 1, *FY2009 Spring Supplemental Appropriations for Overseas Contingency Operations*, coordinated by Stephen Daggett and Susan B. Epstein.

[99] Amount includes $1.85 billion to HHS for the Public Health and Social Services Emergency Fund and $50 million to the President for the Global Health and Child Survival account.

[100] H.Rept. 111-151, pp. 27-28, 34-35, 110, 114-116, 125-126, and 142.

[101] WHO declared the situation to be a flu pandemic, Phase 6, on June 11.

activities, and funding for the CCPF.[102] On September 2, the President requested an additional \$2.7 16 billion of the contingent appropriation, to be used for the Departments of Agriculture, Defense, HHS, State, and Veterans Affairs to support the procurement of vaccine product and supplies, antiviral medications, preparations for a vaccination campaign, and agency preparedness activities.[103]

Prior Funding for Pandemic Flu Preparedness

In the fall of 2005, in the aftermath of Hurricane Katrina, and as H5N1 avian flu was spreading across several continents, Congress provided \$6.1 billion in FY2006 supplemental appropriations for pandemic planning across several federal departments and agencies.[104] Since then, annual funding has been provided to CDC, FDA, and for other activities in HHS to continue work on vaccine development, stockpiling of countermeasures, and assistance to states. In total, from FY2004 through FY2009, HHS has received almost \$13.4 billion for pandemic flu preparedness.[105] (See Table 3.) The U.S. Departments of Agriculture and the Interior have also received annual funding to monitor avian flu in domestic poultry and wild birds, respectively. The U.S. Agency for International Development (USAID) has received funds to assist other countries in managing avian flu transmission to humans, and preparing for a possible pandemic.[106]

In addition to amounts it specifically appropriates, Congress is also interested in how agencies budget for influenza within their existing activities. However, defining such amounts is difficult, for two reasons. First, for many years, domestic public health capacity for infectious disease control has moved away from "categorical" funding and programs (i.e., one disease at a time), and toward the development of flexible capacity that can adapt to new, unanticipated threats. These flexible surveillance systems, laboratory networks, communications platforms, and other capabilities can pivot rapidly to address new threats. But because pandemic planning efforts are tightly woven into the fabric of these flexible capabilities, it is not easy to tease out threads that describe the nation's investment solely for pandemic flu preparedness. Attempt to do so requires making judgments about what is "in" and "out" of scope that are somewhat arbitrary.

Second, for similar reasons, it can be difficult to tease apart investments made for pandemic flu, versus seasonal flu, versus avian or swine flu, versus investments in drug and vaccine development in general. Because different agencies use different methods and assumptions to account for their influenza spending, these amounts are not necessarily

---

[102] The White House, Text of a Letter from the President to the Speaker of the House of Representatives, July 16, 2009, http://www.whitehouse.gov/omb/budget_amendments/.

[103] The White House, Text of a Letter from the President to the Speaker of the House of Representatives, September 2, 2009, http://www.whitehouse.gov/omb/budget_amendments/.

[104] CRS Report RS22576, *Pandemic Influenza: Appropriations for Public Health Preparedness and Response*, by Sarah A. Lister.

[105] This amount includes funds made available through contingent transfer authority as provided in FY2009 supplemental appropriations, discussed in the previous section of this report. This amount excludes funds provided to other federal departments or agencies.

[106] Information can be found in CRS Reports on the applicable appropriations bills, at http://crs.gov/Pages/CLIs.aspx? CLIID=73, and: CRS Report R40239, *Centers for Disease Control and Prevention Global Health Programs: FY2001- FY2010*, by Tiaji Salaam-Blyther.

comparable between agencies, and caution is advised in adding such amounts together as if they were comparable.

HHS has tracked its pandemic influenza funding for the past several fiscal years, using comparable criteria from year to year. These amounts are presented in the department's annual budget requests, in sections designated for pandemic influenza, and are presented in Table 3.

U.S. PANDEMIC INFLUENZA PREPAREDNESS DOCUMENTS

In the George W. Bush Administration, pandemic flu preparedness efforts were coordinated by the Homeland Security Council.[107] Numerous federal and other documents that are specific to preparedness and response for a flu pandemic have been published. Selected documents are listed below. These plans are intended to address a pandemic caused by any so-designated flu strain, but they were written when there was significant global concern about H5N1 avian flu. To date, that flu strain has behaved quite differently from the H1N1 pandemic strain. In particular, the H5N1 strain has not shown the ability to transmit efficiently from person to person, but human infections that result directly from contact with infected poultry have generally been very severe, and there has been a high fatality rate.[108]

Unless otherwise noted, the U.S. pandemic flu plans below can be found on a government-wide pandemic flu website managed by HHS.[109]

- The *National Strategy for Pandemic Influenza,* November 2005, published by the Homeland Security Council, outlines general responsibilities of individuals, industry, state and local governments, and the federal government in preparing for and responding to a pandemic.

- *National Strategy for Pandemic Influenza, Implementation Plan,* May 2006, published by the Homeland Security Council, assigns more than 300 preparedness and response tasks to departments and agencies across the federal government; includes measures of progress and timelines for implementation; provides initial guidance for state, local, and tribal entities, businesses, schools and universities, communities, and non-governmental organizations on the development of institutional plans; provides initial preparedness guidance for individuals and families. One- and two-year implementation status reports have also been published.

- The *HHS Pandemic Influenza Plan,* November 2005, provides guidance to national, state and local policy makers and health departments, outlining key roles and

---

[107] Incident preparedness and response are different functions. At each level of government, they involve different leadership roles, legal authorities, organizational structures, and funding mechanisms. Generally, during an incident, certain conditions must be met before a jurisdiction can implement response activities, or access funds reserved for that purpose. With respect to the current H1N1 pandemic, the U.S. federal government has commenced pandemic flu response activities, under the overall coordination of the Secretary of Homeland Security.

[108] For more information about H5N1 avian flu and related public health concerns, see WHO, *Avian influenza,* http://www.who.int/csr/disease/avian_influenza/en/index.html; WHO, *Confirmed Human Cases of Avian Influenza A(H5N1),* http://www.who.int/csr/disease/avian_influenza/country/en/; and CRS Report RL33 145, *Pandemic Influenza: Domestic Preparedness Efforts,* by Sarah A. Lister (archived).

[109] See http://www.flu.gov/professional/federal/index.html.

responsibilities during a pandemic and specifying preparedness needs and opportunities. This plan emphasizes specific preparedness efforts in the public health and health care sectors.

- The *HHS Pandemic Influenza Implementation Plan, Part I,* November 2006, discusses department-wide activities: disease surveillance; public health interventions; medical response; vaccines, antiviral drugs, diagnostic tests, and personal protective equipment (PPE); communications; and state and local preparedness.

Table 3. HHS Funding for Pandemic Influenza, FY2004-FY2010
(dollars in millions, rounded)

Agency/ Activity	FY 2004	FY 2005	FY 2006[a]	FY 2007	FY 2008	FY 2009 regular[b]	FY2009 supp.[c]	FY 20 10 req.
OS and/or PHSSEF	50	99	5,152	0	75	585	6,391	354
CDC	0	0	400	70	155	156	0	156
FDA	0	0	20	33	35	39	0	39
NIH	0	0	18	35	34	35	0	35
TOTAL, Program Level	50	99	5,590[d]	138	299	815	6,391[c]	584

Source: Compiled by Congressional Research Service from HHS annual "Budget in Brief" documents at http://www.hhs.gov/asrt/ob/docbudget/, unless otherwise noted below.

Notes: OS is Office of the HHS Secretary. PHSSEF is Public Health and Social Services Emergency Fund, an account administered by the Secretary, which Congress has typically used to provide one-time funding for non- routine activities. NIH is the National Institutes of Health.

a. Appropriated in P.L. 109-148, the Department of Defense, Emergency Supplemental Appropriations to Address Hurricanes in the Gulf of Mexico, and Pandemic Influenza Act, 2006, and P.L. 109-234, the Emergency Supplemental Appropriations Act for Defense, the Global War on Terror, and Hurricane Recovery, 2006. Funds are available until expended.

b. Appropriated in P.L. 111-8, the Omnibus Appropriations Act, 2009. Pandemic flu funding was not included in P.L. 111-5, the American Recovery and Reinvestment Act of 2009 (ARRA).

c. Appropriated in P.L. 111-32, the Supplemental Appropriations Act, 2009. The Act provided the Secretary of HHS with $1 .850 billion initially and an additional $5.8 billion contingent upon presidential request and demonstration of need. For more information, see CRS Report R4053 1, *FY2009 Spring Supplemental Appropriations for Overseas Contingency Operations*, coordinated by Stephen Daggett and Susan B. Epstein. Amount includes the initial amount (i.e., $ 1.850 billion) plus $4.54 1 billion in contingent appropriations. (President Obama requested $1.825 billion in contingent appropriations on July 16, and an additional $2.716 billion on September 2. See footnote 102 and footnote 103.)

d. Total does not include $30 million in supplemental funding to HHS that was transferred to the U.S. Agency for International Development (USAID).

- *Interim Pre-pandemic Planning Guidance: Community Strategy for Pandemic Influenza Mitigation in the United States–Early Targeted Layered use of Non-Pharmaceutical Interventions,* February 2007, published by CDC, guidance for "social distancing" strategies to reduce contact between people, with respect to:

closing schools; canceling public gatherings; planning for liberal work leave policies; teleworking strategies; voluntary isolation of cases; and voluntary quarantine of household contacts.

- *Department of Defense Implementation Plan for Pandemic Influenza,* August 2006, provides policy and guidance for the following priorities: (1) force health protection and readiness; (2) the continuity of essential functions and services; (3) Defense support to civil authorities (i.e., federal, state, and local governments); (4) effective communications; and (5) support to international partners.
- *VA Pandemic Influenza Plan*, March 2006, provides policy and instructions for Department of Veterans Affairs (VA) in protecting its staff and the veterans it serves, maintaining operations, cooperating with other organizations, and communicating with stakeholders.
- *Pandemic Influenza Preparedness, Response, and Recovery Guide for Critical Infrastructure and Key Resources*, published by DHS, September 2006, provides business planners with guidance to assure continuity during a pandemic for facilities comprising critical infrastructure sectors (e.g., energy and telecommunications) and key resources (e.g., dams and nuclear power plants).
- *State pandemic plans:* All states were required to develop and submit specific plans for pandemic flu preparedness, as a requirement of grants provided by HHS.[110]

KEY INFORMATION SOURCES

CRS Reports and Experts

2009 H1N1 "Swine Flu": CRS Experts: CRS Report R40845, *2009 H1N1 "Swine Flu": CRS Experts*, by Sarah A. Lister.

Current CRS Reports on public health and emergency preparedness in general: http://apps.crs.gov/cli/cli.aspx?PRDS_CLI_ITEM_ID=3276&from=3&fromId=13

Current CRS Reports on specific aspects of the pandemic influenza threat:

- CRS Report R40560, *The 2009 Influenza Pandemic: Selected Legal Issues*, coordinated by Kathleen S. Swendiman and Nancy Lee Jones.
- CRS Report RS2 1414, *Mandatory Vaccinations: Precedent and Current Laws*, by Kathleen S. Swendiman.
- CRS Report RL34724, *Would an Influenza Pandemic Qualify as a Major Disaster Under the Stafford Act?* by Edward C. Liu.
- CRS Report R4053 1, *FY2009 Spring Supplemental Appropriations for Overseas Contingency Operations*, coordinated by Stephen Daggett and Susan B. Epstein.
- CRS Report R40575, *Potential Farm Sector Effects of 2009 H1N1 "Swine Flu ": Questions and Answers*, by Renée Johnson.

---

[110] For more information, see HHS, *Assessment of States' Operating Plans to Combat Pandemic Influenza: Report to Homeland Security Council,* January 2009, at http://www.pandemicflu.gov/ plan/states/index.html, and CRS Report RL34 190, *Pandemic Influenza: An Analysis of State Preparedness and Response Plans*, by Sarah A. Lister and Holly Stockdale.

- CRS Report R40588, *The 2009 Influenza Pandemic: U.S. Responses to Global Human Cases*, by Tiaji Salaam-Blyther.
- CRS Report R40619, *The Role of the Department of Defense During A Flu Pandemic*, by Lawrence Kapp and Don J. Jansen.
- CRS Report RL33 609, *Quarantine and Isolation: Selected Legal Issues Relating to Employment*, by Nancy Lee Jones and Jon O. Shimabukuro.
- CRS Report RS2 1507, *Project BioShield: Purposes and Authorities*, by Frank Gottron.
- CRS Report R40570, *Immigration Policies and Issues on Health-Related Grounds for Exclusion*, by Chad C. Haddal and Ruth Ellen Wasem.
- CRS Report RL32724, *Mexico-U.S. Relations: Issues for Congress*, by Clare Ribando Seelke, Mark P. Sullivan, and June S. Beittel.
- CRS Report RL33381, *The Americans with Disabilities Act (ADA): Allocation of Scarce Medical Resources During a Pandemic*, by Nancy Lee Jones.
- CRS Report RS22327, *Pandemic Flu and Medical Biodefense Countermeasure Liability Limitation*, by Henry Cohen and Vanessa K. Burrows.
- CRS Report RL31873, *Banking and Financial Infrastructure Continuity: Pandemic Flu, Terrorism, and Other Challenges*, by N. Eric Weiss.
- CRS Report RS22264, *Federal Employees: Human Resources Management Flexibilities in Emergency Situations*, by Barbara L. Schwemle.

Archived CRS Reports on the threat of pandemic influenza: These products generally discuss concerns about a possible human flu pandemic resulting from H5N1 avian influenza, and enhanced federal preparedness efforts during 2005 through 2007.

- CRS Report RL33145, Pandemic Influenza: Domestic Preparedness Efforts, by Sarah A. Lister.
- CRS Report RL33219, U.S. and International Responses to the Global Spread of Avian Flu: Issues for Congress, by Tiaji Salaam-Blyther.
- CRS Report RS22576, Pandemic Influenza: Appropriations for Public Health Preparedness and Response, by Sarah A. Lister.

World Health Organization (WHO) Information

- Information about the current H1N1 pandemic flu situation: http://www.who.int/csr/disease/swineflu/en/index.html (See also the Appendix.)
- Pandemic Influenza Preparedness and Response: A WHO Guidance Document, (April 2009): http://www.who.int/csr/disease/influenza/pipguidance2009/en/index.html
- Current phase of flu pandemic alert: http://www.who.int/csr/disease/avian_influenza/phase/en/index.html
- Pan American Health Organization (PAHO), a regional office of the WHO, H1N1 flu page: http://new.paho.org/hq/index.php?option=com_content&task= blogcategory& id=805&Itemid=569

- International Health Regulations (2005): http://www.who.int/topics/ international _health _regulations/en/

U.S. Federal Government Information

- Government-wide information: http://www.flu.gov/
- DHS, "Department Response to H1N1 (Swine) Flu," with links to information in other federal departments and agencies: http://www.dhs.gov/xprepresp/programs/ swine-flu. shtm
- CDC, H1N1 (swine flu) page: http://www.cdc.gov/h1n1flu/
- CDC Public Health Law Program, 2009 H1N1 Flu Legal Preparedness, http://www2a.cdc.gov/phlp/H1N1flu.asp
- FDA, 2009 H1N1 (Swine) Flu Virus, http://www.fda.gov/NewsEvents/ PublicHealthFocus/ucm1 50305 .htm
- Centers for Medicare and Medicaid Services (CMS), H1N1 information page, http://www.cms.hhs.gov/H1N1/
- U.S. Department of Education, H1N1 Flu Information, http://www.ed.gov/ admins/lead/safety/emergencyplan/pandemic/index.html
- U.S. Department of Agriculture (USDA), H1N1 Flu, http://www.usda.gov/wps/ portal/?navid=USDA_H1N1
- USDA nutrition program policies for pandemic flu, http://www.fns.usda.gov/ disasters/pandemic/default.htm
- Department of Defense Pandemic Influenza Watchboard: http://fhp.osd.mil/ aiWatchboard/
- HHS Pandemic Planning Updates, addressing monitoring and surveillance, vaccines, antiviral medications, state and local preparedness, and communications, through January 2009: http://www.flu.gov/professional/federal/ index.html (Note: much of this information is in the context of planning for the H5N1 avian flu threat.)

Additional Information

- Canada: Public Health Agency of Canada: http://www.phac-aspc.gc.ca/alert-alerte/ swine_200904-eng.php; Canadian Food Inspection Agency: http://www.inspection.gc.ca/english/anima/disemala/swigri/swigrie.shtml
- Security and Prosperity Partnership of North America, *North American Plan for Avian and Pandemic Influenza,* August 2007, http://www.spp-psp.gc.ca/eic/site/spp-psp.nsf/vwapj/pandemic-influenza.pdf/$FILE/pandemic-influenza.pdf
- Center for Infectious Disease Research and Policy (CIDRAP), at the University of Minnesota, frequent updates, including scientific and technical information, http://www.cidrap.umn.edu/cidrap/content/influenza/swineflu/index.html
- Public Health Law and Policy Program at the Sandra Day O'Connor College of Law, at Arizona State University, Global Legal Triage and the 2009 H1N1 Outbreak

(including prior and existing declared emergencies at the federal and state levels), http://www.law.asu.edu/?id=2036

APPENDIX. KEY OFFICIAL ACTIONS BY WHO

Determination of Influenza Pandemic Phase

The World Health Organization is the coordinating authority for health within the United Nations system. It is responsible for providing leadership, guiding a research agenda, setting norms and standards, articulating evidence-based policy options, providing technical support to countries, and monitoring and assessing health trends. WHO does not have enforcement powers.

An influenza pandemic occurs when a novel flu strain emerges and spreads across the globe, causing human illnesses. For that to happen, the virus must have the following features: it must be genetically novel so that there is a lack of preexisting immunity; it must be pathogenic (i.e., capable of causing illness in humans); and it must be easily transmitted from person to person.

WHO, in consultation with experts in member countries, monitors the spread of influenza among human populations, and has developed a scale to monitor pandemic risk. It consists of five "pre- pandemic" phases with increasing incidence of animal and then human illness and transmission, and a sixth phase that represents a full-blown human pandemic, with sustained viral transmission and outbreaks in most or all regions of the world. Historically, flu pandemics have occurred in multiple waves before subsiding. Table A-1 describes the phases of a flu pandemic, as defined by WHO.

As a result of the rapid spread of the new flu strain, WHO raised the pandemic alert level from Phase 3, where it had been for several years because of the threat of H5N1 avian flu, to Phase 4 on April 27, and then to Phase 5 on April 29.[111] Phase 3 meant that a novel flu strain was causing sporadic small clusters of human illness, but was not sufficiently transmissible to sustain community-level outbreaks. Phase 4, by contrast, signaled that human-to-human transmission of the new H1N1 virus was sufficient to sustain community-level outbreaks. According to WHO, raising the alert level to Phase 5 meant that there was sustained community-level transmission in two or more countries within one WHO region, and that a pandemic could be imminent.

On June 11, WHO raised the level to Phase 6, declaring that an influenza pandemic, caused by the new H1N1 strain, was underway. According to WHO Director General Dr. Margaret Chan:

> Spread in several countries can no longer be traced to clearly-defined chains of human-to human transmission. Further spread is considered inevitable.... The world is now at the start of the 2009 influenza pandemic. We are in the earliest days of the pandemic. The virus is spreading under a close and careful watch. No previous pandemic has been detected so early

---

[111] WHO, "Pandemic (H1N1) 2009," http://www.who.int/csr/disease/swineflu/en/index.html.

or watched so closely, in real-time, right at the very beginning. The world can now reap the benefits of investments, over the last five years, in pandemic preparedness.[112]

Table A-1. WHO Influenza Pandemic Phases (current alert level is highlighted)

Phase	Description
Phase 1	No animal influenza virus circulating among animals has been reported to cause infection in humans.
Phase 2	An animal influenza virus circulating in domesticated or wild animals is known to have caused infection in humans and is therefore considered a specific potential pandemic threat.
Phase 3	An animal or human-animal influenza reassortanta virus has caused sporadic cases of small clusters of disease in people, but has not resulted in human-to-human transmission sufficient to sustain community-level outbreaks.
Phase 4	Human-to-human transmission of an animal or human-animal influenza reassortanta virus able to sustain community-level outbreaks has been verified.
Phase 5	The same identified virus has caused sustained community-level outbreaks in two or more countries in one WHO region.[b]
Phase 6	An influenza pandemic. In addition to the criteria defined in Phase 5, the same virus has caused sustained community-level outbreaks in at least one other country in another WHO region.[b]
Post-peak Period	Levels of pandemic influenza in most countries with adequate surveillance have dropped below peak levels.
Possible New	Level of pandemic influenza activity in most countries with adequate surveillance rising again.
Wave	
Post-pandemic	Levels of influenza activity have returned to the levels seen for seasonal influenza in most
Period	countries with adequate surveillance.

Source: Adapted by CRS from WHO, *Pandemic Influenza Preparedness and Response: A WHO Guidance Document*, April 2009, Table 1, p. 13, http://www.who.int/csr/disease/influenza/ pipguidance2009/en/index. html.

a. A reassortant virus results from a genetic reassortment process in which genes from animal and human influenza viruses mix together to create a new strain.

b. WHO governs through six regional offices that do not strictly correspond with the world's continents. The WHO regions are the African Region; the Region of the Americas; the South-East Asia Region; the European Region; the Eastern Mediterranean Region; and the Western Pacific Region. See "WHO–Its People and Offices," http://www.who.int/about/structure/en/index.html.

For several years, WHO urged governments, corporations, and other interests to develop pandemic influenza preparedness and response plans. Generally these plans are staged according to WHO pandemic phases. WHO has noted that under the current definitions, pandemic phases do not reflect the severity of illness, but rather the global extent of sustained community-level outbreaks. Some members of the public, however, had come to think of any

---

[112] WHO, "World Now at the Start of 2009 Influenza Pandemic" (Statement of Dr. Margaret Chan), press release, June 12, 2009, http://www.who.int/csr/disease/swineflu/en/index.html.

flu pandemic as a catastrophic incident on the scale of the one that occurred in 1918, or that many feared could result from the deadly H5N1 avian flu if it became transmissible among humans. Some argued that the definition of a pandemic should be rewritten to take severity into account, and that a Phase 6 pandemic designation for the H1N1 flu situation would trigger over-reactions that were more disruptive than the disease.[113]

International Health Regulations

In 2005, the World Health Assembly adopted revised International Health Regulations (IHR), revising the roles and responsibilities of WHO and member states in the protection of international public health. The IHR(2005) require signatory nations (which include the United States) to notify WHO of all events that may constitute a "Public Health Emergency of International Concern," and to provide relevant information. The IHR(2005) also include provisions regarding designated national points of contact, definitions of core public health capacities, disease control measures such as quarantine and border controls (which are to be no more restrictive than necessary to achieve the desired level of health protection) and others.[114] On April 25, 2009, upon the advice of the Emergency Committee called under the rules of the IHR(2005), the WHO Director-General declared the H1N1 flu outbreak a Public Health Emergency of International Concern, thereby calling upon signatories to provide timely and transparent notification of events to WHO, to collaborate in disease reporting and control, and to adopt effective risk communication strategies to reduce the potential for international disease spread and the unilateral imposition of trade or travel restrictions by other countries.[115]

Travel Guidance

A number of governments have instituted enhanced passenger screening practices at their borders, and policymakers have debated more extensive prohibitions against the entry of travelers from countries or areas affected by the outbreak. The WHO has consistently advised against movement restrictions as a means to control influenza, citing a lack of evidence of their effectiveness, coupled with their potentially harmful effects on public confidence, local economies, and trade.[116]

---

[113] See, for example, Robert Roos, "WHO Drawing Closer to Declaring a Pandemic," *CIDRAP News* (Center for Infectious Disease Research and Policy), June 2, 2009, http://www.cidrap.umn.edu/cidrap/content/influenza/swineflu/ index.html.

[114] For more information, see CRS Report R40560, *The 2009 Influenza Pandemic: Selected Legal Issues*, coordinated by Kathleen S. Swendiman and Nancy Lee Jones.

[115] WHO, *International Health Regulations*, http://www.who.int/ihr/en/. See, also, Rebecca Katz, "Use of Revised International Health Regulations during Influenza A (H1N1) Epidemic," *Emerging Infectious Diseases*, vol. 15, no. 8 (August 2009), http://www.cdc.gov/eid/content/15/8/1165.htm.

[116] WHO, *No Rationale for Travel Restrictions*, May 1, 2009, http://www.who.int/csr/disease/swineflu/ guidance/public_health/travel_advice/en/index.html.

Food Safety Guidance[117]

WHO has published a joint statement with Food and Agriculture Organization of the United Nations (FAO), the World Organization for Animal Health (known by its French acronym, OIE), and the World Trade Organization (WTO), saying:

> In light of the spread of influenza A(H1N1), and the rising concerns about the possibility of this virus being found in pigs and the safety of pork and pork products, we stress that pork and pork products, handled in accordance with good hygienic practices recommended by the WHO, FAO, Codex Alimentarius Commission and the OIE, will not be a source of infection.
>
> To date there is no evidence that the virus is transmitted by food. There is currently therefore no justification in the OIE Terrestrial Animal Health Standards Code for the imposition of trade measures on the importation of pigs or their products.[118]

ACKNOWLEDGMENTS

Legislative Attorneys Kathleen Swendiman, Edward Liu, and Nancy Jones, and Specialists Keith Bea and Frank Gottron, assisted with information in this report regarding federal emergency management authorities, including Figure 1.

---

[117] For more information, see CRS Report R40575, Potential Farm Sector Effects of 2009 H1N1 "Swine Flu ": Questions and Answers , by Renée Johnson.

[118] Joint FAO, OIE, WHO and WTO Statement on A(H1N1) virus, May 2, 2009, http://www.wto.org/english/ news_e/ news09_e/jt_stat_02may09_e.htm.

In: Globalization

Editors: M. G. Massari and K. J. Lutz, 117-149

ISBN: 978-1-61470-327-3

© 2012 Nova Science Publishers, Inc

Chapter 6

UNITED NATIONS REFORM: U.S. POLICY AND INTERNATIONAL PERSPECTIVES*

Luisa Blanchfield

ABSTRACT

Since its establishment in 1945, the United Nations has been in a constant state of transition as various international stakeholders seek ways to improve the efficiency and effectiveness of the U.N. system. Recent controversies, such as corruption of the Iraq Oil-For-Food Program, allegations of sexual abuse by U.N. peacekeepers, and instances of waste, fraud and abuse by U.N. staff, have focused renewed attention on the need for change and improvement of the United Nations. Many in the international community, including the United States, have increased pressure on U.N. member states to implement substantive reforms. The 111th Congress will most likely continue to focus on U.N. reform as it considers appropriate levels of U.S. funding to the United Nations and monitors the progress and implementation of ongoing and previously- approved reform measures.

In September 2005, heads of U.N. member states met for the World Summit at U.N. Headquarters in New York to discuss strengthening the United Nations through institutional reform. The resulting Summit Outcome Document laid the groundwork for a series of reforms that included establishing a Peacebuilding Commission, creating a new Human Rights Council, and enlarging the U.N. Security Council. Member states also agreed to Secretariat and management reforms including improving internal U.N. oversight capacity, establishing a U.N. ethics office, enhancing U.N. whistle-blower protection, and reviewing all U.N. mandates five years or older.

Since the World Summit, U.N. member states have worked toward implementing these reforms with varied degrees of success. Some reforms, such as the creation of the Human Rights Council and the Peacebuilding Commission, have already occurred or are ongoing. Other reforms, such as mandate review and U.N. Security Council enlargement, have stalled or not been addressed. U.N. member states disagree as to whether some proposed reforms are necessary, as well as how to most effectively implement previously agreed-to reforms. Developed countries, for example, support delegating more power to

---

* This is an edited, reformatted and augmented version of CRS Report RL33848, dated December 15, 2009.

the Secretary-General to implement management reforms, whereas developing countries fear that giving the Secretary-General more authority may undermine the power of the U.N. General Assembly and therefore the influence of individual countries.

Congress has maintained a significant interest in the overall effectiveness of the United Nations. Some Members are particularly interested in U.N. Secretariat and management reform, with a focus on enhanced accountability and internal oversight. In the past, Congress has enacted legislation that links U.S. funding of the United Nations to specific U.N. reform benchmarks. Opponents of this strategy argue that tying U.S. funding to U.N. reform may negatively impact diplomatic relations and could hinder the United States' ability to conduct foreign policy. Supporters contend that the United Nations has been slow to implement reforms and that linking payment of U.S. assessments to progress on U.N. reform is the most effective way to motivate member states to efficiently pursue comprehensive reform.

INTRODUCTION

United Nations (U.N.) reform is an ongoing policy issue for the United States, and may be a point of focus during the 111th Congress. As the single largest financial contributor to the U.N. system, the U.S. government has an interest in ensuring the United Nations operates as efficiently and effectively as possible. Congress has the responsibility to appropriate U.S. funds to the United Nations, and can impose conditions on payments. On several occasions, Congress has sought to link U.S. funding of the United Nations to specific reform benchmarks.

In recent years, there has been growing concern among some in the international community that the United Nations has become ineffective and unwieldy in the face of increasing global challenges and responsibilities. In response to these concerns, then-U.N. Secretary-General Kofi Annan and some U.N. member states proposed a series of management, programmatic, and structural reforms to improve the organization. Many of these reforms are in various stages of implementation, while others are still being considered by member states. Secretary-General Ban Ki-moon, who assumed the position of Secretary-General in January 2007, has stated that he will continue to support U.N. reform efforts.

This report focuses on U.N. reform efforts and priorities from the perspective of several key actors, including the U.S. government, the U.N. Secretary-General, selected groups of member states, and a cross-section of groups tasked with addressing U.N. reform. It also examines congressional actions related to U.N. reform, as well as future policy considerations.

BACKGROUND

Reform Trends

Since the establishment of the United Nations in 1945, U.N. member states and past secretaries- general have repeatedly attempted to reform the organization. These reform efforts tend to be cyclical, with member states considering waves of new reform proposals every five to ten years. The reform attempts can be initiated by a member state, groups of member states, and/or the current secretary-general. They generally focus on three areas of concern: (1) perceived inefficiencies and lack of accountability in the U.N. Secretariat; (2) duplication and redundancy of U.N. mandates, missions, and/or programs; and (3) evidence of fraud, waste, abuse and/or mismanagement of U.N. resources.

Proposed reforms often reflect the political, economic, and cultural climate of the time. For example, in the 1950s and 1960s, member states focused on increasing membership on the U.N. Security Council and the U.N. Economic and Social Council (ECOSOC) to account for growing U.N. membership [1] In the 1 970s, as the economic and political gap between developed and developing countries grew more pronounced, the General Assembly requested the Secretary- General to appoint a group of experts to recommend structural changes that would help the United Nations address "problems of international economic co-operation." [2] The most recent wave of U.N. reform is likely driven by a combination of U.N. budgetary and financial issues, controversy over mismanagement of the Iraq Oil-For-Food Program, perceived ineffectiveness of U.N. human rights mechanisms, and recent allegations of sexual abuse committed by U.N. staff and peacekeepers, among other things.

Reform Efforts (1980s and Early 1990s)

U.N. reform initiatives in the 1980s and early 1990s focused primarily on financial and structural issues. In 1986, under pressure from the United States and other industrialized countries, the General Assembly established a high-level group of 18 intergovernmental experts to "review the efficiency of the administrative and financial functioning," of the United Nations. The group made 71 recommendations to the General Assembly, including a revised budgetary process that introduced the use of consensus-based budgeting [3]. In the early 1990s, U.N. Secretary-General Boutros Boutros-Ghali introduced broad reform proposals in reports, "An Agenda for Peace," (1992) and "An Agenda for Development" (1 994) [4] Some of these reform initiatives proposed led to substantive changes to the U.N. structure [5].

Reform Efforts (1997 to 2005)

Kofi Annan ran for Secretary-General on a platform of reform and introduced many reform proposals during his tenure, most notably in 1997, 2002, and 2005. Annan also appointed several independent panels and commissions to propose reforms on specific issues, such as the effectiveness of U.N. peacekeeping operations [6] Annan first proposed a "two track" reform program that recommended cutting Secretariat administrative costs, combining three smaller departments into one large Department of Economic and Social Affairs (DESA), and creating the post of Deputy Secretary-General [7] Over time, some of these early reform initiatives were achieved [8] In September 2002, Annan proposed additional reforms, including a reorganization of the budget and planning system to make it less complex; a thorough review of the U.N. work program; establishing a high-level panel to examine the relationship between the United Nations and civil society; improving U.N. human rights protection; and enhancing U.N. information services [9].

In September 2003, Annan appointed a High-Level Panel on Threats, Challenges and Change to evaluate how the United Nations addressed present-day threats to international peace and security [10]. The Panel recommended enlarging the U.N. Security Council, establishing a Peacebuilding Commission, and enhancing the role of the Secretary-General. Annan drew from many of the Panel's recommendations in his 2005 report, In Larger Freedom: Toward Development, Security, and Human Rights for All [11].

The 2005 U.N. World Summit

In September 2005, U.N. reform efforts seemed to gain momentum as heads of state and government met for the 2005 World Summit at U.N. Headquarters in New York. The Summit convened to review the progress made in the fulfillment of the 2000 Millennium Summit goals and commitments made in other earlier U.N. conferences [12] It provided the groundwork for potentially significant changes to the U.N. system, with a focus on strengthening the United Nations through various reforms. The Summit Outcome Document was negotiated by 191 member states and adopted by consensus on September 16, 2005. The document laid the foundation for reforms such as: establishing a Peacebuilding Commission; strengthening the Central Emergency Response Fund (CERF); [13] establishing a Democracy Fund; strengthening the Security Council; improving U.N. system coordination; and creating a new Human Rights Council. Member states also agreed to Secretariat and management reforms, including (1) establishment of an ethics office; (2) greater whistle-blower protection; (3) strengthening oversight capacity; (4) review of all General Assembly mandates over five years old; and (5) full financial disclosure by U.N. staff [14].

RECENTLY ADOPTED AND/OR IMPLEMENTED REFORMS AND THE NEW SECRETARY-GENERAL

Adopted Reforms

U.N. member states have worked toward implementing reform with varied results since the 2005 World Summit. Some reforms, particularly initiatives related to internal oversight, human resources reform, and Security Council enhancement, are stalled or have not been addressed. Other reforms, such as changes to CERF, the establishment of the Human Rights Council, and the creation of a Peacebuilding Commission, are already completed or are underway. Some management and budget reforms endorsed by heads of state and government at the World Summit were also implemented, including the establishment of a U.N. Ethics Office, enhanced whistle- blower protection policies, and improved financial disclosure policies for U.N. staff [15] On July 7, 2006, the U.N. General Assembly reached consensus on a series of additional management reforms, [16] including:

- establishment of the post of Chief Information Technology Officer to assist in the replacement of an outdated U.N. information system;

- authorization of approximately $700,000 for the Secretary-General to strengthen the U.N. procurement system;
- full operation of a U.N. Ethics Office, with a need for strengthening internal oversight and accountability; [17]
- "experimental" authorization of up to $20 million in discretionary spending for the Secretary-General to meet the needs of the organization; [18] and
- adoption of International Public Sector Accounting Standards. [19]

System-Wide Coherence

The 2005 World Summit Outcome Document also called on the Secretary-General to improve system-wide coherence and coordination by "strengthening linkages between the normative work of the United Nations system and its operational activities." [20].

Accordingly, in February 2006, the Secretary-General announced the creation of a High-Level Panel to examine how the U.N. system can work more effectively, especially in the areas of development, humanitarian assistance, and the environment [21] The Panel's final report emphasized the overall value and progress of the United Nations, but also noted that without substantial reforms the United Nations will be "unable to deliver on its promises and maintain its legitimate position at the heart of the multilateral system." [22]

The Panel recommended the concept of "Delivering as One," to promote greater coherence and consolidation of U.N. departments and agencies at the country, regional, and headquarters level, and also recommended an overhaul of U.N. business practices to bring greater focus on achieving the Millennium Development Goals (MDGs) [23]. In December 2006, the United Nations announced that it would test a Delivering as One pilot program in Vietnam with an aim of ensuring "faster and more effective development." [24] Secretary-General Ban supports the findings of the Panel, emphasizing his "intention to keep implementing those proposals that build on existing intergovernmental processes and reform initiatives." [25]

Overhaul of Internal Justice System

On April 4, 2007, the General Assembly adopted a framework resolution to create a new system of internal justice administration [26]. The system is part of the Secretariat and coordinated through a new Office of the Administration of Justice that operates in two tiers—the U.N. Dispute Tribunal and the U.N. Appeals Tribunal [27]. The resolution establishes formal and informal channels to protect U.N. staff facing disciplinary action, and provides additional accountability among staff, especially managers [28]. The previous internal justice system was criticized by member states for being "slow, cumbersome, ineffective, and lacking in professionalism." [29] The system was backlogged with cases and many of its employees lacked formal legal training or qualifications.

Mandate Review

The Outcome Document negotiated by member states at the 2005 U.N. World Summit called for a systematic review of all U.N. mandates five years or older, a process that has never before been undertaken. Member states are currently reviewing mandates in the Working Group of the Plenary on Secretariat and Management Reform, but progress is slow due to resistance from some countries that fear that mandates important to them will be discarded. If the working group recommends a mandate for removal, the General Assembly would need to amend the resolution that established the mandate.

Secretary-General Ban Ki-moon and U.N. Reform

On December 14, 2006, Ban Ki-moon of South Korea took the oath of office to succeed outgoing U.N. Secretary-General Annan [30]. Ban stated that U.N. reform is "the most pressing and principled issue of today," and that it will be a top priority during his tenure [31] Ban stated that his overall reform priorities include consolidation and better coordination in the U.N. system, improving morale, accountability, and professionalism for U.N. staff, and restoring trust in the United Nations [32].

Proposed Disarmament and Peacekeeping Restructuring

In February 2007, Ban introduced his first set of reform initiatives. He proposed the establishment of a new Department of Field Support to improve the coordination and effectiveness of U.N. field activities. He also called for the Department of Disarmament Affairs (DDA) to become an office under the Secretary-General instead of a stand-alone department. He noted that the U.N. disarmament and non-proliferation agenda needs revitalization, and will require "a greater role and personal involvement of the Secretary-General." [33]. Ban's proposals were met with skepticism by many developing countries, which were concerned with the possible downgrading of DDA and the impact of a new Department of Field Support on current peacekeeping operations [34]

On March 15, 2007, after extensive consultations among the Secretary-General and member states, the General Assembly approved two framework resolutions offering preliminary support for Ban's proposals. The first resolution supported establishment of an Office of Disarmament Affairs (ODA). It stated that DDA will retain its budgetary autonomy and "the integrity of the existing structures and functions." [35] It also stated that the High-Representative for ODA should be appointed at the rank of Under-Secretary-General and report directly to the Secretary-General. The resolution requested that after appointing the High-Representative, the Secretary-General report to the General Assembly on the financial, administrative, and budgetary implications of the reorganization, as well as report on the ODA's activities at the 62nd session of the General Assembly [36]. On July 2, 2007, the Secretary-General appointed Sergio Duarte, a career diplomat from Brazil, as High Representative.

The second General Assembly resolution addressed peacekeeping restructuring and supported establishing a Department of Field Support to be headed by an Under-Secretary General. It requested that the Secretary-General submit "a comprehensive report ... elaborating on the restructuring of the Department of Peacekeeping Operations and the establishment of the Department of Field Support, including functions, budgetary discipline and full financial implications." [37] The General Assembly supported Ban's proposal in principle. In late June 2007, the Assembly approved the restructuring, establishing the Department of Field Support with a new Under-Secretary-General to head the Department [38].

A significant point of contention among some member states during negotiations was the level of autonomy the Secretary-General would have to organize the Secretariat vis-á-vis the Assembly's authority to determine the budget and how it should be spent. Thus, in its initial framework resolution the General Assembly required the Secretary-General to provide comprehensive information on the functions, budgets, and other financial implications of the reorganization.

Other Reform Initiatives

Secretary-General Ban has raised other aspects of U.N. reform, including:

- *Financial Disclosure*—Ban submitted his mandatory personal financial disclosure form and released it to the public. He encouraged other U.N. staff to follow his example of public financial disclosure, but will not make it a requirement [39]
- *Staff Mobility*—Ban announced the availability of several Secretariat positions to be filled by internal U.N. staff. He encouraged other managers to do the same, noting the importance of staff mobility among U.N. agencies and departments.
- *Security Council Reform*—Ban calls Security Council reform "an important and sensitive issue." [40] He supports enlarging the Council, and has stated he will use his position as Secretary-General to facilitate cooperation among member states in order to build a broad consensus for Security Council enhancement.

CONGRESS AND U.N. REFORM

Generally, Congress supports the United Nations and its mission. It authorizes and appropriates U.S. funds to the organization each year and often utilizes U.N. mechanisms to further U.S. foreign policy objectives [41]. Congress can also be critical of the United Nations, however, especially when some Members believe that the organization may not be running as effectively as it could be. When this happens, Congress may use a wide range of legislative tools to influence and direct U.S. policy at the United Nations. Such efforts may include considering "sense of the Congress" resolutions; holding hearings to investigate U.N. programs or oversee Administration policies; and determining U.S. nominees for U.N. posts. Placing financial conditions or limits on U.S. funding to the United Nations is another common congressional policy approach to U.N. reform.

U.S. Funding as a Tool for U.N. Reform

Overview and Options

In the past, Congress has used its authority to limit U.S. funds to the United Nations as a mechanism for influencing U.N. policy [42]. In some cases, Congress withheld a proportionate share of funding for U.N. programs and policies of which it did not approve. Since 1980, it has withheld funds from regular budget programs, including the U.N. Special Unit on Palestinian Rights (for projects involving the Palestine Liberation Organization), and the Preparatory Commission for the Law of the Sea.

The overall impact of withholding a proportionate share of assessed payments depends on the origin of the program's funding. If a program is funded by the U.N. regular budget and the United States withholds a proportionate share of its normal contributions, the cost of the program will most likely be covered by surplus regular budget funds. Some U.N. programs are funded from several budgets that may include the U.N. regular budget, specialized agency budgets, and separate conference and administrative budgets. Because of this, it may be more difficult for U.S. proportionate withholdings to have a significant impact because the program's funding comes from several sources. In such cases, a U.S. withholding would have little or no impact on the program's operation or funding levels. If the United States withholds funds from a program funded primarily by member state contributions, however, the impact of a U.S. withdrawal could be greater. Currently, the only proportionate U.S. withholding from the U.N. regular budget is for some activities and programs related to the Palestine Liberation Organization or entities associated with it [43]. Additionally, the Bush Administration announced in April 2008 that it would withhold a portion of its contributions to the 2008 U.N. regular budget equivalent to the U.S. share of the U.N. Human Rights Council budget [44]

In addition to withholding a proportionate share of U.S. funding, Congress may consider enacting legislation decreasing or increasing U.S. assessment levels or linking payment of U.S. arrears to policies it favors. In October 1993, for example, Congress directed that the U.S. payments of peacekeeping assessments be capped at 25% (lower than the assessment level set by the United Nations) [45]. Congress also used this strategy to further its U.N. reform policies. Enacted legislation such as the Helms-Biden Agreement linked U.S. assessment levels and the payment of U.S. arrears to reform benchmarks (see Appendix A for more information on legislation).

Arguments For and Against Linking U.S. Funding to U.N. Reform

Opponents of linking U.S. funding to progress on U.N. reform are concerned that doing so may weaken U.S. influence at the United Nations, thereby undercutting its ability to conduct diplomacy and make foreign policy decisions [46] Some argue that withholding U.S. assessed payments to the United Nations infringes on U.S. treaty obligations and alienates other U.N. member states. Opponents also note that withholding U.S. funds could have an impact on diplomatic relations outside of the U.N. system. Additionally, some contend that U.N. reform legislation proposals may be unrealistic because the scope and depth of reforms required by the legislation cannot be adequately achieved in the proposed time frames [47]

Supporters of linking U.S. funding to specific reforms argue that the United States should use its position as the largest U.N. financial contributor to push for the implementation of policies that lead to comprehensive reform. They note that despite diplomatic and political pressures from many countries, the United Nations has been slow to implement substantive reform. Advocates also argue that some previously implemented reforms, such as the new Human Rights Council, have proved to be ineffective. They believe that tying U.S. funding to U.N. reform may motivate countries to find common ground on divisive issues. They also emphasize that past legislation that threatened to cut off U.S. funding of the United Nations (such as the Kassebaum-Solomon amendment) was effective, and led to substantive changes in U.N. operations and programs.

Possible Instruments for Furthering U.S. Reform Policy

Congress's influence over U.S. funding of the United Nations is a powerful tool for furthering U.S. reform policy at the United Nations. However, there may be other strategies for Congress to consider when advocating its reform agenda. These strategies have been widely used by many past and current Members of Congress and Administrations, and include, but are not limited to:

- *Resolutions*—Members of Congress may propose and/or enact simple or concurrent resolutions expressing an opinion, fact, or principle in one or both chambers of Congress. Some Members of Congress have used these resolutions to voice an opinion about U.S. policy in the United Nations/or the United Nations itself.
- *Working with the U.N. Secretary-General*—Some previous and current Members of Congress and Administrations have worked to earn the support of U.N. secretaries-general to help advocate their positions. Developing a relationship with the chief administrative officer of the United Nations can be valuable during some negotiations, where the Secretary-General can act as a bridge among member states that disagree on issues. In addition, U.S. citizens have also held key U.N. reform-related posts at the United Nations, which some Members of Congress believe may play a role in furthering U.S. reform policy interests [48] Most recently, Christopher Burnham served as U.N. Under-Secretary for Management [49]
- *Collaborating with U.N. Member States*—The United States may wish to continue to reach out to other U.N. member states to build consensus and form partnerships on reform policies, either within the framework of the United Nations or bilaterally [50] Some observers have noted that U.S. support for certain U.N. reform initiatives can be a liability because some member states may view U.S. support as self-serving. In these cases, the United States may consider allowing like-minded countries advocate its reform agenda.
- *Identifying Key Priorities*—The United States may wish to focus on a small number of reform priorities and pursue them vigorously in both multilateral and bilateral fora. It may also consider compromising with other member states on U.N. reform issues that it has identified as lesser priorities.

Former Secretary-General Kofi Annan often stated that U.N. reform is a process and not an event [51]. With this in mind, the 111th Congress may wish to continue monitoring the implementation and overall progress of recently-approved reform initiatives. It may also consider future reform initiatives proposed by member states and the Administration, as well as by Secretary-General Ban Ki-moon or Members of Congress.

ADMINISTRATION POLICIES

The United States generally supports the mission and mandate of the United Nations. It played a key role in establishing the United Nations in 1945, and serves as one of five permanent members of the Security Council. Some Administrations have been critical of the United Nations, however, and have advocated sweeping reform of the organization.

Obama Administration

Since Barack Obama was sworn in as President on January 20, 2009, representatives of his Administration have commented on various aspects of U.N. reform. During the Senate nomination hearing of Susan Rice to be U.S. Permanent Representative to the United Nations, Rice said that the Administration will "pursue substantial and sustained improvements across the full range of management and performance challenges [in the United Nations]." [52].

She further stated that progress and reform are "essential to address flaws in the institution," and that the United States would work with other countries to "increase the effectiveness and efficiency, the management and accountability of the United Nations," and its "effectiveness in performing those tasks that we [the United States] ask of it." Rice also said that President Obama believes the United States should pay its U.N. dues "in full and on time." In addition, she stated that while the Administration has not taken a position on the issue of Security Council reform, the President recognizes that "the Council of today quite logically ought to be something ... that looks a little bit different from the Council as it was created 60-plus years ago." Rice also maintained that it is "critically important" to ensure that any Security Council reforms do not undermine the operational efficiency and effectiveness of the Council. [53]

On April 29, 2009, the Obama Administration provided further information on its U.N. reform priorities, remarking that that it aimed to "advance reforms that will strengthen the institution and increase accountability." Specifically, it stated that it was working to enhance the effectiveness of U.N. bodies charged with evaluating performance and investigating abuses, including the U.N. Office of Internal Oversight Services (OIOS), the Independent Audit Advisory Committee, and the Board of Auditors. The Administration also highlighted its commitment to reform in the areas of human resources, information technology, procurement, and results-based management. It further emphasized its continuing cooperation with U.N. member states regarding newly established U.N. entities such as the Peacebuilding Commission [54]

George W. Bush Administration

The Bush Administration was an active participant in recent U.N. reform efforts. Prior to and since the adoption of the 2005 World Summit Outcome Document, the Administration attempted to work with like-minded countries and the U.N. Secretary-General to move a reform agenda forward. Some initiatives supported by the Administration, particularly management and oversight reforms, were not approved or considered by the General Assembly. In addition, the Administration expressed its displeasure with the overall effectiveness of some previously implemented reforms [55]. The Administration stated, however, that it would continue to advocate its reform agenda, though it did not support mandatory withholding of U.S. payments to the United Nations [56]. It identified several key priorities that it believed would help the United Nations move towards a goal of a "strong, effective, and accountable organization" [57].

Management, Budget and Secretariat Reform

The Bush Administration viewed management, budget, and secretariat reform as a top U.S. priority for U.N. reform. It contended that substantive change in the United Nation's management and budget structure, particularly within the Secretariat, could contribute to the implementation of more effective U.N. policies and further reforms [58]. In a statement before the General Assembly in 2005, President Bush said that meaningful reforms "include measures to improve internal oversight, identify cost savings, and ensure that precious resources are used for their intended purpose" [59] Bush also emphasized the creation of U.N. structures to "ensure financial accountability and administration and organizational efficiency." [60] Specifically, the Administration advocated:

- *Increased Oversight and Accountability in U.N. Management Structures*— This included enhanced oversight of procurement activities and management in the Secretariat, including the Department of Peacekeeping Operations, as well as a fully independent Office of Internal Oversight Services (OIOS) [61] The Administration also advocated increasing the authority of the Secretary-General to hire and deploy personnel.
- *Review of All U.N. Program Mandates and/or Missions*—The Administration pushed hard for a full mandate review, stressing that the United Nations has over 9,000 mandates and/or programs, some of which may be duplicative or obsolete. It maintained that cost savings resulting from identifying and eliminating these programs could be transferred to fund other reforms [62]
- *Fiscal Discipline*—The Administration believed that the United Nations should implement reforms within existing U.N. budget resources, and encouraged reallocating funds from programs identified as lower priority to those identified as higher priority [63].

The Bush Administration also generally supported some management reform initiatives that were recently approved by the General Assembly and Secretariat, including the establishment of the U.N. Ethics Office, increase in internal oversight funding, improved whistle-blower protections, and stricter U.N. staff financial disclosure requirements [64]. Most recently, the Bush Administration established a "Whistleblower Hotline" for U.N. staff who wish to report "cases of corruption, malfeasance, waste, harassment, and/or retaliation" within the U.N. system [65]

In 2007, the Bush Administration established the U.N. Transparency and Accountability Initiative (UNTAI) at the U.S. Mission to the United Nations, which tracked the adoption of management reforms by U.N. funds and programs. According to the Administration:

> The initial U.N. management reforms authorized by world leaders at the September 2005 World Summit have begun to take shape through the introduction of a number of initiatives relating to increased transparency and accountability in the U.N. Secretariat affairs. Unfortunately, U.N. funds and programs have lagged far behind in the adoption of any such reform measures [66].

To address these issues, the U.S. Mission sent letters to several U.N. funds and programs requesting information on efforts to implement various management reforms. Specifically, the

United States requested information on eight key areas that it maintained would lead to greater oversight and increased transparency and accountability among U.N. entities: (1) availability of internal U.N. audits and other reports to U.N. member states; (2) public access to all relevant documentation related to operations and activities, including budget information and procurement activities; (3) whistleblower protection policies; (4) financial disclosure policies; (5) an effective Ethics Office; (6) independence of the respective internal oversight bodies; (7) adoption of international accounting standards; and (8) establishment of a cap on administrative overhead costs.

The Bush Administration received initial responses from UNDP, the U.N. Children's Fund (UNICEF), and the U.N. Population Fund (UNFPA). The responses, which were part of an ongoing dialogue among the U.S. Mission and these U.N. entities, discussed steps that the organizations are taking to address the issues raised by the United States [67].

Peacebuilding Commission

The United States supported the creation of a U.N. Peacebuilding Commission, which was established by concurrent General Assembly and Security Council resolutions on December 20, 2005 [68] The Commission's mandate is to advise and propose "integrated strategies for post- conflict recovery, focusing attention on reconstruction, institution-building and sustainable development, in countries emerging from conflict." [69]. The Commission operates under the authority of the Security Council and has a 31-member organizational committee [70].

Democracy Initiatives

The Bush Administration identified democracy promotion—particularly the U.N. Democracy Fund (UNDEF)—as a U.S. priority for U.N. reform. On September 21, 2004, President Bush proposed the establishment of UNDEF to provide resources and assistance for projects that promote emerging democracies. The Fund accepts voluntary funding from U.N. member states and promotes activities related to democratic governance, rule of law, electoral assistance, and anti-corruption in new democracies [71]. In 2005, Secretary-General Annan established UNDEF as a U.N. trust fund, and held its inaugural advisory board meeting on March 6, 2006. The United States has contributed over $25 million to UNDEF. Since it was established, 36 U.N. Member States have contributed to the Fund, which has received over $96 million [72].

Convention on Terrorism

The Bush Administration supported the adoption of a Comprehensive Convention on International Terrorism as part of its U.N. reform platform. However, disagreement among U.N. member states regarding the definition of terrorism has delayed progress on the Convention. The Administration agreed with Secretary-General Annan's assertion in his 2005 report, In Larger Freedom, that "the right to resist occupation does not justify the targeting and killing of civilians."[73] Currently, a draft legal framework for the Convention is being considered by the Ad Hoc Committee established by General Assembly Resolution 51/210 of December 17, 1996, which met in February 2007 [74].

Development

The Bush Administration identified economic development as a U.N. reform priority, and aimed to build "healthy institutions and strong economies through trade, foreign investment, and aid," with a focus on "supporting good governance and sound economic policies." [75] At the 2005 U.N. World Summit in New York, the United States joined other member states in agreeing to a $50 billion a year increase in funding (until 2010) to combat poverty, and supported assistance for anti-malaria initiatives, education, and healthcare. The Administration also reaffirmed its commitment to achieving the U.N. Millennium Development Goals (MDGs) by 2015.

Security Council Reform

One of the most discussed issues in the U.N. reform debate is the possibility of modifying the composition and size of the Security Council so that it more adequately reflects present-day political and economic realities. The Bush Administration was generally open to Security Council reform but stressed that the Council should be changed only if it would increase the Council's overall effectiveness [76] It supported Japan as a permanent Security Council member given its democratic and human rights record, and its role as the second largest contributor to the United Nations [77]. The Administration believed that developing countries deserve increased representation in the Council, and maintained that any new potential permanent members should meet specific criteria, including the "size of economy and population; military capacity; contributions to peacekeeping operations; commitment to democracy and human rights; financial contributions to the United Nations; non-proliferation and counter-terrorism records; and equitable geographic balance." [78] The Administration stated that it would remain engaged in the Security Council reform debate, and would continue to be an active participant in the U.N. Working Group on the Question of Equitable Representation on and Increase in the Membership of the Security Council.

It did not support any of the Security Council reform proposals that were submitted for consideration by U.N. member states or former Secretary-General Annan.

REFORM PERSPECTIVES AND PRIORITIES

A significant challenge for advocates of U.N. reform is finding common ground among the disparate definitions of reform held by various stakeholders. The global community has no common definition of U.N. reform and, as a result, there is often debate among some over the scope, appropriateness, and effectiveness of past and current reform initiatives. One method for determining how a stakeholder defines "U.N. reform" may be to identify policy priorities in the U.N. reform debate. In some cases, common objectives among stakeholders have translated into substantive reform policy, though shared goals do not always guarantee successful outcomes.

Recent reform debates in the U.N. General Assembly and its committees drew attention to fundamental differences that exist among some member states, particularly developing countries (represented primarily by the Group of 77 and China), and developed countries (including the United States, Japan, and the United Kingdom). Developed countries, which account for the majority of assessed contributions to the U.N. regular budget, would like the

Secretary-General to have greater flexibility and authority to implement reforms, specifically those related to oversight and human resources. Developing countries, however, generally object to policies that may enhance the power of the Secretary-General and decrease the power of the General Assembly and its budget and administrative committees. Observers are concerned that this difference in reform philosophy will create a deadlock in the General Assembly and significantly delay the implementation of some key management and budget reforms.

Selected International Perspectives

Stakeholders engaged in the U.N. reform debate have different perspectives on how U.N. reform should be implemented and how to prioritize specific U.N. reform issues [79]. Several key actors, including the European Union, the Group of 77 and China, developed countries, and nongovernmental organizations, have weighed in on several reform issues, most notably management and budget reform and development.

European Union (EU)
The EU is composed of 27 countries, accounting for about 13% of the vote share in the U.N. General Assembly and approximately 38% of the U.N. regular budget [80]. The EU's reform initiatives often focus on management reform and increasing the U.N. capacity for development. The EU attaches "great importance to keeping U.N. management reform on track, and "vigorously supports "management reforms such as mandate review [81]. It also views the work of the Secretary-General-appointed Panel on System-Wide Coherence as a high priority, and supports the Panel's efforts to explore how the U.N. system may improve system coordination in the areas of development, humanitarian assistance, and the environment. The EU actively supports the reform of core U.N. organs, including the Security Council, General Assembly and ECOSOC, [82] and it also attaches particular importance to the implementation of the Millennium Development Goals [83].

The Group of 77 and China (G-77)
The G-77 is a loosely affiliated group of 130 U.N. member states representing the interests of developing countries [84] It has played a significant role in recent reform debates due in part to its large membership, which can be a significant voting bloc in the General Assembly. The G-77 generally supports U.N. reform and has long viewed development as a key U.N. reform issue, emphasizing that it should be given the "utmost priority by the United Nations."[85]. The G-77 views reform as a process to examine how the mandates of the United Nations can work through "well-coordinated synergies to achieve the Millennium Development Goals." It believes that U.N. reform should not alter the "intergovernmental nature of our [the United Nations] decision- making, oversight, and monitoring process." Additionally, the G-77 does not view reform as a mechanism to "reduce budget levels ... to fund more activities from within the existing pool of resources, nor to redefine the roles and responsibilities assigned to the various organs." [86]

The G-77 supported some management reforms adopted by the U.N. General Assembly, including the establishment of an ethics office and whistle-blower protection policy. It has, however, actively opposed other initiatives proposed by the Secretary-General, particularly those proposals that it feels may weaken the authority of the General Assembly in the areas of management, budget, and oversight [87]. The G-77 also maintains that the positions of all member countries should be taken into consideration during the reform process. The G-77 has also expressed concern that reform initiatives proposed by the Secretary-General may be influenced by the larger U.N. financial contributors, such as the United States, Japan, and some members of the European Union [88].

Developed Countries

In some cases, the reform priorities of developed countries may not always align with the reform priorities of the G-77 and other developing countries. While the G-77 views development as a top U.N. reform priority, many developed countries tend to focus on management, budget, and structural reform. Generally, developed countries make significantly larger financial contributions to the U.N. system than developing country member states and therefore may want to ensure that their funds are used in what they perceive as the most effective way. For example, the United States and the EU, which together account for a significant portion of the regular budget, view management and budget reform as a top priority. Japan, which contributed approximately 16.6% of the U.N. regular budget in 2007, also views management reform as a priority, particularly Secretariat reform, Security Council reform, and system-wide coherence [89].

The differing perspectives on U.N. reform among developing and developed nations were highlighted in December 2005 when a group of U.N. member states, led primarily by developed countries such as the United States and Japan, sought to link progress on management reforms to the U.N. budget. The countries placed a spending cap of $950 million (about six months of U.N. spending) on the two-year $3.6 billion budget in hopes that the General Assembly would adopt a series of management and budget reform measures proposed by Secretary-General Annan [90]. On May 8, 2006, the General Assembly's Fifth Committee (Administrative and Budgetary) bypassed the traditional practice of budget-by-consensus and voted on a resolution, supported by the G-77, that approved some reforms but delayed the consideration of several others. The developed nations that imposed the budget cap were disappointed with the outcome, and eventually lifted the budget cap in June 2006 because they were unwilling to cause a shutdown of the United Nations [91].

Commissions, Task Forces, and Groups

Since the United Nations was established in 1945, many commissions, panels, committees, and task forces (hereafter referred to collectively as "groups") have been created to examine ways to improve the United Nations [92] These groups are established by a variety of stakeholders, including past secretaries-general, individual member states, groups of member states, NGOs, academic institutions, and others. The following paragraphs will address the findings of a cross- section of these groups—the Volcker Commission, the U.S. Institute of Peace U.N. Reform Task Force, and Secretary-General Kofi Annan's report, In Larger Freedom: Toward Development, Security, and Human Rights for All.

Though the circumstances and mandates for each group are different, they made similar recommendations for improving the United Nations. Notably, each group highlighted the need for enhanced internal oversight and Secretariat reform, including staff buyouts and enhanced financial disclosure requirements. The groups also emphasized the need for overall streamlining and consolidation of the U.N. system (see Appendix B for a side-by-side comparison of the recommendations).

The Volcker Commission

In April 2004, Secretary-General Annan, with the endorsement of the U.N. Security Council, appointed an independent high-level commission to inquire into corruption in the U.N.-led Iraq Oil-for-Food Program [93]. The Commission, led by former Federal Reserve Chairman Paul Volcker, concluded that the failures of the Oil-For-Food Program were evidence of a greater need for "fundamental and wide-ranging administrative reform" in the United Nations [94]. The Commission recommended: establishing an Independent Oversight Board to review U.N. auditing, accounting, and budgeting activities; creating the position of Chief Operating Officer to oversee administrative matters such as personnel and planning practices; providing fair compensation to third parties involved in U.N. programs (while ensuring that the compensation does not lead to inappropriate profit); and expanding financial disclosure requirements to cover a variety of U.N. staff, including those working on procurement.

U.S. Institute of Peace U.N. Reform Task Force

In December 2004, Congress directed the U.S. Institute of Peace to create a bipartisan task force to examine ways to improve the United Nations so that it is better-equipped to meet modern-day security and human rights challenges [95] Congress appropriated $1.5 million to the Task Force and required that it submit a report on its findings to the House Committee on Appropriations [96]. The Task Force identified improving internal oversight as its single most important reform recommendation. It supported the creation of an independent oversight board to direct the budget and activities of the Office of Internal Oversight Services (OIOS). It also recommended several management reforms, including establishing the position of Chief Operating Officer, creating a U.N. Ethics Office, and enhancing whistle-blower protection. It supported broadening the U.N. staff financial disclosure policy, and recommended the review of all U.N. mandates five years or older, as well as the incorporation of sunset clauses into all new mandates. The Task Force supported incorporating results-based budgeting into the U.N. system, and a one-time buyout for all unwanted or unneeded staff. It recommended the creation of a new U.N. Human Rights Council to replace the discredited Commission on Human Rights, but was unable to come to consensus on Security Council reform [97].

In Larger Freedom: Towards Development, Security, and Human Rights for All On March 21, 2005, Secretary-General Annan released his report, In Larger Freedom, in response to the findings of the High-Level Panel on Threats, Challenges and Change [98]. The report was presented to member states as a starting point for discussion at the 2005 U.N. World Summit, and included the following management reform recommendations:

- the review of all U.N. mandates over five years old;
- a one-time staff-buyout to ensure U.N. Secretariat staff meets current needs;

- the establishment of a cabinet-style decision-making body in the Secretariat to improve management and policy activities;
- the review of all budget and human resource operations; and
- a comprehensive review of Office of Internal Oversight Services to examine ways to enhance its authority and effectiveness.

In addition, Secretary-General Annan proposed a broad range of institutional and programmatic reforms, including modifying the composition of the U.N. Security Council so that it more adequately reflects current political realities, and replacing the Commission on Human Rights with a new Human Rights Council. Annan also recommended streamlining the General Assembly agenda and committee structure so that the Assembly can increase the speed of its decision- making and react more swiftly and efficiently to events as they occur [99].

IMPLEMENTING REFORM: MECHANICS AND POSSIBLE CHALLENGES

Mechanics of Implementing Reform

Previous and current U.N. reform initiatives encompass an array of organizational issues that may require different processes for implementation. These reforms might be achieved by amending the U.N. Charter or through various non-Charter reforms. Charter amendment is a rarely used practice and has only occurred on three occasions. Non-Charter reforms are more common and comparatively easier to achieve.

Amending the U.N. Charter

Articles 108 and 109 provide for potential changes to the U.N. Charter. Article 108 of the Charter states that a proposed Charter amendment must be approved by two-thirds of the full General Assembly, and be ratified "according to the constitutional processes" of two-thirds of U.N. member states, including the all permanent members of the Security Council [100] The Charter was first amended in 1963 to increase U.N. Security Council membership from 11 to 15 members, and to increase ECOSOC membership from 18 to 27. It was last amended in 1973, when ECOSOC membership increased from 27 to 54.[101] Examples of possible reform initiatives that might involve amending the U.N. Charter include, but are not limited to: increasing Security Council membership—either permanent or and non-permanent members; increasing membership on ECOSOC; and adding or removing a principal organ [102].

Article 109 of the Charter allows for a convening of a General Conference of U.N. members with the purpose of "reviewing the present Charter." The date and place of the Conference would be determined by a two-thirds vote in the General Assembly, and an affirmative vote from any nine Security Council members. Potential revisions to the Charter would be adopted at the conference by a two-thirds vote (with each country having one vote), and take effect when ratified by the governments of two-thirds of U.N. member states. A Charter review conference has never been held.

Non-Charter Reform Process

Since 1945, the General Assembly has authorized reforms of its own processes and procedures— as well as those of the Secretariat—without Charter amendment. The General Assembly has established various fora for discussing reform issues, including a Committee on the Charter of the United Nations [103] and a Working Group on the Security Council [104]. The General Assembly has also implemented reforms on its own by adopting proposals introduced by member states or the Secretary-General [105] The Secretary-General can also implement reform in his capacity as chief administrative officer. For example, as part of his reform proposal in 1997, Annan established a Senior Management Group to "ensure more integrated and cohesive management of the Secretariat." [106] The Secretary-General can also make administrative decisions regarding the organization of some U.N. departments.

Other non-Charter reforms have included the establishment of consensus-based budgeting in 1986; the creation of an Office of Strategic Planning in the Secretariat, authorized by Kofi Annan in 1997; and the establishment of a Peacebuilding Commission by the Security Council and General Assembly in 2006 [107].

Possible Challenges to Reform

Achieving meaningful and comprehensive U.N. reform is a significant and ongoing challenge for U.N. member states. Congress may wish to take possible reform obstacles into account when considering legislation that exercises oversight or supports a reform agenda.

National Self-Interest and Differing Reform Perspectives

Each U.N. member state has its own political agenda and foreign policy goals, and may also have its own definition of U.N. reform. As a result, member states often hold differing views on how best to implement reform and how to measure the success or failure of a given reform initiative. In some cases, failure to reach consensus can lead to significant delay, or failure, of certain reform initiatives. Some member states package their policy priorities as U.N. reform to further their own policy goals. This can cause distrust among member states as countries question whether reform proposals by other member states are based on self-interest or a genuine desire to improve the U.N. system.

Competing Priorities

Some observers cite the inability of U.N. member states or secretaries-general to effectively prioritize reform initiatives as an obstacle to U.N. reform. When Secretary-General Annan presented his 2005 reform proposals, for example, he requested that they be adopted by the General Assembly not in increments, but as a package of reforms [108]. Instead of considering a large series of reform proposals, some observers argue that member states should select only a few reform priorities and work toward their adoption and implementation. Others contend that the most efficient way to achieve reform may be for member states first to adopt reform initiatives they can agree to and then gradually work toward tackling the more divisive and complicated reform issues.

Organizational Structure and Bureaucracy

The United Nations is a highly complex and decentralized organization, and therefore may be slow to consider or implement potential reforms. Some argue that there is a "culture of inaction"109 in the United Nations, and that U.N. managers and staff are resistant to the implementation of new programs or changes to existing programs. Many contend that prospective and agreed-to reforms lack clear plans for implementation, including deadlines and cost estimates. They stress that this overall lack of planning may affect the progress and ultimate success of reforms already implemented, as well as those reforms currently being considered by the General Assembly [110]. Some also emphasize that without proper implementation plans and follow-up, U.N. member states will be unable to adequately gauge the overall effectiveness of reforms.

Limited Resources

Many observers note that a significant challenge for U.N. reform efforts may be the effective implementation of reforms within the current U.N. budget. Some reform initiatives, such as the Peacebuilding Commission, were established by member states to operate "within existing resources" [111]. Many argue that the existing U.N. budget limits may not be able to support all of the reform initiatives currently being considered. Some member states, including the United States, however, contend that money saved from other reforms, such as mandate review, could create a funding source for further reforms and/or the creation of new U.N. programs or bodies.

External Influences

The complex relationships that exist among member states outside of the U.N. system may be another challenge affecting U.N. reform efforts. These relationships are entirely independent of the United Nations but can affect how countries work together within the U.N. framework to achieve reform objectives. Military conflict, religious and ethnic differences, political conflict, trade and economic issues, and geography can all potentially impact reform cooperation among U.N. member states.

APPENDIX A. PREVIOUS REFORM LEGISLATION

When considering U.N. reform issues, the 111th Congress may wish to explore the nature and effectiveness of past legislative approaches and how or if they may have influenced the adoption of reform measures at the United Nations. There is evidence that legislation such as the Kassebaum-Solomon Amendment and the Helms-Biden Agreement may have led, either directly or indirectly, to substantive changes in U.N. policies. The following paragraphs highlight selected reform legislation from 1986 to the present and note any subsequent changes to internal U.N. policy.

APPENDIX B. KEY U.N. REFORM RECOMMENDATIONS AND PROPOSALS BY INDEPENDENT AND U.N. AFFILIATED GROUPS

Report of the Task Force on the United Nations (June 2004, December 2005)	In Larger Freedom: Towards Development, Security and Human Rights for All (March 2005)	Report of the Independent Inquiry Committee into the United Nations Oil-for-Food Program (October 2005)
Improved management reform, including:	Secretariat reform, including	Strengthen U.N. management practices, including:
Establish an Independent Oversight Board to function as an independent audit committee;	Review of the Office of Internal Oversight Services and general strengthening of internal oversight;	Establish an Independent Oversight Board with responsibility over internal and external audits and investigations;
Establish the role of Chief Operating Officer (COO);	Creation of a cabinet-style decision-making mechanism;	Create the position of Chief Operating Officer (COO);
Establish policies for improved financial disclosure standards, whistle-blower protection; and	Authority/resources for Secretary-General to realign and/or buy-out Secretariat staff; and full review of budget and human resources operations; and Review of all U.N. mandates five years or older.	Expand financial disclosure requirements for U.N. staff, including the Secretary-General, Deputy-Secretary-General, and those involved in procurement and/or disbursement;
Review of all U.N. mandates and sunset clauses for new mandates.		Improve coordination and framework for cross-agency U.N. programs; and Ensure third party agencies involved in U.N. programs are entitled to fair compensation.
Reorganization of the General Assembly;	Streamlining the General Assembly to speed-up decision-making processes;	
Replace the Commission on Human Rights with a new Human Rights Council;	Replace the discredited Commission on Human Rights with a new Human Rights Council;	
Identification of U.N. programs that could be more effective if funded by voluntary contributions; and Improving the Department of Peacekeeping Operations so that it becomes "a more independent program" with its own rules and regulations to address its unique mission.	Modify composition of the Security Council to reflect current political realities; and Reform ECOSOC so it may better coordinate the U.N. development agenda and guide other economic and social agencies in the United Nations.	

Kassebaum-Solomon Amendment (1986-1987) [112]

In the mid-1980s, some Members of Congress expressed concern that U.S. influence over the U.N. budget was not proportionate to its rate of assessment. In 1986 Congress passed legislation, popularly known as the "Kassebaum-Solomon amendment," which required that the U.S. assessed contribution to the U.N. regular budget be reduced to 20% unless the United Nations gave major U.N. financial contributors a greater say in the budget process [113] Subsequently, in 1986 the General Assembly adopted a new budget and planning process that incorporated consensus-based budgeting as a decision-making mechanism, thus giving member states with higher assessment levels a potentially greater voice in the budget process.

U.N. Office of Internal Oversight Services (1993)

In the early 1990s, some Members of Congress and the Administration were concerned with the apparent lack of oversight and accountability within the U.N. system. In 1993, as part of the FY1994 State Department Appropriations Act, Congress directed that 10% of U.S. assessed contributions to the U.N. regular budget be withheld until the Secretary of State certified to Congress that "the United Nations has established an independent office with responsibilities and powers substantially similar to offices of Inspectors General Act of 1978." [114] On July 29, 1994, the U.N. General Assembly established the Office of Internal Oversight Services (OIOS) which reports directly to the Secretary-General and provides "internal auditing, investigation, inspection, programme monitoring, evaluation and consulting services to all U.N. activities under the Secretary-General's authority." [115]

Helms-Biden Agreement (1999)

In the late 1 990s, Congress and the Administration negotiated and agreed to legislation that would further U.S. reform policy at the United Nations. The Helms-Biden bill authorized payment of some U.S. arrears if specific reform benchmarks were met and certified to Congress by the Secretary of State. [116] Under the terms of Helms-Biden, the United States agreed to: (1) pay $819 million in arrearages over fiscal years 1998, 1999, and 2000, and (2) forgive $107 million owed to the United States by the United Nations in peacekeeping costs if the United Nations applied the $107 million to U.S. peacekeeping arrears. For arrearage payments to occur, Congress required that the U.S. assessment for contributions to the U.N. regular budget be reduced from 25% to 22% and that the peacekeeping contribution be reduced from 30% to 25%. [117] In December 2000, the U.N. General Assembly reduced the regular budget assessment level to from 25% to 22%, and the Peacekeeping share from approximately 30.4% to 28%. In subsequent years, the U.S. peacekeeping assessment continued to fall and is now close to 26.5%.

APPENDIX C. ORGANIZATIONAL CHART OF THE U.N. SYSTEM(AS OF DECEMBER 2007)

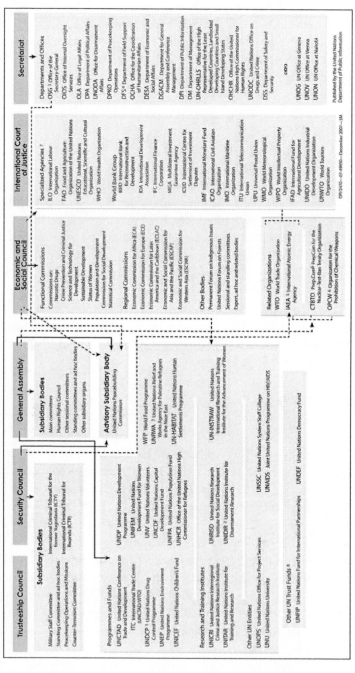

Source: http://www.un.org/aboutun/chart_en.pdf Notes: Solid lines from a Principal Organ (top row) indicate a direct reporting relationship; dashes indicate a non-subsidiary relationship. 1 The UN Drug Control Programme is part of the UN Office on Drugs and Crime. 2 UNRWA and UNIDIR report only to the GA. 3 The United Nations Ethics Office, the United Nations Ombudsman's Office, and the Chief Information Technology Officer report directly to the Secretary-General. 4 In an exceptional arrangement, the Under-Secretary-General for Field Support reports directly to the Under-Secretary-General for Peacekeeping Operations. 5 IAEA reports to the Security Council and the General Assembly (GA). 6 The CTBTO Prep.Com and OPCW report to the GA. 7 Specialized agencies are autonomous organizations working with the UN and each other through the coordinating machinery of the ECOSOC at the intergovernmental level, and through the Chief Executives Board for coordination (CEB) at the inter-secretariat level. 8 UNFIP is an autonomous trust fund operating under the leadership of the United Nations Deputy Secretary-General. UNDEF's advisory board recommends funding proposals for approval by the Secretary-General.

APPENDIX D. ADDITIONAL U.N. REFORM RESOURCES

Websites (NGOs, Think Tanks, U.S. Government, United Nations)

Better World Campaign—U.N. Reform http://www.betterworldcampaign.org/us-un-relations/un-reform.html

Center for U.N. Reform Education http://www.centerforunreform.org/

Eye on the U.N. (joint project of Hudson Institute and the Touro Law Center Institute for Human Rights)

http://www.eyeontheun.org/

Global Policy Forum—U.N. Reform, An Analysis

http://www.centerforunreform.org/

Heritage Foundation—International Organizations http://www.heritage.org/Research/ InternationalOrganizations/ ReformTheUN.org

http://www.reformtheun.org/

United Nations Association of the USA

http://www.unausa.org

U.N. Reform (Official U.N. web page)

http://www.un.org/reform/

U.S. Department of State

http://www.state.gov/p/io/c15031.htm and http://www.un.int/usa/ U.S. Institute of Peace U.N. Reform Task Force and Report http://www.usip.org/un/report/index.html

U.S. Government Reports (CRS and GAO)

CRS Report RL33611, *United Nations System Funding: Congressional Issues*, by Marjorie Ann Browne and Kennon H. Nakamura.

CRS Report RL33608, *The United Nations Human Rights Council: Issues for Congress*, by Luisa Blanchfield.

CRS Report RL33700, *United Nations Peacekeeping: Issues for Congress*, by Marjorie Ann Browne.

CRS Report RL30605, *United Nations Regular Budget Contributions: Members Compared, 1989-2007,* by Marjorie Ann Browne and Luisa Blanchfield.

Governmental Accountability Office (GAO) *Report 08-246, United Nations Management Reforms and Operational Issues,* January 24, 2008.

GAO Report 08-84, *United Nations Progress on Management Reform Efforts Has Varied*, November 2007.

GAO Report 07-5 97, *United Nations Organizations: Oversight and Accountability Could be Strengthened by Further Instituting International Best Practices*, June 2007.

GAO Report 07-14, *United Nations Management Reforms Progressing Slowly with Many Awaiting General Assembly Review*, October 2006.

GAO Report 06-330, *United Nations: Lessons Learned from Oil for Food Program Indicate the Need to Strengthen UN Internal Controls and Oversight Activities*, April 25, 2006.

GAO Report 06-70 1T, *United Nations: Internal Oversight and Procurement Controls and Processes Need Strengthening*, April 27, 2006.

GAO Report 06-577, *United Nations Procurement Internal Controls are Weak*, April 2006.

GAO Report 06-575, *United Nations Funding Arrangement Impede Independence of Internal Auditors*, April 2006.

GAO Report 05-392T, *United Nations Sustained Oversight Is Needed for Reforms to Achieve Lasting Results - Statement of Joseph A. Christoff,* Director, International Affairs and Trade, March 2, 2006.

GAO Report 04-339, *United Nations Reform Progressing, but Comprehensive Assessments Needed to Measure Impact,* February 2004.

REFERENCES

[1]   U.N. membership grew from 51 countries in 1945, to 114 countries in 1963. Currently, the United Nations has 192 member states. Amendments to the Charter related to increased membership are discussed in the "Mechanics of Implementing Reform," section of this report.

[2]   The General Assembly approved some, but not all, of the recommendations in 1977. For more information on this group and other U.N. reform efforts prior to the 1980s, see "Reforming the United Nations: Lessons from a History in Progress," by Edward C. Luck, *Academic Council on the United Nations System—Occasional Papers Series*, 2003.

[3]   U.N. document, A/RES/41/213, December 19, 1986. The group of experts was convened, in part, because of U.S. legislation popularly known as the "Kassebaum-Solomon Amendment," which directed that U.S. contributions to the U.N. regular budget be reduced if larger U.N. financial contributors did not have a more substantial influence in the U.N. budget process. See "Previous Reform Legislation" section of this report.

[4]   In response to the proposals in Boutrous-Ghali's reports, the General Assembly created five open-ended working groups to consider reforms in specific areas, including peace, development, the Security Council, the U.N. financial situation, and strengthening the U.N. system. Only one working group completed its work (the Working Group on Development), and three stopped meeting due to an inability to reach agreement on key issues. The fifth Security Council Working Group still meets regularly. For more information on this working group, see "The Mechanics of Implementing Reform" section of this report.

[5]   Notably, in 1994 the General Assembly established the Office of Internal Oversight Services (OIOS) to enhance and improve oversight in the United Nations.

[6]   Annan appointed a special panel on U.N. Peace Operations in March 2000 to make recommendations for improving the peacekeeping system. The panel's recommendations were consolidated into what is known as the "Brahimi Report." A number of the report's recommendations, such as increasing the number of staff in the Department of Peacekeeping Operations, were implemented. Other recommendations, particularly those involving U.N. member state personnel commitments for deployment, have yet to be achieved.

[7]   Annan subsequently outlined the thematic and technical aspects of these reform proposals in his report, Renewing the United Nations: A Programme for Reform, (A/5

1/950, July 14, 1997) which was endorsed by the General Assembly on December 19, 1997

[8]   Completed reforms include establishment of a strategic planning unit; creation of a senior management group; establishment of a Department for Disarmament and Arms regulation; creation of the Deputy-Secretary-General position; and the establishment of a U.N. Development Group to better coordinate U.N. development mechanisms and programs.

[9]   U.N. document, A/57/387, September 9, 2002, *Strengthening the United Nations: An Agenda for Further Change*. Some of the 2002 reform proposals were implemented, including centralization of U.N. information around regional hubs, starting with Western Europe; strengthening the Office of the High Commissioner for Human Rights; and the establishment of a policy planning unit in the Department of Economic and Social Affairs.

[10] The Panel's report, A More Secure World: Our Shared Responsibility, was released on December 2, 2004, and is available at http://www.un.org/secureworld/.

[11] See "Commissions, Task Forces, and Groups" section for more information on the report, which was released on March 21, 2005. A copy is available at http://www.un.org/largerfreedom/.

[12] The 2000 Millennium Summit was held from September 6-8, 2000, in New York. Its theme was "the role of the United Nations in the 21st Century." More information on the Summit is available at http://www.un.org/millennium/ summit.htm.

[13] CERF was re-launched on March 9, 2006, with an aim of ensuring a more timely and efficient response to humanitarian disasters. The Fund is administered by emergency relief coordinators on behalf of the Secretary-General. Since CERF was established, over $1 billion has been committed and pledged by U.N. member states and NGOs for about 1,400 projects in 66 countries. See http://ochaonline.un.org/cerf/CERF Home/tabid/1705/Default.aspx.

[14] U.N. document, A/RES/60/1, 2005 World Summit Outcome, September 16, 2005.

[15] The improved financial disclosure requirements were expanded to include senior managers, procurement officers, and individuals who invest in U.N. assets. The new requirements lowered the threshold for accepting gifts and provided mechanisms for improving the monitoring of disclosure forms. Secretary-General Ban Ki-moon agreed to submit a disclosure form and release it to the public. Former Secretary-General Annan submitted the form but did not make it publicly available. The whistle-blower protection policy was labeled the "gold standard" for other international organizations. More information is available at http://www.un.org/reform/highlights.shtml.

[16] These reforms were proposed in Secretary-General Annan's March 2006 report, *Investing in the United Nations: For a Stronger Organization Worldwide*, available at http://www.un.org/reform/.

[17] The U.N. Ethics Office was established on January 1, 2006. Initially, some U.N. member states expressed concern that the office was insufficiently staffed. In May 2007, Robert F. Benson of Canada was appointed director of the office, and additional staff were hired. The office has reportedly provided increased ethics training for U.N. staff, including workshops and materials for distribution, such as a May 2007 publication entitled, *Working Together: Putting Ethics to Work*, available at http://www.unescap.org/asd/HRMS/odlu/files/ethics.pdf.

[18] The resolution includes nine criteria for how the money may be spent by the Secretary-General, including a stipulation that if over $6 million is spent per biennium, the Secretary-General must receive prior approval from the U.N. Advisory Committee on Administrative and Budgetary Questions (ACABQ).

[19] U.N. press release, GA/1048 1, General Assembly Approves Reform Measures to Strengthen United Nations, July 7, 2006.

[20] U.N. document, A/RES/60/1, *2005 World Summit Outcome*, September 16, 2005, p. 36.

[21] The 15-member Panel released its report, Delivering as One, on November 9, 2006. The Panel met over a six month period and engaged in a thorough examination of the strengths and weaknesses of the U.N. system. For a list of Panel members, their affiliations, and a copy of the Panel's final report and recommendations, see http://www.un.org/events/ panel/.

[22] U.N. document, A/61/583, *Delivering as One, Report of the Secretary-General's High-Level Panel*, November 9, 2006.

[23] Examples of MDGs include cutting the number of people living on less than a dollar a day by half; ensuring that all children receive primary schooling; reduce the number of people who do not have access to safe drinking water by half; and reverse the spread of diseases such as malaria and HIV, among other things. More information on MDGs is available at http://www.un.org/millenniumgoals/.

[24] The United Nations currently has 11 agencies in ten separate buildings in Hanoi. The One U.N. Initiative would consolidate these agencies into one building to avoid duplication and harmonize management practices. The United Nations announced the establishment of One U.N. initiatives in seven additional countries: Albania, Cape Verde, Mozambique, Pakistan, Rwanda, Tanzania, and Uruguay. For more information, visit http://www.undg.org/?P=7.

[25] U.N. press release, "Secretary-General Gives Priority to Streamlining U.N. with Greater Cohesion," March 29, 2007.

[26] U.N. document, A/RES/61/261, April 4, 2007.

[27] These tribunals replace the Joint Disciplinary Committee and Joint Appeals Board. The current internal justice system was established in the late 1940s and was designed to administer internal justice for only several thousand employees in very few locations

[28] Resolution A/RES/61/261 also abolishes the Panels on Discrimination and Other Grievances, and transfers responsibility to the U.N. Office of the Ombudsman. The office will "encourage staff to seek resolution through the informal system," and will also house a Mediation Division to provide mediation services for the staff in the Secretariat and in U.N. funds and programs.

[29] U.N. documents, A/RES/61/261, April 4, 2007.

[30] Prior to becoming U.N. Secretary-General, Ban was the Minister of Foreign Affairs and Trade for the Republic of Korea. A biography of Secretary-General Ban is available at http://www.un.org/News/Press/docs/2006/sg21 18.doc.htm.

[31] "U.N. Security Council Reform is Most Pressing Issue—New Secretary-General," *ITAR-TASS Russian News Agency*, November 1, 2006.

[32] U.N. press release, SG/21 19, GA/10558, Speech of Secretary-General Ban Ki-moon on Taking Oath of Office, December 14, 2006.

[33] For detailed information on Ban's restructuring proposals, see U.N. document, A/61/749, February 15 2007.

[34] Farley, Maggie, "Ban's U.N. Peacekeeping Reforms Rejected," *Los Angeles Times*, February 6, 2007.

[35] U.N. document, A/61/L.55, March 13, 2007.

[36] U.N. document, A/RES/61/257.

[37] U.N. document, A/RES/61/256, March 15, 2007. For more information on the peacekeeping restructuring, see CRS Report RL33700, *United Nations Peacekeeping: Issues for Congress*, by Marjorie Ann Browne.

[38] The framework resolution, A/RES/61/256 was adopted March 15, 2007 and the Assembly adopted A/RES/61/279 on June 29, 2007.

[39] Some critics of Secretary-General Ban's policy maintain that the financial disclosures of all high-level staff should be made public. Ban has stated that public disclosure is "an important voluntary initiative," that "demonstrates that U.N. staff members understand the importance of the general public and U.N. Member States being assured that... staff members will not be influenced by any consideration associated with his/her private interests." The U.N. Secretariat maintains a public list of financial disclosures by senior U.N. officials, which is available at http://www0.un.org/sg/Public Disclosure. shtml.

[40] U.N. press release, SG/2 120, Transcript of Press Conference by Secretary-General-Designate Ban Ki-moon, December 14, 2006.

[41] Congress has enacted laws supporting U.N. policies and/or requiring that U.N. member states comply with U.N. Security Council resolutions or the directives of other U.N. bodies. For example, the John Warner National Defense Authorization Act for FY2007 (P.L. 109-3 64, §3 02) states, "Congress urges ... in the event Iran fails to comply with United Nations Security Council Resolution 1696 (July 31, 2006), the Security Council to work for the adoption of appropriate measures under Article 41 of Chapter VII of the Charter of the United Nations."

[42] For a more detailed examination of U.S. funding of the United Nations, see CRS Report RL33611, *United Nations System Funding: Congressional Issues*, by Marjorie Ann Browne and Kennon H. Nakamura

[43] Foreign Assistance Act of 1961 (P.L. 87-195; Sec. 307; 22 USC 2227), as amended.

[44] For more information, see CRS Report RL33608, *The United Nations Human Rights Council: Issues for Congress*, by Luisa Blanchfield.

[45] Foreign Affairs Authorization Act for FY1994 and 1995 (P.L. 103-236), April 30, 1994. On September 30, 2002, Congress lifted the 25% cap on Peacekeeping assessment to allow the United States to pay its current assessments (P.L. 107-228, section 402). For more information on U.N. Peacekeeping funding, see CRS Report RL33700, *United Nations Peacekeeping: Issues for Congress*, by Marjorie Ann Browne.

[46] Additionally, some observers contend that if the United States were to delay or stop payment of its arrears, it may risk losing its vote in the General Assembly—a generally undesirable outcome for many Members of Congress and the Administration. In 1999, for example, the United States came very close to losing its General Assembly vote. Under Article 19 of the U.N. Charter, a U.N. member state with arrears equaling or

exceeding the member states's assessments for the two preceding years will have no vote in the General Assembly.

[47] "The Right Approach to Achieving U.N. Reform," *Better World Campaign Fact Sheet,* available at http://www.betterworldcampaign.org.

[48] Article 100 of the U.N. Charter states, "In the performance of their duties the Secretary-General and the staff shall not seek or receive instructions from any government or from any other authority external to the Organization. They shall refrain from any action which might reflect on their position as international officials responsible only to the Organization." A copy of the U.N. Charter is available at http://www.un.org/aboutun/charter/.

[49] Under-Secretary-General Burnham stepped down before Secretary-General Annan's term ended in 2007. Prior to Christopher Burnham, the post was held by Catherine Bertini, also a U.S. citizen. The current U.N. Under-SecretaryGeneral for Management for Secretary-General Ban is Angela Kane of Germany.

[50] In the 1970s and 1980s, for example, the "Geneva Group" was formed to encourage dialogue and cooperation among like-minded U.N. member states. It was composed mostly of Western countries that were the United Nations' largest financial contributors. The group focused mainly on financial and budgetary issues, and some contend it was instrumental in bringing about budgetary restraint in some of the U.N. specialized agencies. For more information, see *The United States and Multilateral Institutions,* edited by Margaret P. Karns and Karen A. Mingst, Unwin Hyman Publishers, 1990, p. 313; and *United Nations: Law, Policies and Practice,* edited by Rudiger Wolfrum, Martinus Nijhoff Publishers, 1995, pp. 70-71.

[51] U.N. press release, SG/SM/10089, "Transcript of Press Conference by Secretary-General Kofi Annan at United Nations Headquarters," September 13, 2005. This is a view shared by many who are involved in formulating U.N. reform policy.

[52] Congressional Transcripts, Congressional Hearings, "Senate Foreign Relations Committee Holds Hearing on the Nomination of Susan Rice to be the U.S. Representative to the United Nations," *Congressional Quarterly,* January 15, 2009."

[53] Ibid.

[54] "Progress Report by the United States Mission to the United Nations, A New Era of Engagement, Advancing America's Interests in the World,'" U.S. Mission to the United Nations press release # 082(09), April 29, 2009.

[55] Testimony by then-U.S. Ambassador to the United Nations John Bolton before the Senate Foreign Relations Committee, Challenges and Opportunities in Pushing Ahead on U.N. Reform, May 25, 2006. Available at http://www.state.gov/p/io/rls/rm/66904.htm.

[56] Testimony by then-U.S. Ambassador to the United Nations John Bolton before the Senate Foreign Relations Committee, Challenges and Opportunities in Moving Ahead on U.N. Reform, October 18, 2005, available at http://www.state.gov/p/io/rls/rm/55341.htm.

[57] Drawn from U.S. Department of State Fact Sheet, "U.S. Priorities for a Stronger, More Effective United Nations," June 17, 2005, available at http://www.state.gov/documents/organization/53104.pdf.

[58] Testimony by then-U.S. Ambassador to the United Nations John Bolton before the Senate Foreign Relations Committee, May 25, 2006.

[59] "President Addresses United Nations High-Level Plenary Meeting," Office of the Press Secretary, The White House, September 14, 2005.

[60] The National Security Strategy of the United States of America, Executive Office of the President, March 2006, p. 45.

[61] OIOS is dependent on much of its funding from the U.N. programs that it audits, which some believe creates a conflict of interest. For more information, see U.S. Government Accountability Office Report GAO-05-392T, *United Nations: Sustained Oversight is Needed for Reforms to Achieve Lasting Results*, March 2, 2006, and GAO Report 08-84, *United Nations Progress on Management Reform Efforts has Varied*, November 2007.

[62] "Statement by Ambassador Mark D. Wallace, U.S. Representative for U.N. Management and Reform, on 'Investing in the U.N.: For a Stronger Organization Worldwide,'" U.S. Mission to the United Nations press release, July 7, 2006.

[63] Testimony by then-U.S. Ambassador to the United Nations John Bolton before the Senate Foreign Relations Committee, May 25, 2006.

[64] Ibid.

[65] The U.S. Mission assures confidentiality for whistleblowers who use the hotline. More information is available at http://www.usunnewyork.usmission.gov/Issues/reform_whisleblow.html.

[66] As evidence of this, the Administration cites abuses by the government of North Korea involving U.N. Development Program (UNDP) humanitarian and development activities. See "United Nations Transparency & Accountability Initiative," U.S. Mission to the United Nations, available at http://www.usunnewyork.usmission.gov/Issues/reform _untai.html

[67] Copies of the correspondences between the U.S. Mission and U.N. funds and programs are available at http://www.usunnewyork.usmission.gov/Issues/reform_untai_let.php.

[68] U.N. documents, A/RES/60/180 and S/RES/1645(2005), December 20, 2005.

[69] Further information on the Peacebuilding Commission is available at http://www.un.org/peace/peacebuilding/.

[70] The United States is a member of the organizational committee. For a list of members, see http://www.un.org/peace/ peacebuilding/mem-orgcomembers.shtml.

[71] For further information on UNDEF, see http://www.unfoundation.org/features/un_democracy_fund.asp.

[72] Top UNDEF donors include Australia, India, Japan, Qatar, and the United States. For a list of all donors, see http://www.un.org/democracyfund/XFinancialContributions.htm.

[73] "Statement by Ambassador Anne W. Patterson, Acting U.S. Ambassador to the United Nations, on U.S. Proposals for U.N. Reform in the General Assembly," U.S. Mission to the United Nations press release, June 22, 2005.

[74] More information on the activities of the Ad Hoc Committee is available at http://www.un.org/law/terrorism/ index.html.

[75] "U.S. Priorities for a Stronger, More Effective United Nations," *U.S. Department of State Fact Sheet*, June 17, 2005.

[76] Statement by then-Ambassador John Bolton on Security Council reform and expansion, to the General Assembly, U.S. Mission to the United Nations press release, July 21, 2006.

[77] In 2007, Japan contributed 16.624% (approximately $332.2 million) of the U.N. regular budget. For more information on individual member state contributions to the United Nations, see CRS Report RL30605, *United Nations Regular Budget Contributions: Members Compared, 1989-2007*, by Marjorie Ann Browne and Luisa Blanchfield.

[78] Statement by Ambassador Mark Wallace, December 11, 2006, available at http://www.un.int/usa/06_393.htm.

[79] The groups of U.N. member states discussed in this report are only a few of many political and geographical alliances in the United Nations. Others include the Non-Aligned Movement, the Organization of the Islamic Conference, and the African Union. Israel is a temporary member of the Western European and Others Group (WEOG), but it is excluded from the system of regional groups outside of U.N. Headquarters in New York. The United States is not a member of any regional group but participates in WEOG as an observer and is "considered part of that group for the electoral purposes." For more information, see Chapter 3, "Groups and Blocs," in Politics and Process as the United Nations: The Global Dance, by Courtney B. Smith, Lynne Rienner Publishers, London, 2006, p. 64. A list of U.N. alliances is available at http://www.eyeontheun.org/view.asp?1=11&p=55.

[80] Each U.N. member state has one vote in the U.N. General Assembly regardless of its affiliations. For more information, see "The EU at the U.N.—Overview," at http://www.europa-eu-un.org/documents/infopack/en/EUUNBrochure-1_en.pdf.

[81] "EU Priorities for the 61st U.N. General Assembly," July 18, 2006, available at http://www.europa-eu-un.org/articles/ en/article _6242 _en.htm.

[82] An October 25, 2005 EU paper on ECOSOC reform is available at http://www.europa-eu-un.org/articles/en/ article_5350_en.htm.

[83] "EU Priorities for the 61st U.N. General Assembly," July 18, 2006, available at http://www.europa-eu-un.org/articles/ en/article _6242 _en.htm.

[84] The G-77 was established in 1964 and represents approximately 69% of U.N. member states. For more information and records of G-77 statements made at the United Nations, see http://www.g77.org/index.html.

[85] U.N. document, A/60/879, Statement Adopted by the Special Ministerial Meeting of the Group of 77 and China, Putrajaya (Malaysia), June 7, 2006.

[86] U.N. document, A/60/907, June 27, 2006.

[87] For example, the G-77 opposed proposals by Secretary-General Annan that gave the Secretariat more power to move, hire, and fire U.N. Secretariat staff, as well as to modify and consolidate the budgeting process.

[88] "Statement on Behalf of the Group of 77 and China on Secretariat and Management Reform: Report of the Secretary- General entitled 'Investing in the United Nations'" New York, April 3, 2006, available at http://www.g77.org/ Speeches/040306.htm. Also see "U.N. Management Reform: The Role and Perspective of the G-77," by Irene Martinetti, *Center for U.N. Reform,* September 10, 2007.

[89] The foremost institutional reform priority for Japan is changing the composition of the Security Council to "reflect the realities of the international community in the 21st Century." For more information on Japanese U.N. reform priorities, see the Japanese Ministry of Foreign Affairs publication, "Japan's Efforts for Reform of the U.N.," available at http://www.mofa.go.jp/policy/un/reform/pamph0608.pdf.

[90] Annan's reforms were proposed in his March 2006 report, Investing in the *United Nations: For a Stronger Organization World Wide.*

[91] On July 7, 2006, the General Assembly approved the reforms recommended by the Fifth Committee. (See U.N. document, A/RES/60/283, July 7, 2006.) A list of the approved reforms is available in the "Recently Adopted Reforms and the New Secretary-General" section of this report. For more information and additional resources on the six-month budget cap controversy, http://www.globalpolicy.org/ finance/docs/unindex.htm.

[92] For a discussion on the effectiveness of various U.N. reform groups, see keynote speech at University of Waterloo made by Edward C. Luck, Director of the Center on International Organization at Columbia University, "U.N. Reform Commissions: Is Anyone Listening?" May 16, 2002, available at http://www.sipa.columbia. edu/cio/cio/projects/ waterloo.pdf.

[93] U.N. document, A/RES/1538, April 21, 2004. The Committee was chaired by Paul Volcker and included Professor Mark Peith of Switzerland, an expert on money laundering from the Organization for Economic Cooperation and Development (OECD); and Justice Richard Goldstone of South Africa, a former prosecutor with the International Criminal Tribunals for the former Yugoslavia and Rwanda. The Commission's final report was released on October 27, 2005. For more detailed information on the functioning of the Iraq Oil-For-Food Program, see CRS Report RL3 0472, *Iraq: Oil-For-Food Program, Illicit Trade, and Investigations*, by Christopher M. Blanchard and Kenneth Katzman.

[94] "Briefing by Paul A. Volcker Chairman of the Independent Inquiry Committee into the U.N. Oil-For-Food Program for the Permanent Subcommittee on Investigations of the U.S. Senate," Washington, DC, October 31, 2005.

[95] Consolidated Appropriations Act, 2005 (P.L. 108-447, December 8, 2004). In the report accompanying the act, conferees stated that they were "deeply troubled by the inaction of the United Nations on many fronts, especially in regard to the genocide in Darfur, Sudan and the allegations of corruption regarding the United Nations Oil-For-Food Program." Conferees directed that the task force should include experts from the American Enterprise Institute, Brookings Institution, Council on Foreign Relations, Center for Strategic and International Studies, Hoover Institution, and the Heritage Foundation.

[96] The Task Force was co-chaired by former Speaker of the House Newt Gingrich and former Senate Majority Leader George Mitchell, and released its first report, American Interests and U.N. Reform in June 2005. Following the 2005 U.N. World Summit in New York, the Task Force released an updated report entitled, The Imperative for Action, in December 2005. The USIP Task Force reports are available at http://www.usip.org/un/report/.

[97] The Task Force stated that any Security Council reform should "enhance the effectiveness of the Security Council and not in any way detract from the Council's efficiency and ability to act in accordance with the U.N. Charter." (See page 7 of the Task Force's report, American Interests and U.N. Reform.)

[98] See "Reform Efforts (1997-2005)" section of this report for more information on the High-Level Panel.

[99]   Annan also supported reforming the U.N. Economic and Social Council (ECOSOC) so that it may better coordinate with economic and social agencies and departments within the U.N. system. More information on ECOSOC reform is available at http://www.centerforunreform.org/node/186 and http://www.globalpolicy.org/socecon/un/reform/articlesindex.htm.

[100] Article 108 of the U.N. Charter states, "Amendments to the present Charter shall come into force for all Members of the United Nations when they have been adopted by a vote of two-thirds of the members of the General Assembly and ratified in accordance with their respective constitutional processes by two thirds of the members of the United Nations, including all the permanent members of the Security Council." A copy of the U.N. Charter is available at http://www.un.org/aboutun/charter/.

[101] Simma, Bruno, *The Charter of the United Nations: A Commentary.* Second Edition, Vol. II. New York, Oxford University Press, 2002, p. 1367-1357.

[102] Principal organs of the United Nations include the Trusteeship Council (TC); Security Council; General Assembly; Economic and Social Council; International Court of Justice; and the Secretariat. There is an ongoing effort to abolish the TC, a system that was designed to administer and supervise U.N. trust territories. The TC suspended its operations on November 1, 1994, with the independence of its last trust territory, Palau.

[103] The "Special Committee on the Charter of the United Nations and on the Strengthening of the Role of the Organization," was established in 1974 to consider "any specific proposals that Governments might make with a view to enhancing the ability of the U.N. to achieve its purposes," as well as "suggestions for the more effective functioning of the U.N. that might not require amendments to the Charter." The Committee also makes recommendations for possible Charter amendments. Most recently, in 1995 it proposed an amendment to delete "enemy state" clauses in the Charter. For more information on the Committee, see http://www.un.org/law/chartercomm/.

[104] The "Working Group on the Question of Equitable Representation on and Increase in the Membership of the Security Council and Other Matters Related to the Security Council," was established in 1993, and a copy of its most recent report is available at http://www.reformtheun.org/index.php?module=uploads&func=download&fileId=1757

[105] For example, on March 15, 2006, the Assembly negotiated and approved a resolution replacing the previous U.N. Commission on Human Rights with a new Human Rights Council, which was considered a key component of U.N. reform by many member states and NGOs.

[106] U.N. document, A/52/684, November 10, 1997.

[107] An example of a possible non-Charter reform could be the redistribution of regional seats on the Security Council or ECOSOC. For further discussion on possible non-Charter reforms, see article by Louis B. Sohn, "Important Improvements in the Functioning of the Principal Organs of the United Nations that Can be Made Without Charter Revision," *American Journal of International Law,* October, 1997.

[108] "The Secretary-General's Statement to the General Assembly," New York, March 21, 2005, available at http://www.un.org/largerfreedom/sg-statement.html.

[109] "Annan's 'Culture of Inaction.'" *The Chicago Tribune,* December 12, 2006.

[110] U.S. Government Accountability Office Report, GAO-07-14, *United Nations Management Reforms Progressing Slowly with Many Awaiting General Assembly Review*, October 2006.

[111] U.N. document, A/RES/60/1, *2005 World Summit Outcome*, September 16, 2005.

[112] For a more detailed account of the Kassebaum-Solomon Provisions, see CRS Report RL33611, *United Nations System Funding: Congressional Issues*, by Marjorie Ann Browne and Kennon H. Nakamura.

[113] Foreign Relations Authorization Act, FY1986 and 1987 (H.R. 2608, P.L. 99-93), Section 143, August 16, 1985.

[114] U.S. Department of State Appropriations Act, 1994 (H.R. 2519, P.L. 103-121), October 27, 1993.

[115] More information on OIOS is available at http://www.un.org/depts/oios/. See U.N. document, A/RES/48/218 B, August 12, 1994, for a detailed description of its mandate.

[116] The Helms-Biden Agreement was incorporated into the Consolidated Appropriations Act for FY2000 (H.R. 3194, P.L. 106-113), November 19, 1999.

[117] See CRS Report RL33700, *United Nations Peacekeeping: Issues for Congress*, by Marjorie Ann Browne for further information

In: Globalization

Editors: M. G. Massari and K. J. Lutz, pp. 151-178

ISBN: 978-1-61470-327-3

© 2012 Nova Science Publishers, Inc

Chapter 7

UNITED NATIONS ASSISTANCE MISSION IN AFGHANISTAN: BACKGROUND AND POLICY ISSUES[*]

Rhoda Margesson

ABSTRACT

The most serious challenge facing Afghans and Afghanistan today remains the lack of security. Recent moves by the Taliban and other insurgents to reestablish control of some areas of the country have slowed the pace and extent of economic development and the expansion of the Afghan government, an essential part of the peacebuilding process in Afghanistan. On December 1, 2009, the Obama Administration laid out its strategy for Afghanistan in response to a battlefield assessment from General McCrystal and reemphasized an earlier commitment to civilian efforts in cooperation with the United Nations. The December 1 policy announcement was a follow-on to a March 2009 Obama Administration statement that identified Afghanistan as a top national security priority. It also highlighted the unsatisfactory status of progress to date and need to find a way forward. Congress has focused on Afghanistan as a critical concern during the first session of the 111th Congress.

The United Nations has had an active presence in Afghanistan since 1988. Since the Bonn Agreement of December 2001, international donor activity and assistance has been coordinated primarily through the United Nations Assistance Mission in Afghanistan (UNAMA), though there are other coordinating institutions tied to the Afghan government. Most observers agree that continued, substantial, long-term development is key, as is the need for international support, but questions have been raised about aid effectiveness (funds required, priorities established, impact received) and the coordination necessary to achieve sufficient improvement throughout the country.

The international recovery and reconstruction effort in Afghanistan is immense and complicated and, in coordination with the Afghan government, involves U.N. agencies, bilateral donors, international organizations, and local and international non-governmental organizations (NGOs). The international community and the Afghan

---

[*] This is an edited, reformatted and augmented version of CRS Report R40747, dated December 14, 2009.

government have sought to establish coordinating institutions and a common set of goals in order to use donor funds effectively.

The international donor community has put great emphasis on Afghan "ownership"—meaning leadership and control—of reconstruction and development efforts by the country itself. Although the Afghan government is taking on an increasingly central role in development planning and the management of aid funds, the international community remains extensively involved in Afghan stabilization, not only in diplomacy and development assistance, but also in combating insurgents and addressing broader security issues. The coordinated aid programs of the United States and its European allies focus on a wide range of activities from strengthening the central and local governments of Afghanistan and its security forces, to promoting civilian reconstruction, reducing corruption, and assisting with elections.

This report examines the central role of UNAMA in Afghanistan. It discusses the obstacles the organization faces in coordinating international efforts and explores related policy issues and considerations for the 111th Congress. This report will be updated as events warrant.

INTRODUCTION

The United States and the international community have turned greater attention to the central role of the United Nations Assistance Mission in Afghanistan (UNAMA) as coordinator of international donor activity and assistance. This shift has been brought about by a broader, ongoing debate focused on U.S. and other assessments of efforts to stabilize Afghanistan. UNAMA's role has been emphasized in different contexts. For example, U.N. Security Council Resolution 1806 (2008) significantly expanded UNAMA's authority. The Declaration of the International Conference in Support of Afghanistan, which took place in Paris in June 2008, also underlined UNAMA's role in leading all aspects of civilian coordination. In unveiling a new strategy for Afghanistan and Pakistan in March 2009, the Obama Administration highlighted the need for coordination and burdensharing among donors in building Afghan capacity and providing the necessary civilian expertise. It also emphasized the importance of a leadership role for UNAMA on these issues and as part of its coordination role. The Chairman's statement of the International Conference on Afghanistan (The Hague, March 31, 2009) also emphasized UNAMA's coordination role and urged its expansion into as many provinces as possible. Most recently, on December 1, 2009, the Obama Administration laid out a strategy for Afghanistan in response to a battlefield assessment from General McCrystal and reestablished previous commitments to civilian efforts in cooperation with the United Nations.

Some observers contend that progress has been achieved so far in Afghanistan. U.S. embassy officials in Kabul have noted progress on reconstruction, governance, and security in many areas of Afghanistan and report that violence is higher than previous levels and accelerating in certain areas. Experts argue that recent progress on civilian reconstruction and development in Afghanistan needs to be understood in the context out of which Afghanistan has emerged since 2001 following more than two decades of conflict that resulted in significant political, economic, and social decline. Reconstruction efforts must cope with the destructive impact of war and with the distortions in the Afghan economy, in which the war and drugs compete with agriculture and other economic activities. Despite the deteriorating security situation, some progress in Afghanistan's reconstruction continues to be made, and when considered over time, is not insignificant.

Other assessments are more pessimistic. Critics say that slow reconstruction, corruption, and the failure to extend Afghan government authority into rural areas and provinces, particularly in the south and east, have contributed to continuing instability and a Taliban resurgence. Afghan officials in the more stable northern part of the country have expressed concerns about the limited progress on reconstruction. Narcotics trafficking persists, despite counter-measures, and independent militias remain a problem throughout the country, although many have been disarmed. Some experts raise concerns about increased insecurity in previously stable areas and the challenges this creates in providing humanitarian and development assistance [1]

UNAMA has been given a lead role in the civilian reconstruction effort. Some contend that UNAMA's role in the flawed August 2009 elections and aftermath may have undermined its credibility. Still, many experts agree that the international effort in Afghanistan is at a critical period. The international community's expectations of UNAMA may in part reflect the impact UNAMA might have on the success or failure of international efforts in Afghanistan. This report provides an analysis of UNAMA's role in Afghanistan and the key policy issues it faces on civilian reconstruction.

SETTING THE CONTEXT

The United States, other countries, and international relief organizations have long been active in providing assistance to the Afghan people. Afghanistan was admitted as a member of the United Nations on November 19, 1946, and has had a relationship with the United Nations that goes back more than 60 years. During the 1980s, the United States, along with other countries, funded the mujahedin forces fighting against the Soviet Union, as well as provided humanitarian aid to Afghans who fled to refugee camps in Pakistan. In 1988, the Geneva Peace Accords were signed, which led to the Soviet withdrawal nearly a decade after its invasion [2]

With the peace accord in place, the United Nations established an active presence in Afghanistan. It generally maintains separate offices for (1) political and peace processes (Pillar I) and (2) humanitarian and reconstruction operations (Pillar II) [3]. During the violent civil war that lasted through the 1990s, the United Nations continued to seek a peace agreement that would allow for sustained reconstruction. However, with the failure of several peace agreements, the international donor community focused primarily on humanitarian aid because the conditions were not stable for long-term development [4]. Donors also did not want to provide assistance to the Taliban, an Islamic fundamentalist movement that ruled Afghanistan between 1996 and 2001, when it was ousted by U.S.-backed Afghan factions [5]

Afghanistan was one of the least developed countries in the world even prior to the outbreak of war in 1978 [6]. The assistance situation changed dramatically once the Taliban was removed from power following the U.S.-led military intervention in 2001. The implementation of humanitarian assistance and the development of reconstruction plans quickly took shape when Afghans met under U.N. auspices to decide on a governance plan, which resulted in the Bonn Agreement, signed on December 5, 2001. On December 22, 2001, an interim government was formed with Hamid Karzai as its leader. This paved the way for a constitution, considered the most progressive in Afghan history, which was approved at a "constitutional loya jirga" (traditional Afghan assembly) in January 2004. Hamid Karzai was elected president in October 2004, and parliamentary and provincial elections were subsequently held in September 2005. The presidential and provincial elections were held on August 20, 2009 (details discussed later in the report), with parliamentary elections likely to follow in 2010. The Afghan government has been working with the international donor community on reconstruction programs and plans since a major donor conference in January 2002 in Tokyo.

The Afghan government and the international community face a daunting task. Many problems remain in every sector. Strategic challenges are numerous and continue to put the institution- building effort in Afghanistan at risk. In conjunction with security, reconstruction is seen by many as the single most important factor for sustaining peace. According to many observers, successful development could stem public disillusionment with the international effort in Afghanistan, sustain Afghan participation in the reconstruction process, and help keep Afghanistan from again becoming a permanent haven for terrorists.

MANDATE, STRUCTURE, AND FUNDING

The role of UNAMA is to promote peace and stability in Afghanistan and to lead the international community in this effort. In support of the Government of Afghanistan, UNAMA coordinates efforts to rebuild the country and strengthen governance, development, and stability.

Mandate

On March 28, 2002, U.N. Security Council Resolution 1401 (2002) established the United Nations Assistance Mission in Afghanistan (UNAMA) as a political and "integrated" mission, directed and supported by the U.N. Department of Peacekeeping Operations, to help implement the Bonn Agreement. UNAMA aims to bring together two key elements—one with a political focus and the other dealing with humanitarian and development efforts. Lakhdar Brahimi, then Special Representative for the U.N. Secretary-General to Afghanistan, organized the Bonn Agreement and directed UNAMA until December 2004. UNAMA's mandate is renewed annually in March. U.N. Security Council Resolution 1868 (2009) extends UNAMA's mandate for another year until March 23, 2010 [7]

Significantly, U.N. Security Council Resolution 1806 (2008) expanded the mandate to include a "super envoy" concept that would represent the United Nations, the European Union, and the North Atlantic Treaty Organization (NATO) in Afghanistan. U.N. Security Council Resolution 1868 (2009) incorporates UNAMA's increased scope, which includes leading international civilian efforts to support the Afghan government, increasing cooperation with the International Security Assistance Force (ISAF), and developing greater political outreach with Afghan leaders [8]

Organization

Beginning in March 2008, the head of UNAMA, and Special Representative of the U.N. Secretary-General (SRSG) for Afghanistan, with expanded powers over his predecessors, is Norwegian diplomat Kai Eide [9]. On December 11, 2009, Eide was reported to have said he would leave his post in March 2010 when his two-year contract expires [10]

There are two Deputy Special Representatives of the Secretary-General (DSRSG) for Afghanistan: Wolfgang Weisbrod-Weber (of Germany) is acting DSRSG and covers Political Affairs [11] Robert Watkins (of Canada) covers Relief, Recovery, and Reconstruction (RRR). Mr. Watkins also serves as the U.N. Development Program (UNDP) Resident Representative, Resident Coordinator and Humanitarian Coordinator in Afghanistan.

UNAMA has approximately 1,500 staff, of which about 80% are Afghan nationals (see organizational chart in Appendix B.) It coordinates all activities of the U.N. system in Afghanistan, which includes the participation of 18 U.N. agencies and several other organizations considered to be part of the U.N. country team (see Appendix C) [12]. UNAMA has eight regional offices and 12 provincial offices. The participants at the International Conference on Afghanistan in March 2009 emphasized that UNAMA should expand its presence into as many provinces as possible [13]

Budget

The total Calendar Year (CY) 2008 expenditures for UNAMA were $86.34 million, which was $10.2 million above the approved budget amount. With an expanded mandate, the U.N. General Assembly agreed to an increase of 91.5% in the Mission's CY2009 budget to $168 million. This number reflects an increase in staff, the opening of four additional provincial offices, and the strengthening of regional offices in Tehran and Islamabad. UNAMA is funded through assessed contributions to the U.N. regular budget. The U.S. assessment is 22% (the same level as for the U.N. regular budget) or approximately $36.96 million for CY2009. The General Assembly approved a 70% increase in UNAMA's budget for 2010, which reflects an increase in staff and the number of field offices.

FRAMEWORK FOR AFGHANISTAN'S RECONSTRUCTION STRATEGY

UNAMA was established in part to facilitate the implementation of the 2001 Bonn Agreement. In addition to this landmark document, two subsequent agreements between the Afghan government and the international community outline the overall Afghanistan reconstruction strategy: The 2006 Afghanistan Compact and the 2008 Afghanistan National Development Strategy (ANDS). The Joint Coordination and Monitoring Board (JCMB), of which UNAMA is co-chair, serves as a coordinating and monitoring mechanism for the implementation of these agreements. In addition, several international conferences, such as the Paris Conference in 2008, have provided guidance and built international support for the way forward in Afghanistan.

Bonn Agreement—Bonn 2001

The Agreement on Provisional Arrangements in Afghanistan Pending the Re-establishment of Permanent Government Institutions, or Bonn Agreement, was signed in Bonn, Germany, on December 5, 2001. It was endorsed by U.N. Security Council Resolution 1385 (2001). Under U.N. auspices, Afghan participants met to outline a process for the political transition in Afghanistan. The Bonn Agreement established an Afghan Interim Authority (AIA) on December 22, 2001, which was made up of 30 members and headed by Chairman Hamid Karzai. An Emergency *"loya jirga"* (traditional Afghan assembly) held in June 2002 replaced the AIA with a *Transitional Authority* (TA).

The TA brought together a broad transitional administration to lead the country until a full government could be elected. A constitution, considered the most progressive in Afghan history, was approved at a *"constitutional loya jirga"* in January 2004. Hamid Karzai was elected president in October 2004, and parliamentary and provincial elections were subsequently held in September 2005.

The Bonn Agreement also called for the establishment of a Supreme Court of Afghanistan and a Judicial Commission. It requested the U.N. Security Council to consider authorizing the deployment of a U.N.-mandated security force, outlined the role of the United Nations during the interim period, and referred to the need for cooperation with the international community on a number of issues, including reconstruction, elections, counternarcotics, crime, and terrorism. The Bonn Agreement was fully implemented in 2005.

Afghanistan Compact—London 2006

Donor countries and the Afghan government met at the London Conference in February 2006 to adopt the Afghanistan Compact (Compact), which provided a five-year time line (2006-2011) for addressing three main areas of activity, each with identified goals and outcomes: Security, Governance (Rule of Law and Human Rights), and Economic and Social Development. It also highlighted the cross-cutting issue of narcotics. The Compact acknowledged the need for Afghanistan to become more self-reliant while affirming the responsibilities required to achieve that goal. The international community agreed to monitor implementation of the Compact and the outlined benchmarks, and to improve aid effectiveness and accountability [14]

Afghanistan National Development Strategy (ANDS)—Paris 2008

The Afghanistan National Development Strategy (ANDS), which was signed by President Karzai in April 2008 and later presented as the "blueprint for the development of Afghanistan" at the donors conference in Paris, France, on June 12, 2008, is a policy paper created by the Afghan government. It builds on the Compact and follows a plan for establishing goals and measurable targets that is similar to the U.N. Millennium Development Goals [15]

Focusing on the three issue areas identified in the Compact (security, governance, economic growth/poverty reduction), it looks ahead to a vision for Afghanistan in the year 2020 while identifying specific goals to be achieved over five years between 2008 and 2013 [16] The ANDS envisions that most of the funding required would be provided by donors and that these funds would be distributed through the central government.

Joint Coordination and Monitoring Board (JCMB)

The Joint Coordination and Monitoring Board (JCMB) was established in 2008 and is the coordination body between the Afghan government and the international community. UNAMA is co-chair of the JCMB and has a central role in helping implement the development strategies outlined in the Compact and the monitoring activities put forward in ANDS. U.N. Security Council Resolution 1806 (2008) and U.N. Security Council Resolution 1868 (2009) direct UNAMA, in that capacity, to coordinate the work of international donors and organizations with an emphasis on aid effectiveness. The JCMB co-chairs reviewed the Compact and presented their findings at the June 2008 conference in Paris, stating that significant progress had been made in health and education, infrastructure and economic growth, and strengthening of Afghan national security forces.

INTERNATIONAL DONOR CONFERENCES AND TRUST FUNDS

The international donor community has established a series of institutional mechanisms for developing and coordinating reconstruction for countries emerging from conflict. Though adapted to specific situations, these mechanisms are generally similar. In November 2001, with the possibility of the fall of the Taliban and a potential opening for sustainable reconstruction work, the international donor community quickly established and implemented new initiatives. In addition to providing their own assistance to Afghanistan, international organizations and international financial institutions administered donor conferences, trust funds, and humanitarian and reconstruction programs. A brief summary of the main international donor conferences demonstrates the ongoing challenges that remain in Afghanistan and the repeated articulation of some of the issues. At the same time, it also shows increased participation by international stakeholders, perhaps, many contend, as a barometer of the importance that has now been ascribed to Afghanistan's future [17].

International Donor Conferences [18]

- *Bonn Conference (December 22, 2001)*—With the Bonn Agreement and interim government in place, UNDP organized a donor conference in which the interim government presented its reconstruction plans and country representatives and international NGOs made pledges in order to show international support for those plans.

- *Tokyo Conference (January 21-22, 2002)*—A ministerial conference, co-hosted by Japan, the United States, the European Union, and Saudi Arabia, was convened in Tokyo to discuss aid to Afghanistan. Donors pledged $4.5 billion.
- *Berlin Conference (April 1, 2004)*—The conference brought together 65 representatives from countries and international organizations to focus on reconstruction in Afghanistan. Pledges exceeded $8.2 billion.
- *London Conference (February 1, 2006)*—At the conference in London, the government of Afghanistan and the international community signed the Compact that outlined the principles of their cooperation over the next five years. Donors pledged $10.5 billion.
- *Paris Conference (June 12, 2008)*—The Afghan government and international community met in Paris in June of the same year to reiterate their partnership, with guidance from the Compact and the Afghan government's assigned leadership role in the implementation plan outlined in ANDS. The conferees affirmed the expanded role of UNAMA in all aspects of coordination. Key priorities identified at the conference included a wide range of activities: strengthening democracy and governance; investing in infrastructure and the private sector; improving aid effectiveness and reducing corruption; improving counter-narcotics measures; and ensuring the needs of all Afghans would be addressed through government services, greater civil society participation, and respect for human rights.
- *The Hague Conference (March 31, 2009)*—More than 80 countries met in The Hague for the "International Conference on Afghanistan: A Comprehensive Strategy in a Regional Context," which was hosted by the government of the Netherlands and UNAMA. The conference reinforced the central role outlined for UNAMA as coordinator of international action and assistance [19]. It also generated consensus on several points, including the need for a more directed agenda for Afghanistan, emphasizing the civilian capacity and institution- building, with sustained priority areas: security, governance, economic growth, and regional cooperation.

Proposed Conferences for 2010

At the Commonwealth Summit in Trinidad and Tobago, on Saturday, November 28, 2009, Prime Minister Gordon Brown and U.N. Secretary General Ban Ki-moon jointly announced plans to host an international conference at the ministerial level on Afghanistan to be held in London on January 28, 2010. Along with Prime Minister Brown, German Chancellor Angela Merkel and French President Nicolas Sarkosy have taken the lead in proposing the conference, the purpose of which is to find ways to strengthen the Afghan government and security forces as they take on responsibilities currently carried out by the international community. President Obama linked the need for this transition to the possible withdrawal of international troops in his December 1 speech. The United States is likely to be represented by Secretary of State Hillary Clinton. It is reported that a second high-level conference will be convened in Kabul, Afghanistan, several months after the London conference to further outline the framework for the phases of such a transition.

Trust Funds

At the start of the civilian reconstruction effort in Afghanistan in 2002, the international community placed great emphasis on paying the Afghan government's current expenditures, most importantly the salaries of government employees to enhance government capacity. Toward this end, several trust funds were established. Trust funds allow for rapid distribution of monies because they centralize funding and remove the administrative requirements of drawing from multiple funds. Donor countries decide to contribute to these trust funds and urge others to make contributions. The Afghan Interim Authority Fund (AIAF), for example, was created for donor contributions to the first six months during governmental operations and other related activities. On July 22, 2002, the Afghanistan Reconstruction Trust Fund (ARTF) succeeded the AIAF. In addition, the Law and Order Trust Fund for Afghanistan (LOTFA) was established to cover the rehabilitation of police facilities, salaries, training and capacity-building, and the procurement of non-lethal equipment. Following on these trust funds, the Counter-Narcotics Trust Fund was also established.

Administered by the World Bank, the ARTF continues to provide funds for the government's budget, investment activities and programs including quick-impact recovery projects, government training programs for Afghans, and support for the National Solidarity Program. ARTF has also expanded into other sectors such as education, agriculture, justice, and urban infrastructure. ARTF currently provides approximately half of the government's non-security operating costs and over a quarter of its development expenditures [20]. Recently, donors agreed to extend the ARTF until 2020. In part this reflects an ongoing commitment by donors to utilize the ARTF mechanism, and in part it is an acknowledgement of the development challenges that remain in Afghanistan. According to the World Bank, as of September 20, 2009, 30 international donors have contributed $3 billion to the ARTF since 2002 [21]

U.S. ASSISTANCE

Before 2001, U.S. aid to Afghanistan flowed mainly through U.N. agencies and NGOs, but the U.S. role increased dramatically after the start of Operation Enduring Freedom (OEF). U.S. government funding for assistance has come from three main agencies—the Department of Defense (DOD), the U.S. Agency for International Development (USAID), and the State Department [22]. Military and security assistance since 2001 represents more than half of U.S. funding for Afghanistan and has been provided through DOD, mainly through the Afghan Security Forces Fund, the Commander's Emergency Response Program (CERP), and other funds appropriated for counternarcotics and other programs. Funds provided for development and humanitarian-related activities and implemented mainly through USAID and the State Department are distributed to international organizations and non-governmental organizations, which provide services in Afghanistan, or directly to the Afghan government. Afghanistan also receives U.S. aid through multilateral institutions. The most important avenue is through the United Nations and its affiliated agencies and through international financial institutions, such as the World Bank and the International Monetary Fund (IMF). Some U.S. funding for Afghanistan comes from U.S. dues and additional voluntary donations to the United Nations through the State Department's International Organizations account or through the State Department's Migration and Refugee Assistance (MRA) account [23]

UNAMA's 2009 MANDATE FOR THE INTERNATIONAL CIVILIAN EFFORT IN AFGHANISTAN

In deciding to extend the mandate of UNAMA until March 23, 2010, the U.N. Security Council emphasized specific priorities for UNAMA [24]. It also asked the U.N. Secretary-General to report to the Security Council every three months on developments in Afghanistan. In addition, it requested the U.N. Secretary-General to establish benchmarks (drawing on the mandate and identified priorities) to determine progress in their implementation. The Secretary-General's June 2009 report was supposed to provide an update on the status of the benchmarks; instead, the U.N. Secretary-General requested a delay in finalizing the benchmarks, which were then outlined in the September 22, 2009, report [25]

U.N. Security Council Resolution 1868 (2009) — UNAMA Priorities

The priorities below are outlined in U.N. Security Council resolution 1868 (2009) as key areas of UNAMA's work in Afghanistan: [26]

- promote more coherent support by the international community to the Afghan government;
- strengthen cooperation with ISAF;
- provide political outreach through a strengthened and expanded presence throughout the country;
- provide good offices in support of Afghan-led reconciliation programs;
- support efforts to improve governance and the rule of law and to combat corruption;
- play a central coordinating role to facilitate the delivery of humanitarian aid;
- monitor the human rights situation of civilians and coordinate human rights protection;
- support the electoral process through the Afghan Independent Electoral Commission;
- support regional cooperation in working for a more stable and prosperous Afghanistan [27]

UNAMA's Benchmarks

The strategic benchmarks are outlined below. [28]

- Governance and Institution Building

Benchmark: Extension of Government authority throughout the country through the establishment of democratic, legitimate, accountable institutions, down to the local level, with the capacity to implement policies and to be increasingly capable of sustaining themselves.

- Security

Benchmark: Development of a sustainable Afghan security structure that is capable of ensuring peace and stability and protecting the people of Afghanistan.

- Economic and Social Development

Benchmark: Government policies backed by international support to promote sustainable economic growth that contributes to overall stability.

- Human Rights

Benchmark: Improved respect for the human rights of Afghans, in line with the Afghan Constitution and international law, with particular emphasis on the protection of civilians, the situation of women and girls, freedom of expression and accountability based on the rule of law.

- Counter-narcotics

Benchmark: Sustained trend in the reduction of poppy cultivation, narcotics production and drug addiction.

In his September 2009 report, the U.N. Secretary-General clarified that the benchmarks to measure progress on UNAMA's priorities would focus on broad areas in UNAMA's mandate and incorporate goals outlined in the agreed national strategies. The benchmarks would be results- based rather than tied to specific target dates, except where required under the constitution. While UNAMA has the capacity to monitor progress in some areas, the Secretary-General noted that this responsibility would also need to be shared with the Afghan government and other members of the international community. Furthermore, developing benchmarks in a comprehensive way would depend on creating an appropriate consultation process with the Afghan government and other international stakeholders.

Some experts believe that on the one hand, regular reports on benchmarks could help UNAMA execute its mandate in a more effective manner and would provide an opportunity to demonstrate the strengths and weaknesses of its strategy on a regular basis. On the other hand, others have questioned whether this is the most efficient way of measuring and tracking implementation of the mandate, whether it is possible to see progress in three-month intervals, and whether this may narrow the scope of how UNAMA's success or failure may be judged, which could have a significant impact on the perception of UNAMA's performance during a critical year.

POLICY ISSUES AND RECENT DEVELOPMENTS

Afghanistan remains a key priority in the 111th Congress. It is at the top of the Obama Administration's national security agenda, as reinforced by President Obama's December 1 speech outlining his strategy and resources decision at West Point military academy. As congressional concerns about the strategy in Afghanistan unfold, UNAMA's role as a key player in coordinating international donor activity and assistance may be of particular interest, in part because the extent to which UNAMA is successful may reduce the need for relief and reconstruction activities currently conducted by the United States and other members of the international community. Congress may also raise questions related to the budget, oversight of benchmarks and activities, and its role in overseeing aid effectiveness and the elections process in 2010.

The following sections address areas where UNAMA is playing a significant role.

Deteriorating Security Situation and Limited Progress on Development

There are several issues of concern for the international community, the Afghan government, and observers. First, the increasing lack of security has threatened the progress of development. According to the U.N. Secretary-General, violence has increased in parts of the country to levels not seen since 2001 [29] In 2009, the monthly average of security incidents increased by 43%. Targeted attacks on unarmed civil servants and the aid community, including the United Nations, have also risen. Second, although progress has been made on development (see Appendix H for a list of key achievements since 2002), some observers argue that Afghans have become frustrated with what they perceive as little evidence of development. There are many possible explanations for the perceived lack of progress, including lack of security, lack of human and physical capacity to implement substantial development, inadequate funding levels, and a focus on other funding priorities.

It is well understood that both security and progress on development are necessary in order to maintain international donor interest in Afghan development, encourage private investment in Afghanistan, and maintain Afghans' hope in improvement in their country and their own lives. The deteriorating security situation continues to take center stage as the key issue in Afghanistan while international stakeholders try to find ways to enable civilian efforts to take hold and be sustained. As part of this effort, for example, UNAMA is coordinating with the Independent Directorate of Local Governance and ISAF on a pilot project to fashion local approaches to securing communities.

August 2009 Presidential and Provincial Elections

Many experts placed significant emphasis on the need for credible, free, and fair presidential and provincial elections on August 20, 2009. The elections were seen as a potential benchmark in the promotion of good governance, and as an indicator of the confidence of the Afghan people in and consolidation of democracy in Afghanistan. The elections were front and center in Afghan politics and in international community circles. Of particular concern to the United Nations were questions about corruption (with some evidence that there had been some problem in the registration of candidates), finding ways to handle electoral irregularities, and ensuring the safety and security of civilians prior to and during the elections. Approximately 15.6 million voters (38% of whom are women) updated their registrations. The final list of candidates included 32 presidential candidates and 3,178 provincial council candidates, 328 of whom were women. UNAMA assisted with the registration and candidate nomination process and worked to resolve controversies such as the date of the elections and questions about the powers of the President when the Presidential term expired. UNAMA contributed technical support for the election process and worked closely with the U.N. Development Program (UNDP) on its project called Enhancing Legal and Electoral Capacity for Tomorrow (ELECT), which was the primary vehicle through which the international community supported the Afghan elections. UNAMA also provided guidance to a range of actors, including the Independent Election Commission (IEC), the Electoral Complaints Commission (ECC), the Afghanistan Independent Human Rights Commission, and members of civil society.

The Post Election Period

The August 20, 2009, presidential and parliamentary elections were the first elections run entirely under the auspices of the Afghan authorities in 30 years. Nevertheless, voting was unquestionably marred by irregularities, fraud, intimidation, and violence, all of which greatly affected turnout and results. The IEC released vote results slowly. Final, but uncertified, results released on September 16, 2009, showed Karzai at 54.6% and Dr. Abdullah at 27.7%. Other candidates received single-digit vote counts. The ECC ordered a recount of 10% of the polling stations as part of its investigations of fraud. On October 20, 2009, the ECC determined, based on its investigations, that about 1 million Karzai votes and about 200,000 Abdullah votes were considered fraudulent and were deducted from their totals. The final, certified results of the first round were as follows: Karzai, 49.67% (according to the IEC, with a lightly lower total of about 48% according to the ECC determination); Abdullah, 30.59%; and considerably lower figures for the remainder of the field [30]. Thus, Karzai did not legitimately exceed the 50% + threshold to claim a first-round victory. On October 21, 2009, the IEC accepted the ECC finding and Karzai conceded the need for a runoff election; Dr. Abdullah initially accepted the runoff. A date was set for November 7, 2009, for the runoff election.

In an attempt to produce a clean second round, UNAMA ordered about 200 district-level election commissioners be replaced. In addition, it recommended eliminating about 400 polling stations where few votes were expected to be cast. Security procedures were to be similar to those of the first round.

The End Result

On November 1, 2009, Dr. Adullah said he would not compete in the runoff on the grounds that the conditions that enabled the fraud had not been adequately addressed. On November 2, the IEC issued a statement saying that, by consensus, the body had determined that Karzai, being the only candidate remaining in a two-person runoff, should be declared the winner and the second round should not be held. The United States, U.N. Secretary General Ban Ki-moon, and several governments congratulated Karzai on the victory. U.S. officials, including Secretary of State Clinton, praised Dr. Abdullah for his relatively moderate speech announcing his withdrawal and refusing to call for demonstrations or violence by his supporters. President Karzai was inaugurated on November 19, 2009.

U.S. and international officials publicly called on President Karzai to choose his next cabinet based on competence, merit, and dedication to curbing corruption. A major U.S. and international concern remains focused on questions about the strength and legitimacy of Karzai's government and what kind of a partnership is possible, particularly with regard to President Obama's recent proposed strategy for the way forward.

The UNAMA Dispute

Within weeks of the August election and lead-up to the release of the initial results, a dispute ensued within UNAMA between SRSG Kai Eide and DSRSG Peter Galbraith, which ended in the departure of Galbraith from his post at the end of September. The main issues appear to have been focused on the degree of fraud that had taken place during the election and how to deal with it.

On the one hand, Eide's position was to let process run through Electoral Complaints Commission (ECC) and Independent Election Commission (IEC) to ensure adherence to the constitution and electoral laws of Afghanistan. Some also say that he was willing to encourage an Afghan compromise to avoid a second round. On the other hand, concerned with rule of law and election legitimacy, Galbraith argued that the United Nations had the responsibility to intervene, and he questioned whether it would intervene, and to what extent if he did not speak out. This issue played out very publicly and there were allegations of support by Eide to Karzai and Galbraith to Abdullah. U.N. Secretary General Ban Ki-moon removed Galbraith from his post on the grounds that the dispute was compromising UNAMA's overall mission. Several Galbraith supporters subsequently resigned from UNAMA and morale within UNAMA was reported to be low. For Afghans, the concern was less about the fraud in the election itself (which many expected) but rather concerns over U.S. influence and unnecessary international interference in their election.

To what degree the dispute will affect UNAMA's overall standing and credibility remains to be seen. On December 11, 2009, SRSG Eide was reported to have said he would leave his post in March 2010 as planned when his two-year contract expires. Eide maintains that this decision is unrelated to his handling of the controversy over the August election or the deadly attack on U.N. staff in October (discussed later in this report.) A search for a replacement is reportedly underway. [31] There had already been some calls for Eide's resignation [32]. Others have suggested the need for a super envoy outside the UNAMA structure, a revival of a previous proposal that was rejected by Karzai. NATO officials are reportedly considering the possibility of sending their own civilian envoy [33] Most agree that there has been a loss of momentum and that UNAMA will have to reassert itself as a voice in the transition strategy proposed by President Obama or risk being sidelined.

Parliamentary Elections in 2010

Parliamentary elections are scheduled to be held in 2010. The recent presidential and provincial elections raise many questions about how the problems encountered in 2009 should be addressed and by whom. Clearly there is a need for overall electoral reform and perhaps a need to reassess expectations of the capacity of the electoral process in Afghanistan. It remains to be seen what impact the recent Obama Administration's strategy will have on election planning and how the Afghan government will view this responsibility in the evolution of its democratic process.

UNAMA's Security

On October 28, 2009, in the lead-up to the second round, an attack on a U.N. guest house in Kabul killed five U.N. workers, most of whom were assisting election teams. UNAMA then decided to withdraw or relocate up to 600 of its 1,100 international staff temporarily for security reasons. This raises several questions, including UNAMA's ability to implement its mandate, the impact on other aid groups which may rethink their presence in Afghanistan, and the overall view of the United Nations in Afghanistan. The United Nations is not considered neutral because it supports the government of Afghanistan in its overall mandate. But it is also not always seen as impartial. The guest house incident appears to have been election related—perhaps meant as a deterrent for participation in the then scheduled second round or possibly a comment on UNAMA's role in the election process overall.

Civilian Casualties from Air Strikes

UNAMA reported that 1,013 civilian casualties occurred between January and June 2009, mostly in the south and eastern parts of the country, an increase of 24% over the same time last year [34]. Of these casualties, 59% were caused by anti-government elements and 30.5% were attributed to international and Afghan forces (12% could not be attributed). Most civilian casualties result from targeted attacks by the Taliban and terrorist groups. At the same time, extensive press coverage from bombing campaigns in Afghanistan reveals that there have been a number of innocent victims of erroneous U.S. bombings. While the effort to combat Taliban and other militants continues, the potential for mistaken targets remains a risk. In recent months, claims of erroneous bombing targets have highlighted the difficulty of intelligence gathering and security problems on the ground. The issue is blurred by the recognition that the end result may not be a matter of simple human error, but rather a complex combination of factors for which it is more difficult to determine responsibility. Collateral damage includes civilian losses, considered to be a byproduct of war, despite efforts to minimize innocent loss of life. Concerns about civilian casualties from air strikes, particularly in populated areas, have also focused on the degree to which this affects the Afghan population's perception of the ISAF and U.S.-led forces, and whether the international forces are doing enough to protect civilians. UNAMA has been outspoken over its concerns regarding civilian casualties [35]. Afghans have raised concerns that increased troops may mean an increase in civilian casualties.

Organizational Issues

Resources and Expansion of UNAMA

The U.N. Security Council, and most recently the participants at the March 2009 conference in The Hague, have called for the expansion of UNAMA's presence to each of Afghanistan's 34 provinces. UNAMA's regional and provincial offices are viewed by many as a means to help support the civilian surge, to further the work of national programs (such as ANDS), and to foster participation at the subnational level by the local government and civil society. In order to expand into each province, UNAMA would need additional resources and funding to open another 11 offices. The U.N. Secretary-General has stated that to meet the expectations outlined in its mandate and to sustain its progress so far, the mission will need to be strengthened in 2010 [36]

Afghan Participation

Experts emphasize the need to create Afghan jobs and to build Afghan capacity. Nevertheless, very little has been said about the mechanics of doing so or discerning the differing views that exist within the Afghan community. The international donor community has put great emphasis on "ownership"—meaning leadership and control—of reconstruction efforts by the country itself. The degree to which Afghans feel a part of what is at stake in their country and to what has been achieved so far is unclear. Some argue that the people and government of Afghanistan are increasingly taking the lead and that the international community is moving toward a supporting role, while others argue just the opposite is taking place. Some are concerned that not enough aid gets directly to the people and that Afghans see little improvement in their lives. It is recognized by many that Afghans are a critical piece of the puzzle in their country's success. Finding ways to empower Afghans in Afghanistan emphasizes the importance of an integrated approach and one that builds needed capacity on multiple levels.

Donor Aid Effectiveness

In his June 2009 report, the U.N. Secretary-General commented on three "interlinked strategic shifts" in Afghanistan that point to the emergence of an "aid effectiveness framework." With UNAMA as the coordinator, these included (1) an emphasis on civilian efforts, (2) a focus on subnational governance and service delivery, and (3) signs that the international efforts are beginning to line up behind comprehensive government programs that, by agreement, serve as the basis for moving forward [37]

International Donors

President Hamid Karzai and his ministers have complained that virtually all international aid is decided and provided directly by international donors. Karzai has called the international development efforts a "parallel government" that is not serving the needs of Afghans. He publicly called for a higher percentage of international aid to be channeled through the Afghan government, or at least for development priorities to be determined in partnership with the Afghan government. This Afghan sentiment was supported in the Compact and the strategy outlined in ANDS. To some extent, the Afghan government remains in a weak position to insist on greater input in setting development priorities because it is so dependent on the international community for security and development funds. In addition, the international donor community provides direct budgetary support to the Afghan government through the ARTF.

International donors, for their part, have complained about widely reported corruption, waste and abuse within the Afghan bureaucracy that have hampered implementation of projects. On the one hand, UNAMA is expected to take the lead on ensuring that donors honor their commitments and align their efforts in a transparent manner behind the financing and implementation of ANDS. To sustain international support, it needs to explain both the achievements and challenges.

Nevertheless, on the other hand, UNAMA is also keen to see the capacity of government institutions strengthened with accountability measures in place to provide donors with the confidence to commit funds to Afghanistan's central budget, and to ensure the Afghan government is able to tackle the problem of corruption. Aid effectiveness is a central part of

UNAMA's mandate and an area where it places great emphasis in its work with the Afghan government and international donors.

Aid Coordination

The international community continues to struggle with establishing effective coordinating mechanisms and institutions to help move the development process forward. The institutional networks have altered over time, with UNAMA taking on the main coordinating role in March 2002 and, under its recent mandates, a renewed emphasis on expanding that role. The international community and the Afghan government have sought to establish a common set of goals in order to coordinate activities and utilize donor funds most effectively.

Some observers argue that the Afghan government, international organizations, NGOs, donor countries, and others are following their own priorities and programs, and therefore do not coordinate their efforts as effectively as possible. Some, however, have suggested that complete coordination may be both unnecessary and ineffective, especially when different organizations do not share common goals or strategies. For example, the United Nations, the United States, and others have in the past supported a specific strategy intended to bolster the Karzai government through development. For those in Afghanistan and the region who did not support this goal of Karzai empowerment or for those who were marginalized by regime change (such as former supporters of the Taliban regime), supposedly neutral, non-partisan humanitarian assistance could appear partisan. Coordination is a complicated matter, but some would argue that there should be coordination only among like-minded organizations, such as among humanitarian groups, separate from the coordination of political groups, and separate from the coordination of military oriented groups. The SRSG for Afghanistan, Kai Eide, has said that additional capacity-building resources are needed, and that some efforts by international donors duplicate each other or are tied to purchasing decisions by Western countries.

Sustained Support from the United States

With the Obama Administration's latest strategy for Afghanistan, other key international stakeholders are also refocusing their efforts. Some experts argue there needs to be greater U.S., including congressional, attention to the United Nation's role in Afghanistan and the implementation of its expanded priorities. Other experts say that sustained (and increased) support from the United States in the form of public statements, reporting, transparency, and oversight is critical to UNAMA and to the importance attached to its mission. And yet some are concerned that UNAMA not become "Americanized" or controlled by the United States [38]

Negative views about the United Nations itself could also undermine U.S. support for UNAMA. In general, Congress supports the United Nations, but it has also been critical of the organization, particularly with regard to perceived inefficiencies and insufficient accountability, duplication of efforts across agency mandates and missions, and allegations of waste, fraud, and abuse of U.N. resources. The 111th Congress is likely to continue to focus on broad U.N. reform efforts and priorities in general, and with increased attention toward Afghanistan, could decide to conduct greater oversight of UNAMA's activities and progress.

Other questions that have raised tensions in the past, such as how much of U.S. foreign assistance to Afghanistan should be provided bilaterally and how much through multilateral organizations like the United Nations, may also prove challenging as UNAMA manages the complexities of donor relations and policy objectives in Afghanistan.

APPENDIX A. MAP OF AFGHANISTAN

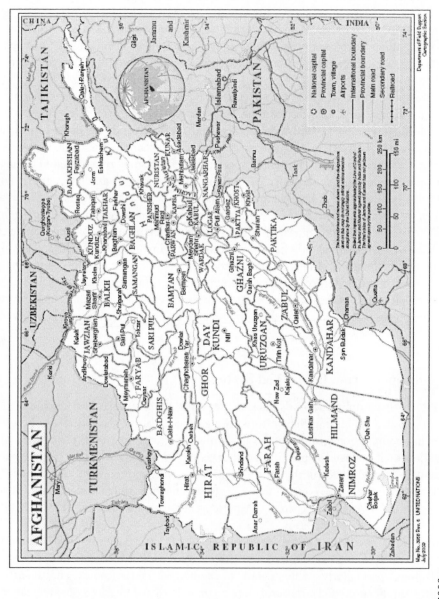

Source: UNAMA, 2009.

Figure A-1. Map of Afghanistan.

APPENDIX B. UNAMA ORGANIZATIONAL CHART

Organization charts

A. United Nations Assistance Mission in Afghanistan

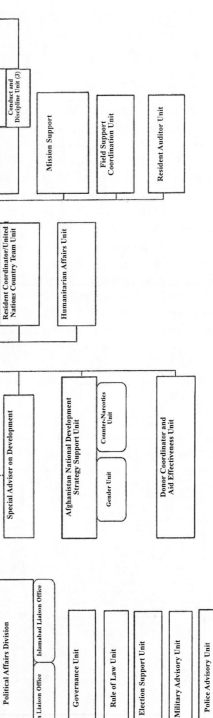

Source: UNAMA, 2008.

Figure B-1. UNAMA Organization Chart.

Appendix C. The U.N. Country Team

The following organizations and U.N. agencies make up the county team in Afghanistan [39]

Afghanistan's New Beginnings Programme

Asian Development Bank (ADB)

International Labor Organization (ILO)

International Organization for Migration (IOM)

Mine Action Coordination Centre for Afghanistan (MACCA) Office of the High Commissioner for Human Rights (UNHCR) United Nations Children's Fund (UNICEF)

United Nations Office for the Coordination of Humanitarian Affairs (OCHA)

United Nations Development Programme (UNDP)

United Nations Development Fund for Women (UNIFEM)

United Nations Educational, Scientific and Cultural Organization (UNESCO)

United Nations Environment Programme (UNEP)

United Nations Food and Agriculture Organization (FAO) United Nations High Commissioner for Refugees (UNHCR) United Nations Human Settlements Programme (Habitat) United Nations Industrial Development Organization (UNIDO) United Nations Integrated Regional Information Network (IRIN) United Nations Population Fund (UNFPA)

United Nations Office for Project Services (UNOPS) United Nations Office on Drugs and Crime (UNODC) United Nations World Food Programme (WFP)

United Nations World Health Organization (WHO) World Bank (WB)

Appendix D. Map of U.N. Presence in Afghanistan

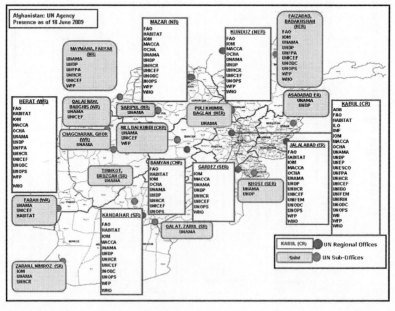

Source: UNAMA, July 2009.

Figure D-1. Map of U.N. Presence in Afghanistan.

APPENDIX E. MAP OF UNAMA OFFICES

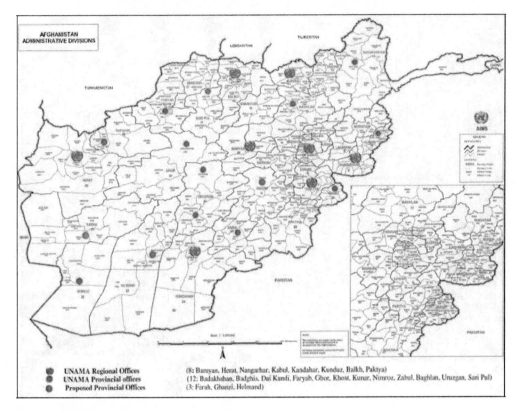

Source: UNAMA, 2009.

Figure E-1. Map of UNAMA Offices.

APPENDIX F. AFGHANISTAN INTERNATIONAL
COMMUNITY DONORS LIST

(in $ millions)				
Pledges at the Paris Conference to support the Afghanistan National Development Strategy				
Donor	Fresh	Old	Total Pledge	Total Pledges—4Q FY1380 to FY1389 (January 2002-March 2011)
ADB	500.00	800.00	1,300.00	2,200.00
Aga Khan	100.00		100.00	200.00
Australia	232.36		232.36	440.23
Austria				14.00
BelgiumBrazil	46.80 1.00		46.80 1.00	86.80 1.00
Canada	600.00		600.00	1,479.75
China	7.50		7.50	196.50

Appendix F. (Continued)

Donor	Fresh	Old	Total Pledge	Total Pledges—4Q FY1380 to FY1389 (January 2002-March 2011)
Croatia	28.10		28.10	28.10
Czech Republic	22.00		22.00	22.00
Denmark	430.00	0.00	430.00	683.04
EC		780.00	780.00	1,768.65
ECHO	0.00	0.00	0.00	268.20
Egypt	2.00		2.00	2.00
Estonia			0.00	.30
Finland	30.00	45.00	75.00	152.00
France	126.80	38.70	165.50	208.00
Germany	280.80	374.40	655.20	1,108.32
Global Fund				11.48
Greece	3.10		3.10	12.70
Hungary	3.00		3.00	3.00
India	450.00		450.00	1,200.00
Iran	350.00		350.00	1,164.00
Ireland	13.50		13.50	33.40
Islamic Dev Bank			0.00	70.00
Italy	234.00		234.00	637.36
Japan	550.00		550.00	1,900.00
Kazakhstan	0.00		0.00	4.00
Korea(Rep of)	30.00		30.00	86.20
Kuwait	30.00		30.00	75.00
Luxembourg	0.00		0.00	7.20
Malta	0.30		0.30	0.30
Netherlands	1,209.00		1,209.00	1,697.00
New Zealand	15.00		15.00	30.85
Norway	669.00	6.00	675.00	977.00
Oman	3.00		3.00	9.00
Org Islamic Conf	0.00		0.00	15.00
Pakistan	20.00		20.00	305.00
Poland	1.30		1.30	6.33
Portugal	0.00		0.00	1.20
Qatar	4.00		4.00	24.00
Russian Federation	0.00	0.00	0.00	141.00
Saudi Arabia	0.00	0.00	0.00	533.00
Slovakia	1.00		1.00	1.00
Spain	234.00		234.00	486.47
Sweden	0.00		0.00	288.60

Donor	Fresh	Old	Total Pledge	Total Pledges—4Q FY1380 to FY1389 (January 2002-March 2011)
Switzerland			0.00	134.00
Taiwan	0.00		0.00	28.60
Turkey	100.00		100.00	190.00
UAE	250.00		250.00	323.70
UK	1,200.00		1,200.00	2,897.00
UN Agencies	0.00	0.00	0.00	252.40
USA	7,095.40	3,104.60	10,200.00	31,851.86
Vietnam	0.01		0.01	0.01
World Bank	433.00	667.00	1,100.00	2,803.00
Other Donors	0.00	0.00	0.00	92.77
Total	15,305.97	5,815.70	21,121.87	57,149.62

Source: Office of the SIGAR, October 30, 2008 Report to Congress.

APPENDIX G. PRIORITIES IN UNAMA'S 2009 MANDATE

The priorities below were identified by the U.N. Security Council in resolution 1868 (2009) as key areas of UNAMA's work in Afghanistan: [40]

- promote more coherent support by the international community to the Afghan Government;

    Promote, as co-chair of the Joint Coordination and Monitoring Board (JCMB), more coherent support by the international community to the Afghan Government and the adherence to the principles of aid effectiveness enumerated in the Afghanistan Compact, including through mobilization of resources, coordination of the assistance provided by international donors and organizations, and direction of the contributions of United Nations agencies, funds and programmes, in particular for counter-narcotics, reconstruction, and development activities;

- strengthen cooperation with ISAF;

    Strengthen the cooperation with ISAF at all levels and throughout the country, in accordance with their existing mandates, in order to improve civil-military coordination, to facilitate the timely exchange of information and to ensure coherence between the activities of national and international security forces and of civilian actors in support of an Afghan-led development and stabilization process, including through engagement with provincial reconstruction teams and engagement with non-governmental organizations;

- provide political outreach through a strengthened and expanded presence throughout the country;

    Through a strengthened and expanded presence throughout the country, provide political outreach, promote at the local level the implementation of the Compact, of the ANDS and of the National Drugs Control Strategy, and facilitate inclusion in and understanding of the Government's policies;

- provide good offices in support of Afghan-led reconciliation programs;

  Provide good offices to support, if requested by the Afghan Government, the implementation of Afghan-led reconciliation programmes, within the framework of the Afghan Constitution and with full respect for the implementation of measures introduced by the Security Council in its resolution 1267 (1999) and other relevant resolutions of the Council;

- support efforts to improve governance and the rule of law and to combat corruption;

  Support and strengthen efforts to improve governance and the rule of law and to combat corruption at the local and national levels, and to promote development initiatives at the local level with a view to helping bring the benefits of peace and deliver services in a timely and sustainable manner;

- play a central coordinating role to facilitate the delivery of humanitarian aid;

  Play a central coordinating to facilitate the delivery of humanitarian assistance in accordance with humanitarian principles and with a view to building the capacity of the Afghan government, including by providing effective support to national and local authorities in assisting and protecting internally displaced persons and to creating conditions conducive to voluntary, safe, dignified and sustainable return of refugees and internally displaced persons;

- monitor the human right situation of civilians and coordinate human rights protection;

  Continue, with the support of the Office of the United Nations High Commissioner for Human Rights, to cooperate with the Afghan Independent Human Rights Commission (AIHRC), to cooperate also with relevant international and local non-governmental organizations, to monitor the situation of civilians, to coordinate efforts to ensure their protection and to assist in the full implementation of the fundamental freedoms and human rights provisions of the Afghan Constitution and international treaties to which Afghanistan is a State party; in particular those regarding the full enjoyment by women of their human rights;

- support the electoral process through the Afghan Independent Electoral Commission;

  Support, at the request of the Afghan authorities, preparations for the crucial upcoming presidential elections, in particular through the IEC, by providing technical assistance, coordinating other international donors, agencies and organizations providing assistance and channeling existing and additional funds earmarked to support the process;

- support regional cooperation in working for a more stable and prosperous Afghanistan.

  To work towards a stable and prosperous Afghanistan.

APPENDIX H. KEY EFFORTS IN AFGHANISTAN, 2002-2008

UNAMA has outlined the following key indicators of progress between 2002 and 2008:

- *Health:* 85% of the population has been given access to a basic package of health services.
- *Social Protection*: 2.5 million Afghans have received social support.
- *Education and Culture*: More than 6 million children are enrolled in school.
- *Agriculture and Rural Development*: 32,000 villages have benefitted from development projects.
- *Natural Resources Management*: More than 3 million have benefitted from rural water and sanitation projects.
- *Infrastructure*: 13,150 km of roads have been rehabilitated, improved, or built.
- *National Army and Police*: More than 140,000 policemen and soldiers have been recruited and trained since 2003.
- *Disarmament and Demining:* More than 7.7 million unexploded ordnances have been cleared since 2001.
- *Democracy and Governance*: 75% of voters participated in Afghanistan's first democratic elections in 2004.
- *Justice and Human Rights*: The Constitution adopted in 2004 calls for the protection of human rights.
- *Economy and Trade*: Gross Domestic Product (GDP) per capita has increased by over 70% since 2002.
- *Media and Telecoms:* 75% of Afghans have access to telecommunications, including over 5 million cell phones now in use [41]

REFERENCES

[1] For background information, see CRS Report RL3 0588, *Afghanistan: Post-Taliban Governance, Security, and U.S. Policy*, by Kenneth Katzman. For a map of Afghanistan, see Appendix A. CRS interviews in Kabul, October 2009.

[2] After the Soviet Union left Afghanistan, the United States sharply reduced its aid programs to Afghanistan.

[3] Since 1988, these offices received a series of different names, but most recently until 2002, the political office was run by the United Nations Special Mission to Afghanistan (UNSMA) and the humanitarian and reconstruction office was run by the United Nations Office for Coordination of Humanitarian Affairs (UNOCHA).

[4] Usually, the international donor community is considered to be made up of international organizations and individual donor countries.

[5] From FY1994 through FY2001, the United States Agency for International Development (USAID) did not have a mission in Afghanistan, but continued to provide aid mainly through U.N. agencies and NGOs.

[6]   In 2007, Afghanistan placed 174th out of 178 countries on global rankings of the Human Development Index (HDI), which fell slightly under that of 2004 and well behind its regional neighbors. See *Afghanistan Human Development Report 2007*, U.N. Development Programme and the Center for Policy and Development, Kabul University, 2007.

[7]   The priorities of the Mission are outlined in detail in Appendix D, and some are discussed in the policy section of this report.

[8]   ISAF is a NATO-led operation in Afghanistan authorized by the U.N. Security Council under a peace enforcement mandate (Chapter VIII of the U.N. Charter) and established to assist the Government of Afghanistan in maintaining security. See U.N. Security Council Resolutions 1386 (2001), 1413 (2002), 1444 (2002), 1510 (2003), 1563 (2004), 1623 (2005), 1707 (2006), 1776 (2007) and 1833 (2008). Its current mandate extends the authorization for a period of 12 months beyond October 13, 2008. ISAF has been deployed in Afghanistan since the end of 2001. In 2003, NATO took over leadership of ISAF.

[9]   In January 2008, with U.S. support, U.N. Secretary-General Ban Ki-moon tentatively appointed British diplomat Paddy Ashdown to this "super envoy" position, but President Karzai rejected the appointment reportedly over concerns about the scope of authority of such an envoy, in particular its potential to dilute the U.S. role in Afghanistan. Some contend that for political purposes, Karzai might have also sought to show independence from the international community. Ashdown withdrew his name on January 28, 2008.

[10]   Mr. Eide says he is not resigning and contends that he never planned to renew his contract beyond March 2010. Criticized for his handling of the flawed Afghan presidential election in August, it is unclear whether this factored into the timing of his decision to step down. Possible successors reportedly include Jean-Marie Guehenno (of France), who was the U.N. Undersecretary General for Peacekeeping Operations from 200 1-2008, and Saffan de Mistura (of Sweden), who was head of the U.N. Mission in Iraq (UNAMI) from 2007-2009. See Richard A. Oppel, Jr., "U.N. Afghan Mission Chief to Resign," *New York Times*, December 12, 2009; and Ben Farmer, "U.N. Chief Kai Eide to Step Down After Criticism," Telegraph.co.uk.

[11]   Mr. Weisbrod-Weber is Director of the Asia and Middle East Division in the Department of Peacekeeping Operations (DPKO) at U.N. Headquarters in New York. He is temporarily dispatched to serve as the acting Deputy Special Representative of the Secretary-General. The former deputy, U.S. diplomat Peter Galbraith, was fired by U.N. Secretary General Ban Ki-moon in September 2009 after an open disagreement with the SRSG about how the United Nations handled the first round of Afghanistan's August 20, 2009 presidential election. This issue is discussed in greater detail later in this report.

[12]   For a map of the U.N. presence across Afghanistan, see Appendix D.

[13]   Chairman's Statement of the International Conference on Afghanistan, The Hague, March 31, 2009. For a map of UNAMA offices, see Appendix E.

[14]   The Afghanistan Compact, London 31 January-1 February 2006.

[15]   Examples of MDGs include cutting the number of people living on less than a dollar a day by half; ensuring that all children receive primary schooling; reducing the number of people who do not have access to safe drinking water by half; and reversing the

spread of diseases such as malaria and HIV, among other things. More information on MDGs is available at http://www.un.org/milleniumgoals/.

[16] See Islamic Republic of Afghanistan, Afghanistan National Development Strategy, Executive Summary, 1387 – 1391 (2008 – 2013), A Strategy for Security, Governance, Economic Growth and Poverty Reduction. ANDS also serves as Afghanistan's Poverty Reduction Strategy Paper (PRSP).

[17] Pledges represent amounts that countries have been willing to earmark for Afghanistan. See the first U.S. Special Inspector General for Afghanistan Reconstruction (SIGAR), Quarterly Report to the United States Congress, October 2008. For a list of donor country pledges 2002-2008, see Appendix F. Many inside and outside the Afghan government have criticized donors for not following through on their pledges. However, donor conferences in general exhibit problems, such as slow disbursement of funds, weak mechanisms for pledging and mobilizing assistance, inadequate devices for tracking aid flows, inappropriate forms of aid conditionality, poor articulation between relief and development efforts, and weak coordination within the donor community. Donors over-pledge, pledge already allocated funds, and slowly or never fulfill their pledges. In the case of Afghanistan, the international community has sought to avoid some of these problems through the creation of an aid database, which has made pledging, tracking, and monitoring more transparent. Whether donor conferences and trust funds are the best way to fund reconstruction has been questioned by some observers. (The latest SIGAR Quarterly Report to the United States Congress was published on October 30, 2009, but does not contain information on donor country pledges.)

[18] Several other meetings and conferences with an Afghanistan focus have taken place, including the Shanghai Cooperation Organisation March 27, 2009, in Moscow, Russia; the third Regional Economic Cooperation Conference on Afghanistan, May 13-14 in Islamabad, Pakistan; a summit with the leaders of Afghanistan and Pakistan on May 19, 2009; and a meeting between NATO heads of state and government in Strasbourg on April 3-4, 2009.

[19] Chairman's Statement of the International Conference on Afghanistan, The Hague, March 31, 2009. See also U.N. document, Report of the Secretary-General to the General Assembly and Security Council, *The Situation in Afghanistan and its Implications for International Peace and Security*, A/63/892, S/2009/323, June 23, 2009

[20] Along with the World Bank, the Asian Development Bank, Islamic Development Bank and United Nations Development Program make up the ARTF Management Committee. The latest report on the ARTF is at http://siteresources. worldbank.org/INTAFGHANISTAN/Resources/Afghanistan-Reconstructional-Trust-Fund/ ARTF_Annual_ReportSY1387.pdf

[21] Office of the SIGAR, October 30, 2009 Report to Congress.

[22] Other funds are distributed through U.S. Department of Agriculture (USDA) and the Centers for Disease Control and Prevention (CDC).

[23] For more information on these efforts, see CRS Report R40699, *Afghanistan: U.S. Foreign Assistance*, by Curt Tarnoff.

[24] These priorities were initially set out in paragraph 4 of resolution 1806 (2008) and then restated in paragraph 4 of resolution 1868 (2009).

[25] U.N. document, Report of the Secretary-General to the General Assembly and Security Council, *The Situation in Afghanistan and its Implications for International Peace and Security*, A/64/364, S/2009/475, September 22, 2009.

[26] See Appendix G for more information on these priorities.

[27] Bullet points from UNAMA Fact Sheet, March 28, 2008.

[28] The text covering the benchmarks is drawn directly from U.N. document, Report of the Secretary-General to the General Assembly and Security Council, *The Situation in Afghanistan and its Implications for International Peace and Security*, A/64/364, S/2009/475, September 22, 2009, where information about the indicators of progress and metrics are discussed.

[29] Report of the U.N. Secretary General, *The Situation in Afghanistan and its Implications for International Peace and Security*, A/63/892, S/2009/323, June 23, 2009.

[30] See IEC website at http://www.iec.org.af/results.

[31] Possible successors reportedly include Jean-Marie Guehenno (of France), who was the U.N. Undersecretary General for Peacekeeping Operations from 200 1-2008, and Saffan de Mistura (of Sweden), who was head of the U.N. Mission in Iraq (UNAMI) from 2007-2009. See Richard A. Oppel, Jr., "U.N. Afghan Mission Chief to Resign," New York Times, December 12, 2009; and Ben Farmer, "U.N. Chief Kai Eide to Step Down After Criticism," Telegraph. co.uk.

[32] See, for example, International Crisis Group, Afghanistan: Elections and the Crisis of Governance, November 25, 2009: http://www.crisisgroup.org/library/documents/ asia/south_asia/ b96_afghanistan___elections_and_the_crisis_of_governance.pdf

[33] Ben Farmer, "U.N. Chief Kai Eide to Step Down After Criticism," Telegraph.co.uk.

[34] Report of the U.N. Secretary General, *The Situation in Afghanistan and its Implications for International Peace and Security*, A/63/892, S/2009/323, June 23, 2009; UNAMA, Human Rights Unit, *Afghanistan: Mid Year Bulletin on Protection of Civilians in Armed Conflict*, 2009, July 2009.

[35] U.N. Security Council, Extending Mandate of U.N. Assistance Mission in Afghanistan, Security Council Condemns All Attacks on Civilians, Recruitment of Child Soldiers, SC/9624, March 23, 2009; Highlights of the Noon Briefing, U.N. Headquarters, New York, June 30, 2009.

[36] Report of the U.N. Secretary General, *The Situation in Afghanistan and its Implications for International Peace and Security*, A/63/892, S/2009/323, June 23, 2009.

[37] Report of the U.N. Secretary General, *The Situation in Afghanistan and its Implications for International Peace and Security*, A/63/892, S/2009/323, June 23, 2009.

[38] When Peter Galbraith was appointed as DSRSG for Afghanistan, he was viewed as controversial because of fears of undue influence by the Americans.

[39] Source: UNAMA, June 2009.

[40] Text in italics is taken directly from U.N. Security Council resolution 1868 (2009). Bullet points from UNAMA Fact Sheet, March 28, 2008

[41] U.N. Assistance Mission in Afghanistan, International Conference in Support of Afghanistan, Set of Fact Sheets, Paris, 24 May, 4 June, 12 June 2008.

In: Globalization
Editors: M. G. Massari and K. J. Lutz, pp. 179-200

ISBN: 978-1-61470-327-3
© 2012 Nova Science Publishers, Inc

Chapter 8

THE UNITED NATIONS HUMAN RIGHTS COUNCIL: ISSUES FOR CONGRESS[*]

Luisa Blanchfield

ABSTRACT

On March 15, 2006, the U.N. General Assembly passed a resolution replacing the Commission on Human Rights with a new Human Rights Council (the Council). The U.N. Secretariat and some governments, including the United States, view the establishment of the Council as a key component of comprehensive U.N. reform. The Council was designed to be an improvement over the Commission, which was widely criticized for the composition of its membership when perceived human rights abusers were elected as members. The General Assembly resolution creating the Council, among other things, increased the number of meetings per year and introduced a "universal periodic review" process to assess each member state's fulfillment of its human rights obligations.

One hundred seventy countries voted in favor of the resolution to create the Council. The United States, under the George W. Bush Administration, was one of four countries to vote against the resolution. The Administration maintained that the Council structure was no better than the Commission and that it lacked mechanisms for "maintaining credible membership." It initially stated that it would fund and support the work of the Council. During the Council's first two years, however, the Administration expressed concern with the Council's focus on Israel and lack of attention to other human rights situations. In April 2008, the Bush Administration announced that the United States would withhold a portion of its contributions to the 2008 U.N. regular budget equivalent to the U.S. share of the Human Rights Council budget. In June 2008, it further announced that the United States would engage with the Council "only in matters of deep national interest."

The Barack Obama Administration participated as an observer in the 10th regular session of the Human Rights Council (held in March 2009). The Administration stated that it furthers the United States' interest "if we are part of the conversation and present at the Council's proceedings." At the same time, however, it called the Council's trajectory

---

[*] This is an edited, reformatted and augmented version of CRS Report RL33608, dated December 14, 2009.

"disturbing," particularly its "repeated and unbalanced" criticisms of Israel. In March 2009, the Obama Administration announced that it would run for a seat on the Council. The United States was elected as a Council Member by the U.N. General Assembly on May 12, 2009, and its term began on June 19, 2009.

Since its establishment, the Council has held 12 regular sessions and 12 special sessions. The regular sessions addressed a combination of specific human rights abuses and procedural and structural issues. Six of the 12 special sessions addressed the human rights situation in the Occupied Palestinian Territories and in Lebanon. Other special sessions focused on the human rights situations in Burma (Myanmar), Darfur, Sri Lanka, and Democratic Republic of the Congo.

Congress maintains an ongoing interest in the credibility and effectiveness of the Council in the context of both human rights and broader U.N. reform. In the Omnibus Appropriations Act, 2009 (Division H, the Department of State, Foreign Operations, and Related Programs Appropriations Act, 2009 of P.L. 111-8), for example, Congress prohibited U.S. contributions to support the Council unless (1) the Secretary of State certifies to the Committees on Appropriations that funding the Council is "in the national interest of the United States" or (2) the United States is a member of the Council. A similar provision was included in Division J of the Consolidated Appropriations Act, 2008 (P.L. 110-161). Withholding Council funds in this manner would be a largely symbolic policy action because assessed contributions finance the entire U.N. regular budget and not specific parts of it. This chapter will be updated as events warrant.

BACKGROUND

Overview of the U.N. Commission on Human Rights [1]

The U.N. Human Rights Commission (the Commission) was the primary intergovernmental policymaking body for human rights issues before it was replaced by the U.N. Human Rights Council (the Council) in 2006. Created in 1946 as a subsidiary body of the U.N. Economic and Social Council (ECOSOC), [2] the Commission's initial mandate was to establish international human rights standards and develop an international bill of rights. One of the Commission's notable successes was the Universal Declaration of Human Rights, adopted by the U.N. General Assembly on December 10, 1948 [3]. During its tenure, the Commission played a key role in developing a comprehensive body of human rights laws and regulations [4]. Over time, its work evolved to address specific human rights violations and complaints as well as broader human rights issues. It developed a system of special procedures to monitor, analyze and report on human rights violations. The procedures addressed country-specific human rights violations, as well as "thematic" crosscutting human rights abuses such as racial discrimination, religious intolerance, and denial of freedom of expression [5].

In recent years, controversy developed over the human rights records of Commission members. Countries widely perceived as systematic abusers of human rights were elected as members. In 2001, Sudan, a country broadly criticized by governments and human rights groups for ethnic cleansing in its Darfur region, was elected. Sudan was reelected in 2004, prompting outrage from human rights organizations and causing the United States to walk out of the Commission chamber in protest. These instances significantly affected the Commission's credibility. Critics claimed that countries used their membership to deflect attention from their own human rights violations by questioning the records of others. Some members were accused of bloc voting and excessive procedural manipulation to prevent debate of their human rights abuses [6]. In 2005, the collective impact of these controversies led U.N. Secretary-General Kofi Annan to propose the idea of a new and smaller Council to replace the Commission. On March 15, 2006, the U.N. General Assembly approved a resolution to dissolve the Commission and create the Council in its place. The Commission held its final meeting in Geneva, Switzerland, on June 16, 2006, where, among other actions, it transferred its reports and responsibilities to the new Council.

The Office of the High Commissioner for Human Rights (OHCHR) is a department within the U.N. Secretariat headed by a High Commissioner for Human Rights, currently Navanethem Pillay of South Africa [7]. Its mandate is to promote and protect human rights worldwide through international cooperation, and through the coordination and streamlining of human rights efforts within the U.N. system. The OHCHR provided general support to the Commission and will continue to do so for the Council, working specifically with Council experts to document human rights violations.

The United States and U.N. Human Rights Efforts

The United States is generally supportive of human rights mechanisms at the United Nations. It played a key role in creating the Commission on Human Rights in 1946, and was a member and active participant of the Commission until it lost its first election in 2001. It was restored to the Commission the following year by election. In 2005, the United States supported doubling the U.N. regular budget resources of OHCHR. This increased the U.N. regular budget for human rights activities from $64 million in 2004-2005 to $83 million in 2006-2007. Congress has also demonstrated continued support for U.N. human rights bodies, often using the mechanisms and special procedures of the Commission to call attention to the human rights abuses of countries such as Cuba and China [8]. In addition, Congress receives annual Country Reports on Human Rights Practices from the Secretary of State as mandated by the Foreign Assistance Act of 1961 [9]. The Secretary of State is required, among other things, to submit reports on countries that are members of the United Nations.

There were instances when both Congress and the executive branch had been critical of the Commission. In 1997, controversy emerged between the U.S. government and the Commission when the Commission appointed a Special Rapporteur on Extrajudicial, Summary, and Arbitrary Executions who, among other things, analyzed how the death penalty is implemented in the United States [10]. The Rapporteur reported that economic status, ethnicity, and racial discrimination were indicators for death penalty verdicts, reportedly prompting then-Senator Jesse Helms to declare the Special Rapporteur's mission "an absurd U.N. charade." [11]

In 2001, more controversy followed when the United States was not elected to the Commission and widely perceived human rights violators such as Pakistan, Sudan, and Uganda were elected.

The Bush Administration and Congress were frustrated and disappointed by the election outcome. The House of Representatives reacted with a Foreign Relations Authorization Act amendment that linked payment of U.S. arrears to the U.N. regular budget with the United

States regaining a seat on the Commission [12]. The Administration, however, stated it would not link U.S. payment of U.N. dues and arrears to the outcome of the Commission elections. [13] Given the controversy over the Commission, both Congress and the Administration supported the U.N. Secretary-General's 2005 proposal that the Commission be disbanded and a new Council created.

The U.N. Human Rights Council and U.N. Reform

The establishment of the U.N. Human Rights Council was part of a comprehensive U.N. reform effort by former U.N. Secretary-General Annan and member states. In March 2005, the Secretary- General outlined a plan for U.N. reform in his report, In Larger Freedom: Towards Development, Security, and Human Rights for All. He presented human rights, along with economic and social development and peace and security, as one of three "pillars" on which to base the work of the United Nations. In September 2005, heads of state and other high-level officials met for the World Summit at U.N. Headquarters in New York to address issues of development, security, human rights, and reform. The Summit Outcome document listed several mandates for "Strengthening the United Nations," including reform of the U.N. Security Council, management structure, and human rights bodies. In particular, the Outcome document mandated the creation of a new Council as part of broader U.N. reform.

The United States also viewed the Council as a critical element of overall U.N. reform. The Bush Administration identified the establishment of a new Council as a key reform priority necessary to achieve a "strong, effective, and accountable organization." [14] Congress also identified U.N. human rights reform as a significant component of overall U.N. reform. Recent proposed legislation has linked payment of U.N. assessed dues with the fulfillment of specific reforms, including those involving human rights.

COUNCIL MANDATE, STRUCTURE AND PROCEDURES

Mandate and Responsibilities

On March 15, 2006, the U.N. General Assembly passed resolution A/RES/60/25 1, which established the Council and outlined its purpose and responsibilities [15]. Under the resolution, the Council is responsible for "promoting universal respect for the protection of all human rights and fundamental freedoms for all, without distinction of any kind and in a fair and equal manner."

The Council will "address situations of violations of human rights, including gross and systematic violations, and make recommendations thereon." It may also promote and coordinate the mainstreaming of human rights within the U.N. system. In order to achieve the above goals, the Council undertakes a universal periodic review of each U.N. Member State's fulfillment of its human rights obligations and commitments. (See the "Universal Periodic Review" section for more information.)

The resolution also ensures adequate transition of responsibilities from the Commission on Human Rights to the new Council. Like the Commission, the Council continues to collaborate with OHCHR. It works to maintain and improve the system of special mandates, expert advice, and complaint procedures instituted by the Commission. Under the resolution, the Council also:

- promotes human rights education, advisory services, technical assistance, and capacity building with relevant member states;
- serves as a forum for dialogue on thematic human rights issues and recommend opportunities for the development of international human rights law to the U.N. General Assembly; and
- promotes the full implementation of human rights obligations by member states, and follow-up on human rights commitments from other U.N. conferences and summits [16]

Structure and Composition

On June 18, 2007, the Council adopted a resolution entitled "Institution-Building of the United Nations Human Rights Council" that addressed many critical details related to the work of the Council, including its mechanisms, procedures, framework, and system of universal periodic review [17]. Some aspects of the Council's work, however, continues to be debated and determined by Council members. This section addresses current structural elements of the Council. Key differences between the Council and the Commission are noted where relevant.

Status Within U.N. Framework

The Council is designated a subsidiary body of the General Assembly, whereas the Commission was a subsidiary body of ECOSOC. This change enhances the standing of human rights within the U.N. framework. In its new capacity, the Human Rights Council reports directly to the General Assembly's 192 members instead of to ECOSOC's 54 members.

Membership

The Council comprises 47 members apportioned by geographic region as follows: 13 from African states; 13 from Asian states; six from Eastern Europe states; eight from Latin America and the Caribbean states; and seven from Western European and other states. Members are elected for a period of three years and may not hold a Council seat for more than two consecutive terms. If a Council member commits "gross and systematic violations of human rights," the General Assembly may suspend membership with a two-thirds vote of members present. For comparison, the Commission was composed of 53 member states elected by members of the ECOSOC. Countries served three year terms with no term limits. Like the Commission, the Council created a formula to ensure equitable distribution of seats by region [18]

Elections

All U.N. member states are eligible to run for election to the Council. Countries are elected through secret ballot by the General Assembly with an absolute majority (97 out of 192 votes) required. The resolution instructs countries to consider "the contribution of candidates to the promotion and protection of human rights and their voluntary pledges and commitments" when voting for Council members. A country submitting its name for election must affirm its commitment to the promotion and protection of human rights with a written pledge.

A key difference between the Council and the Commission is the direct election of Council members by the U.N. General Assembly. Under the Commission, candidates were first nominated by their regional groups and then the nominees were submitted for election by members of ECOSOC. Regional groups often sent the same number of nominees to the election as there were seats available. This meant some member states might cast votes for countries with questionable human rights records in order to fill all regional group seats. The next election will be held in May or June of 2010, and 14 of the 47 Council seats will be open.

Structure

The Council holds an organizational meeting at the beginning of each Council year. The Council president presides over the election of four vice-presidents representing other regional groups in the Council [19]. The president and vice-presidents form the Council Bureau, which is responsible for all procedural and organizational matters related to the Council. At the meeting, members elect a president from among Bureau members for a one-year term. The current president is Ambassador Alex Van Meeuwen of Belgium. Under the Commission, the role of president was held by a chairperson.

Meetings

The Council is headquartered in Geneva, Switzerland, and meets for three or more sessions per year for a total of 10 weeks or more, including a high-level session. It can hold special sessions at the request of any Council member with the support of one-third of the Council membership. By contrast, the Commission on Human rights met in Geneva once a year for approximately six weeks, and since 1990 special sessions were held on request [20]

Reporting

The Council submits annual reports directly to the General Assembly. At the end of its first five years, the Council is also required to review and report to the General Assembly on its work and functioning. The Commission submitted reports primarily to ECOSOC, a limited membership body, which reported Commission activities to the General Assembly. In some instances, a special rapporteur addressing a specific human rights situation or issue might report directly to both the Commission and the General Assembly.

Rules of Procedure

The Council follows the rules of procedure created for committees of the General Assembly [21]. Procedures that relate to the participation of observer states, international organizations, nongovernmental organizations (NGOs), specialized agencies, and human rights institutions fall under the practices that were observed by the Commission. These rules encourage consultation and interaction at Council sessions among Council members, observing U.N. member states, NGOs, and other relevant organizations. Countries that are not Council members do not have voting rights.

Universal Periodic Review

All Council members and U.N. member states are required to undergo a universal periodic review (UPR) that examines a state's fulfillment of its human rights obligations and commitments. The review is an intergovernmental process that facilitates an interactive dialogue between the country under review and the UPR working group, which is composed of the 47 Council members and chaired by the Council President. The first UPR cycle lasts four years, with Council members evaluating 48 states per year during three two-week sessions (six weeks total). Observer states may attend and speak at the working group, and relevant stakeholders (such as NGOs) may also attend the meetings and present information that is assembled by OHCHR. All Council members will undergo a review during the term of their membership.

UPR is based on the principles of the U.N. Charter, the Universal Declaration of Human Rights, and the human rights instruments to which the state under review is party. Voluntary pledges by states are also taken into account, as is input from the U.N. Office of the High Commissioner for Human Rights and relevant stakeholders, such as NGOs and national human rights institutions. During the review cycles, which began in April 2008, the UPR working group makes initial recommendations, with subsequent reviews focusing on the implementation of recommendations from the previous review. The full Council also addresses any cases of consistent non-cooperation with the review. After the first four-year UPR cycle is completed, the Council will review the process to identify best practices and lessons learned.

Special Procedures

The Council, like the previous Commission, maintains a system of special procedures that includes country and thematic mandates. Country mandates, which last for one year and can be renewed, allow for special rapporteurs to examine and advise on human rights situations in specific countries. Thematic mandates, which last for three years and can also be renewed, allow special rapporteurs to analyze major human rights phenomena globally [22]. Similar to the Commission, the special rapporteurs serve in an independent, personal capacity and conduct in- depth research and site visits pertaining to their issue area or country. They can be nominated by U.N. member states, regional groups within the U.N. human rights system, international organizations, NGOs, or individuals. A newly established "consultative group" nominates rapporteurs for country and thematic mandates. Based on the consultative group's input, the Council president submits a list of possible candidates to Council members, who then consider each appointment [23]

Complaint Procedure

The Council maintains a complaint procedure that allows individuals and groups to report human rights abuses in a confidential setting. The goal of the procedure is to objectively and efficiently facilitate dialogue and cooperation among the accused state, Council members, and the complainant(s). A working group on Communications and a working group on Situations evaluate the complaints and bring them to the attention of the Council [24]. The groups hold two five-day meetings per year to consider complaints and replies from concerned states. The full Council determines whether to take action on the complaints based on recommendations from the working groups. The Council's complaint procedure is very similar to the complaint procedure under the Commission on Human Rights, which also allowed for confidential reporting of human rights abuses.

Human Rights Council Advisory Committee

The Advisory Committee replaces the Council's previous Sub-Commission on the Promotion and Protection of Human Rights. Similar to the Sub-Commission, the Advisory Committee is a subsidiary body of the Council and functions as a "think-tank" for Council members. The committee is composed of 18 experts nominated or endorsed by U.N. member states and elected by Council members through a secret ballot. Upon the Council's request, the Committee provides research-based advice that focuses on thematic human rights issues. The Committee meets twice a year for a maximum of 10 days, and can schedule meetings on an ad hoc basis with approval from Council members [25]. The previous Sub-Commission came under criticism for duplicating the work of the Council and disregarding the Council's guidance and direction. The Sub-Commission consisted of 26 independent experts elected for four-year terms, and held an annual four-week session in Geneva [26]

OVERVIEW OF THE COUNCIL'S WORK AND ELECTIONS

Since it was established in March 2006, the Council has held 12 regular sessions and 12 special sessions [27]. The regular sessions addressed a mixture of procedural and substantive issues, with a focus on improving working methods of the Council. The Council has also held 12 special sessions, six of which have focused on Israeli human rights violations in the Occupied Palestinian Territory, Lebanon, or East Jerusalem. Others have addressed the human rights situation in the Democratic Republic of the Congo, Sri Lanka, Sudan, and Burma (Myanmar), as well as the impact of the world food crisis and the global economic crisis on human rights (see Table 1).

Institution-Building Framework: Controversial Issues and the Secretary-General's Response

In June 2007, Council members adopted an institution-building resolution to address the Council's working methods. In the resolution, Council members identified the "Human rights situation in Palestine and other occupied Arab territories," as a permanent part of the Council's agenda and framework for its future program of work. The Council also established a mechanism for confidential complaint procedures, as well as Council rules of procedure. In addition, the text stated the need for "proposers of a country resolution to secure the broadest possible support for their initiatives (preferably 15 members), before action is taken." [28]

Council members also terminated the mandates of the special rapporteur for Belarus and Cuba [29]

Many U.N. member states and Council observers objected to the Council singling out human rights violations by Israel while terminating the Council's country mandates of widely perceived human rights abusers [30]. At the conclusion of the Council's fifth regular session in Geneva in June 2007, a U.N. spokesperson noted Secretary-General Ban Ki-moon's "disappointment" with the Council's decision to "single out only one specific regional item, given the range and scope of allegations of human rights violations throughout the world." [31]. In response to the Council's decision to terminate the country mandates of Cuba and Belarus, Ban released a statement that emphasized "the need to consider all situations of possible human rights violations equally," and noted that "not having a Special Rapporteur assigned to a particular country does not absolve that country from its obligations under the Universal Declaration of Human Rights and every other human rights treaty." [32] Ban, however, welcomed and supported the new procedures for universal periodic review, calling them "strong and meaningful," and noting that they "send a clear message that all countries will have their human rights record and performance examined at regular intervals." [33]

Table 1. Special Sessions of the Human Rights Council

Session/Subject	Dates
1st Special Session: Human rights situation in the Occupied Palestinian Territory	July 5-6, 2006
2nd Special Session: Grave situation of Human Rights in Lebanon caused by Israeli Military Operations	August 10-11, 2006
3rd Special Session: Israeli Military Incursions in the Occupied Palestinian Territories	November 15, 2006
4th Special Session: Human Rights Situation in Darfur	December 12-13, 2006
5th Special Session: Human Rights Situation in Myanmar (Burma)	October 2, 2007
6th Special Session: Violations Stemming from Israeli Incursions in the Occupied Palestinian Territory	January 24, 2008
7th Special Session: Negative Impact on the Realization of the Rights to Food of the Worsening of the World Food Crisis, Caused inter alia by the Soaring Food Prices	May 22, 2008
8th Special Session: Situation of the Human Rights in the East of the Democratic Republic of the Congo	November 28, 2008
9th Special Session: The Grave Violations of Human Rights in the Occupied Palestinian Territory including the recent aggression in the occupied Gaza Strip	January 9, 2009
Session/Subject	Dates
10th Special Session: The Impact of the Global Economic and Financial Crises on the Universal Realization and Effective Enjoyment of Human Rights	February 20, 2009
11th Special Session: The human rights situation in Sri Lanka	May 26, 2009
12th Special Session: The human rights situation in the Occupied Palestinian Territory and East Jerusalem	October 15-16, 2009

Source: U.N. Office of the High Commissioner for Human Rights.

Election Results

The Human Rights Council has held four elections. The most recent Council elections were held on May 12, 2009. Eighteen countries were elected, five of which will be serving on the Council for the first time. Re-elected members include Bangladesh, Cameroon, China, Cuba, Djibouti, Jordan, Mauritius, Mexico, Nigeria, Russian Federation, Saudi Arabia, Senegal, and Uruguay. The new Council members are Belgium, Hungary, Kyrgyzstan, Norway, and the United States [34]. The new members will begin their term on June 19, 2009. (See the Appendix for a full list of Council members broken down by region and term.)

U.S. RESPONSE

The United States has generally supported the Human Rights Council's overall mission. Past and current Administrations and Members of Congress, however, have disagreed as to whether the Council is an effective or credible mechanism for addressing human rights.

Barack Obama Administration

On March 31, 2009, the Obama Administration announced that it would run for a seat on the Human Rights Council. The United States was elected as a Council Member by the U.N. General Assembly on May 12, 2009, receiving a total of 167 General Assembly votes. Its term will begin on June 19, 2009. After the vote, U.S. Permanent Representative to the United Nations Susan Rice stated that the Administration is "looking forward to working from within a broad cross section of member states to strengthen and reform the Human Rights Council." Rice recognized the Council as a "flawed body that has not lived up to its potential," and emphasized that the Administration views the five-year review of the Council's activities in 2011 as "an important opportunity to strengthen and reform the Council." [35]

Previously, in February 2009, the Obama Administration had announced that it would participate as an observer in the 10th regular session of the Human Rights Council (held from March 2 to 27, 2009). The Administration stated that it "furthers our interest if we are part of the conversation and present at the Council's proceedings." [36] At the same time, however, the it stated that the Council's trajectory was "disturbing," particularly its "repeated and unbalanced" criticisms of Israel [37].

George W. Bush Administration

The Bush Administration opposed the Human Rights Council structure agreed to in March 2006, and consequently the United States was one of four countries to vote against the U.N. General Assembly resolution creating the Council. The Bush Administration stated that it did not have confidence that the new Council would be better than its predecessor, but at the same time indicated that it would work with other member states to ensure the Council was strong and operated as effectively and efficiently as possible [38]. In April 2006, the

Bush Administration announced that it would not run for a Council seat in the first election. A State Department spokesperson stated, "There are strong candidates in our regional group, with long records of support for human rights, that voted in favor of the resolution creating the Council. They should have the opportunity to run." [39]

The Bush Administration was generally disappointed with the work of the Council during its first two years. A main point of contention was the Council's focus on Israeli human rights violations while failing to address human rights abuses in other parts of the world. The Administration maintained that the legitimacy of the Council would be undermined if some Council members continue to push such "imbalanced" views [40]. Citing these concerns, the Administration announced that it would not run for a Council seat in the May 2007 elections [41]. It expressed similar concerns when it announced its decision to not run for a seat in the third Council election, held in May 2008.

In July 2007, the Bush Administration stated that it remained committed to supporting human rights in the multilateral system, though it was "deeply skeptical that the U.N. 's Human Rights Council will, in the near future, play a constructive role in our efforts."42 The Administration also maintained that despite its concerns, it would continue to support U.S. funding of the Council [43]. In April 2008, however, then-U.S. Permanent Representative to the United Nations, Zalmay Khalilzad, stated that the United States would withhold a portion of its contributions to the 2008 U.N. regular budget equivalent to the U.S. share of the Human Rights Council budget [44]

In June 2008, a State Department spokesperson announced that the United States would engage with the Council "only when we [the United States] believe that there are matters of deep national interest before the Council and we feel compelled; otherwise, we are not going to." [45]. According to the official, instead of focusing on human rights situations around the world, the Council "turned into a forum that seems to be almost solely focused on bashing Israel." The official added that future U.S. participation would be "ad hoc" [46] According to Bush Administration officials,

the United States continued to work with other multilateral human rights mechanisms, such as the U.N. Office of the High Commissioner for Human Rights and the General Assembly's Third Committee (Social, Humanitarian, and Cultural) [47]

Congressional Actions Regarding Council Funding

Some Members of Congress have sought to limit U.S. contributions to the Human Rights Council because of concerns over the Council's effectiveness [48]. On March 11, 2009, Congress enacted H.R. 1105, the Consolidated Appropriations Act, 2009 (P.L. 111-8), which included a provision on Human Rights Council funding. Section 7053 of Division H, the Department of State, Foreign Operations, and Related Programs Appropriations Act, 2009, specified that "none of the funds appropriated by this Act may be made available for a United States contribution to the United Nations Human Rights Council." The provision specified that it shall not apply if (1) the Secretary of State certifies to the Committees on Appropriations that funding the Council is "in the national interest of the United States" or (2) the United States is a member of the Human Rights Council. Because the United States was elected as a Human Rights Council member on May 19, 2009, the provision will likely not apply. Similar legislation was enacted in FY2008 [49].

CONGRESSIONAL ISSUES

The 111th Congress will likely remain interested in the work of the Council both as a mechanism for addressing human rights abuses and as an element of broader U.N. reform. Ultimately, future U.S. policy toward the Council will depend on whether the United States views the Council's work as effective and credible.

U.S. Funding of the Council

Comprehensive U.N. reform is a pressing issue for Congress, and the Human Rights Council is a component of this broader U.N. reform effort. As a result, there is continued congressional interest in U.S. funding of the Council. Specifically, some Members of Congress have proposed that the United States withhold a proportionate share of its assessed contributions, approximately 22%, from the U.N. regular budget, which is used to fund the Council. Since 1980, the United States has withheld proportionate shares of its contributions to the U.N. regular budget for U.N. programs and activities it has opposed. However, withholding Council funds in this manner would be a largely symbolic policy action because assessed contributions finance the entire U.N. regular budget and not specific parts of it [50]

On December 26, 2007, the President signed into law H.R. 2764, the Consolidated Appropriations Act, 2008 (P.L. 110-161), which prohibits U.S. contributions to support the Human Rights Council unless (1) the Secretary of State certifies to the Committees on Appropriations that funding the Council is "in the national interest of the United States" or (2) the United States is a member of the Council (Sec. 695) [51]

In April 2008, then-U.S. Permanent Representative to the United Nations, Zalmay Khalilzad, announced that the United States would withhold a portion of U.S. contributions to the 2008 U.N. regular budget equivalent to the U.S. share of the Human Rights Council budget. In 2007, the Congressional Budget Office estimated that under current law U.S. contributions to the Human Rights Council for 2008 and 2009 would be approximately $1.5 million per year [52]

Effectiveness of the Council

Since its establishment, the Council has faced considerable criticism from governments, NGOs, and other observers who contend that it does not effectively address human rights issues. Many contend that this apparent ineffectiveness stems from a number of political and organizational issues.

Focus on Specific Countries/Bloc Voting

The Council's focus on Israel during its regular and special sessions alarmed many countries and human rights organizations. After the first elections, the Organization of the

Islamic Conference (OIC) [53] held 17 seats on the Council—accounting for about one-third of the votes needed to call a special session [54]. Some observers believe that consequently the Council held more special sessions on Israel than on any other country or human rights situation.

Role of Regional Groups in Council Elections

Some Council members and observers are worried that the process of elections by regional group does not allow for competition among member states running for Council seats. In the May 2007 elections, for example, three out of five regional groups nominated the same number of countries as there were seats available.

This limited the number of choices and guaranteed the election of nominated member states regardless of their human rights records.

Leadership from Democratic Countries

Some have noted that the Council lacks leadership, particularly from democracies and countries with positive human rights records [55]. Many observers have speculated that pro-democracy Council members are not promoting their initiatives as they have in the past because they need support from other Council members, particularly from the Non-Aligned Movement, in negotiations on Council structure and mechanisms [56]

Alternately, some observers maintain that the Council can still change its current course and improve. They emphasize that the Council has yet to fully implement some of the mechanisms that differentiate it from the Commission—most notably the universal periodic review process.

Council supporters also maintain that the composition of Council membership is a significant improvement over the composition of Commission membership. They emphasize that the most egregious human rights abusers did not attempt to run in Council elections because of the new criteria and process. Some supporters also point out that widely perceived human rights violators that announced their candidacy, such as Belarus, failed to win a seat in the second election.

Proponents further highlight the Council's recent adoption of resolutions on the human rights situation in Sudan, Myanmar (Burma), and the Democratic Republic of the Congo as examples of the Council's continued improvement. Moreover, some advocates suggest that the May 2009 election of the United States to the Council could increase the Council's credibility and enhance its ability to effectively address human rights issues [57]

The "Goldstone Report" on Human Rights in Palestine and Other Occupied Arab Territories

On September 15, 2009, a report entitled Human Rights in Palestine and Other Occupied Arab Territories, Report of the United Nations Fact-Finding Mission on the Gaza Conflict (also referred to as the "Goldstone Report") was published [58]. The report, which was mandated by a U.N. Human Rights Council resolution, concluded there is "evidence of serious violations of international human rights and humanitarian law" by Israel during the

Gaza conflict and that Israel committed actions amounting to war crimes, and possibly crimes against humanity.

The report also found evidence that Palestinian armed groups committed war crimes, as well as possibly crimes against humanity, in their repeated launching of rockets and mortars into Southern Israel [59]. The Goldstone Report has generated considerable debate among the international community and U.S. policymakers, including Members of Congress. On November 3, 2009, for example, the House of Representatives passed a resolution calling on the President and Secretary of State to oppose unequivocally any endorsement or further consideration of the Goldstone Report in multilateral for a [60]

The Council and Alleged U.S. Human Rights Abuses

When considering the work of the Council, Members of Congress will likely monitor its activities related to the United States. The following sections address recent instances of the Council's investigations of human rights situations in the United States.

Council Report on Detainees in Guantanamo Bay

On February 16, 2006, the U.N. Commission on Human Rights released a report on the "situation of detainees at Guantanamo Bay." [61] The report was written by five independent rapporteurs appointed by the Chairperson of the Commission on Human Rights [62]. It alleges, among other things, that the United States violated the human rights of detainees held at the Guantanamo Bay Detention Center in Cuba, and that consequently the facility should be closed. According to the report, the United States is responsible for the alleged "force-feeding of detainees on hunger strike," and using "excessive violence" when transporting detainees.

The report also alleges that detainees are denied the right to "challenge the legality of their detention before a judicial body," which violates the Convention Against Torture and Other Cruel, Inhuman or Degrading Treatment or Punishment [63]. It requests that the five U.N. rapporteurs be granted full and unlimited access to the facility, and allowed private interviews with detainees.

When researching the report, the rapporteurs collected their information from interviews with former detainees, reports from nongovernmental organizations (NGOs), media reports, and a questionnaire answered by the United States. The rapporteurs were not permitted to visit the detention facility in Guantanamo Bay.

In its rebuttal to the report, the Bush Administration wrote that it was "engaged in a continuing armed conflict against Al Qaida, and that the law of war applies to the conduct of that war and related detention operations." [64] The Administration maintained that detainees at Guantanamo Bay were treated "humanely," and that potential human rights violations were thoroughly investigated by the U.S. government [65].

On July 7, 2006, the U.N. special rapporteurs, acting in their new capacity as Council experts, renewed their call for the closing of the Guantanamo Detention Center. They encouraged the United States to develop a timeline for closing the facility, and urged U.N. member states, the International Committee for the Red Cross (ICRC), and other relevant agencies and organizations to "collaborate actively, constructively, and urgently with the United States," to ensure the closure of the detention center [66]

Inquiry of the Council's Special Rapporteur on Human Rights while Countering Terrorism

In October 2006, the Council's Special Rapporteur on the Promotion and Protection of Human Rights and Fundamental Freedoms while Countering Terrorism, Martin Scheinin of Finland, wrote a letter of inquiry to the United States regarding its counter-terrorism practices [67]

In December 2006, the Administration invited Scheinin to visit the United States to discuss his concerns [68] Scheinin hoped to engage in a dialogue with U.S. officials and groups to discuss a variety of issues, including "U.S. counter-terrorism laws, policies and practices ... issues regarding detention, arrest and trial of terrorist suspects and the rights of victims of terrorism or persons negatively impacted by counter terrorism measures." [69]

Scheinin visited the United States from May 16 to 25, 2007. [70] He met with officials from the Departments of State, Homeland Security, Defense, and Justice, and traveled to Miami to observe the trial against Jose Padilla. He was not allowed access to the detention center at Guantanamo Bay to interview detainees. Scheinin met with some Members of Congress, as well as academics and NGOs.

In his preliminary findings, Scheinin dismissed criticism by some that the United States had become an enemy of human rights and complimented its judicial system, rule of law, and respect for individual rights [71] Scheinin emphasized, however, that he did not consider the U.S. fight against terrorism to be a "war"—though he recognized that the United States views itself as "engaged in an armed conflict with Al Qaeda and the Taliban." [72] He also stated that the United States violated international law by detaining prisoners in Guantanamo Bay for several years without charges, thereby "undermining the right of fair trial." [73]

In addition, he highlighted reports from the Central Intelligence Agency (CIA) that noted the use of enhanced interrogation techniques by the United States. These activities, according to Scheinin, violated international law, particularly the International Covenant on Civil and Political Rights [74] He also noted with regret that laws such as the USA PATRIOT Act of 2001, the Detainee Treatment Act of 2005, and the Military Commissions Act of 2006 eliminated important legal mechanisms that protect individual rights.

Then-U.S. Ambassador to the United Nations Zalmay Khalilzad disagreed with Scheinin's findings, stating, "We have a different point of view." [75] Khalilzad emphasized that the United States followed U.S. laws, procedures, and decision-making authorities. He stated, "We are a rule of law country and our decisions are based on rule of law." [76]

Inquiry of the Special Rapporteur on the Human Rights of Migrants

The Council's Special Rapporteur on the Human Rights of Migrants, Jorge Bustamante, traveled to the United States from April 30 to May 17, 2007. [77] He visited the Arizona and California borders to observe U.S. Border Patrol and Immigration and Customs Enforcement operations. He also met with migrants in Florida, New York, Georgia, and Washington, DC, and visited the Florence Detention Center in Florence, Arizona, to observe the living conditions of migrant detainees.

Bustamante's preliminary findings highlighted (1) the lack of a centralized system for tracking information on detained migrants, (2) the lack of representation for migrants being deported (many of whom are often forced to represent themselves in judicial proceedings), and (3) poor working and living conditions for migrants affected by Hurricane Katrina [78].

In addition, Bustamante recommended that the United States work to ensure that its domestic laws and immigration activities are "consistent with its international obligations to protect the rights of migrant workers," especially in the context of international agreements such as the International Covenant on Civil and Political Rights.

He also stated that the United States "overly-relies" on local law enforcement for its immigration activities, which could potentially impact the federal government's ability to effectively address migrant issues and ensure compliance with international law [79].

APPENDIX. HUMAN RIGHTS COUNCIL MEMBERSHIP

Table A-1. Human Rights Council Membership, by Regional Group

African States (13)	Asian States (13)	Latin American and Caribbean States (8)	Eastern European States (6)	Western European and Other States (7)
Angola (2010)	Bangladesh (2012)	Argentina (2011)	Bosnia & Herzegovina (2010)	Belgium (2012)
Cameroon (2012)	Bahrain (2011)	Bolivia (2010)	Hungary (2012)	France (2011)
Burkina Faso (2011)	China (2012)	Brazil (2011)	Slovakia (2011)	Italy (2010)
Djibouti (2012)	India (2010)	Chile (2011)	Russian Federation (2012)	Netherlands (2010)
Egypt (2010)	Indonesia (2010)	Cuba (2012)	Slovenia (2010)	Norway (2012)
Gabon (2011)	Japan (2011)	Mexico (2012)	Ukraine (2011)	United Kingdom (2011)
	Jordan (2012)	Nicaragua (2010)		United States (2012)
		Uruguay (2012)		
Ghana (2011)	Kyrgyzstan (2012)			
Madagascar (2010)	Pakistan(2011)			
Mauritius (2012)				
Nigeria (2012)	Philippines (2010)			
Senegal (2012)	Qatar (2010)			
South Africa (2010)	Republic of Korea (2011)			
	Saudi Arabia (2012)			
Zambia (2011)				

Source: U.N. Office of the High Commissioner for Human Rights.

Notes: Council membership is staggered by year. All Council members are eligible for reelection for a full second term. Dates represent year of term end.

REFERENCES

[1] For further information on the background and evolution on the Commission on Human Rights, see CRS Report RS20110, *The United Nations Commission on Human Rights: Background and Issues*, by Vita Bite (archived; available from the author of this chapter).

[2] ECOSOC is a principal organ of the United Nations that coordinates the economic and social work of the specialized U.N. agencies. It is comprised of 54 member governments elected to three-year terms by the U.N. General Assembly.

[3] The Universal Declaration of Human Rights was adopted by General Assembly resolution 217 A (III), December 10, 1948, and can be viewed at http://www.un.org/Overview/rights.html.

[4] This includes the International Covenant on Civil and Political Rights, which entered into force on March 23, 1976, and the International Covenant on Economic, Social, and Cultural Rights, which entered into force on January 3, 1976. The United States signed both treaties on October 5, 1977, and ratified the Covenant on Civil and Political Rights on June 8, 1992.

[5] Other examples of thematic mandates include the right to development; the right to education; the rights of migrants; and the right to food.

[6] "A New Chapter for Human Rights: A handbook on issues of transition from the Commission on Human Rights to the Human Rights Council," *International Service for Human Rights* and *Friedrich-Ebert-Stiftung*, June 2006.

[7] Pillay's appointment was confirmed by consensus on July 28, 2008, and her term began on September 1, 2008. She succeeded the previous High Commissioner, Louise Arbour of Canada. Pillay is the fifth U.N. High Commissioner for Human Rights since the office was established 15 years ago. The OHCHR has just under 1,000 staff working in 50 countries with a budget of approximately $150 million.

[8] Examples include H.Con.Res. 83, introduced on March 3, 2005 [109th], Urging the appropriate representative of the United States to the 61st session of the U.N. Commission on Human Rights to introduce a resolution calling on the Government of the People's Republic of China to end its human rights violations; and H.Res. 91 [107th], passed/agreed to in the House of Representatives on April 3, 2001, urging the President to make all necessary efforts to obtain passage during the 2001 meetings of the Commission on Human Rights of a resolution condemning the Cuban government for its human rights abuses.

[9] Country Reports on Human Rights Practices are submitted to Congress in compliance with Sections 116(d) and 502B(b) of the Foreign Assistance Act of 1961, as amended.

[10] Bacre Waly Ndiaye, *Report of the Special Rapporteur on Extrajudicial, Summary or Arbitrary Executions,* U.N. document E/CN.4/1998/68/Add.3, January 22, 1998.

[11] Elizabeth Olson, "U.N. Report Criticizes U.S. for 'Racist' Use of Death Penalty," *The New York Times*, April 7, 1998.

[12] For more information on this congressional action, see CRS Report RS201 10, *The United Nations Commission on Human Rights: Background and Issues*, by Vita Bite, pp. 3-4 (archived; available from the author of this chapter).

[13] Press Conference of the President, Office of the Press Secretary, The White House, May 11, 2001.

[14] "U.S. Priorities for a Stronger, More Effective United Nations," U.S. Department of State publication, June 17, 2005. Other Administration reform priorities included budget, management, and administrative reform, Democracy initiatives, and the creation of a comprehensive Convention on Terrorism.

[15] One hundred seventy countries voted in favor of the U.N. General Assembly resolution creating the Council; four voted against (Israel, Marshall Islands, Palau, and the United States), and three abstained (Belarus, Iran, and Venezuela).

[16] The mandates and responsibilities are drawn from U.N. document, A/RES/60/251, March 15, 2006.

[17] During its first year, the Council established four working groups (WGs) to address its working methods: (1) WG to Develop the Modalities of Universal Periodic Review; (2) WG on the Review of Mechanisms and Mandates on the Future System of Expert Advice; (3) WG on the Review of Mechanisms and Mandates and Special Procedures; and (4) WG on the Agenda, Annual Program of Work, Working Methods, and Rules of Procedures. WG members met throughout the year to negotiate and recommend Council procedures and mechanisms. Based on the recommendations, then-Council President Luis Alfonso de Alba proposed a draft institution-building text that was subsequently negotiated and adopted by Council members in Human Rights Council resolution 5/1 (June 18, 2007). See U.N. document, A/HRC/5/L. 11, *Report to the General Assembly on the Fifth Session of the Human Rights Council*, June 18, 2007

[18] Regional distribution of seats on the Commission on Human Rights was as follows: 15 members from African states; 12 from Asian states; five from Eastern European states; 11 from Latin America and Caribbean states; and 10 from Western Europe and other states.

[19] Current Vice-Presidents are Hisham Badr (Egypt), Dian Triansyah Djani (Indonesia), Carlos Portales (Chile), and Andrej Logar (Slovenia)

[20] Examples of Special Sessions under the Commission included Situation of human rights in Rwanda (1994); Situation in East Timor (1999); and "Grave and massive violations" of the human rights of the Palestinian people by Israel (2000).

[21] General Assembly Rules of Procedure can be viewed at http://www.un.org/ga/ 60/ga_rules.html. The Commission on Human Rights followed ECOSOC rules of procedure.

[22] For more information on Council special procedures, see http://www2.ohchr. org/english/bodies/chr/special/ index.htm.

[23] On June 18, 2007, the Council adopted a new Code of Conduct for special procedure mandate holders. See Human Rights Council resolution 5/1, in U.N. document, A/HRC/5/L. 11, *Report to the General Assembly on the Fifth Session of the Human Rights Council*, June 18, 2007, pp. 45-55.

[24] For more information on the newly-established complaint procedures, see U.N. document, A/HRC/5/L. 11, *Report to the General Assembly on the Fifth Session of the Human Rights Council*, June 18, 2007, pp. 19-24.

[25] For more information on the Advisory Committee, see U.N. document, A/HRC/5/L. 11, *Report to the General Assembly on the Fifth Session of the Human Rights Council*, June

18, 2007, pp. 15-18. The first meeting of the Committee is scheduled from August 4 to 15 in Geneva, Switzerland.

[26] Additional information on the Sub-Commission for the Promotion and Protection of Human Rights can be found at http://www2.ohchr.org/english/bodies/subcom/index.htm.

[27] A synopsis of the Human Rights Council regular and special sessions is available from the author of this chapter. Information on these sessions is also available at http://www2.ohchr.org/english/bodies/hrcouncil/.

[28] U.N. document A/HRC/5/L. 11, p. 29. This provision was a point of contention among Council members. During negotiations, China maintained that a two-thirds majority should be required to take action on country-specific resolutions—a position that EU countries did not accept. Multiple credible sources confirm that the European Union (EU) agreed to terminate the Council's Cuba and Belarus mandates if China would agree to the language in the adopted text.

[29] Council members maintained country mandates for countries such as Burma, Democratic Republic of the Congo, Haiti, North Korea, Somalia, and Sudan. The mandates for Cuba and Belarus were not included in the final list of renewed mandates in Appendix I of the institution-building text. (U.N. document A/HRC/5/L. 11, June 18, 2007, p. 38).

[30] For a synthesis of U.N. member state views, see U.N. press release, "Human Rights Council Hears Praise and Criticism About Adopted Text on Institution Building of Council," June 19, 2007. See also, "Conclusion of the United Nations Human Rights Council's Institution Building," Amnesty International External Document, No. 115, June 20, 2007.

[31] Daily Press Briefing by the Office of the Spokesperson for the Secretary-General, June 21, 2007, available at http://www.un.org/News/briefings/docs/2007/db070621.doc.htm.

[32] U.N. press release, "Secretary-General Urges Human Rights Council to Take Responsibilities Seriously, Stresses Importance of Considering All Violations Equally," June 20, 2007, available at http://www.un.org/News/Press/docs/ 2007/sgsm1 1053.doc.htm.

[33] U.N. press release, SG/SM/1 1053, HRC/8, June 20, 2007.

[34] For more information on the fourth election, see http://www.un.org/News/Press/docs// 2009/ga10826.doc.htm.

[35] U.S. Mission to the United Nations press release #095(09), "Remarks by Ambassador Susan E. Rice, U.S. Permanent Representative, Regarding the Election of the U.S. to the Human Rights Council at the General Assembly Stakeout," May 12, 2009, available at http://www.usunnewyork.usmission.gov/press_releases/20090512_095.html.

[36] Department of State press release, "U.S. Posture Toward the Durban Review Conference and Participation in the U.N. Human Rights Council," February 27, 2009, available at http://www.state.gov/r/pa/prs/ps/2009/02/119892.htm.

[37] Ibid.

[38] In a statement made after the vote, then-U.S. Ambassador to the United Nations John Bolton called the U.S. position a "matter of principle," and said the United States could not support the resolution because it lacked "stronger mechanisms for maintaining credible membership." Drawn from Ambassador Bolton's statement in the U.N. provisional verbatim record. U.N. document, A/60/PV. 72, March 15, 2006, p. 6.

[39] Press Statement by Sean McCormack, Spokesman, U.S. Department of State, April 6, 2006.

[40] It further stated it did not object to discussing potential Israeli human rights abuses as long as violations by other countries were also discussed. U.S. Statement on the Third Special Session of the Human Rights Council, Tom Casey, Deputy Spokesman, U.S. Department of State, Washington, DC, November 15, 2006.

[41] Press Statement by Sean McCormack, Spokesperson, U.S. Department of State, March 6, 2007.

[42] Remarks by Assistant Secretary for International Organization Affairs Kristin Silverberg, before the Senate Committee on Foreign Relations Subcommittee on International Operations and Organizations, Democracy, and Human Rights, July 26, 2007.

[43] Drawn from a press briefing of Mark Lagon, Deputy Assistant Secretary of State for International Organization Affairs, U.S. Department of State, April 25, 2006, and remarks by Assistant Secretary for International Organization Affairs Kristin Silverberg, before the Senate Committee on Foreign Relations Subcommittee on International Operations and Organizations, Democracy, and Human Rights, July 26, 2007

[44] U.S. Mission to the United Nations press release #075(08), "Statement by Zalmay Khalilzad on the Durban II Conference and the Human Rights Council," April 8, 2008, available at http://www.usunnewyork.usmission.gov/ press_releases/20080408 _075.html.

[45] Daily Press Briefing, Sean McCormack, Spokesperson, U.S. Department of State, June 6, 2008, available at http://www.state.gov/r/pa/prs/dpd/2008/jun/105716.htm.

[46] Ibid.

[47] Remarks by Assistant Secretary for International Organization Affairs Kristin Silverberg, before the Senate Committee on Foreign Relations Subcommittee on International Operations and Organizations, Democracy, and Human Rights, July 26, 2007.

[48] For information on possible political and budget implications of withholding Council funds, see the "U.S. Funding of the Council", under the "Congressional Issues" section.

[49] On December 26, 2007, Congress agreed to H.R. 2764, the Consolidated Appropriations Act, 2008 (P.L. 110-161), which included an identical provision on Human Rights Council funding

[50] In the past, the United States withheld certain amounts from U.N. activities and/or programs pending clarification on the exact cost or the program or activity. This was done in order to determine a more appropriate measure of the proportionate figure to withhold.

[51] Consolidated Appropriations Act 2008, (P.L. 110-161, December 26, 2007; 121 Stat. 1844).

[52] For more information, see Congressional Budget Office Cost Estimate for S. 1698 (1 10th), July 16, 2007, available at http://www.cbo.gov/ftpdocs/83xx/doc8328/s1698.pdf.

[53] The OIC is an intergovernmental group composed of 57 states with a goal of combining their efforts and resources to "speak with one voice to safeguard the interest and ensure the progress and well-being of... Muslims in the world over." For more information, see http://www.oic-oci.org/.

[54] After the second elections, OIC members occupied 15 of 47 Council seats. This includes a majority in both the African and Asian regional groups, which together account for over half of the Council membership. After the third election, OIC members accounted for 16 of 47 Council seats.

[55] "Human Rights Hoax," *Wall Street Journal*, June 21, 2007.

[56] "Dawn of a New Era? Assessment of the U.N. Human Rights Council and its Year of Reform," *U.N. Watch,* May 7, 2007, p. 7.

[57] Nick Amies, "Human Rights Organizations Welcome U.S. Bid for U.N. Council Seat," *Deutsche Welle,* February 4, 2009.

[58] See U.N. document A/HRC/12/48, September 25, 2009

[59] For the Human Rights Council resolution mandating the report, see U.N. document, A/HRC/S-9/L. 1, January 12, 2009. United Nations Press Release, "UN Fact Finding Mission finds strong evidence of war crimes and crimes against humanity committed during the Gaza conflict; calls for end to impunity," September 15, 2009. More information on the Goldstone Report is available at http://www2.ohchr.org/ english/bodies/hrcouncil/specialsession/9/ FactFindingMission.htm.

[60] H.Res. 867 [11 1th], introduced on October 23, 2009, by Rep. Ileana Ros-Lehtinen.

[61] U.N. document, E/CN.4/2006/120, February 15, 2006.

[62] The special rapporteurs include Leila Zerrougui, Chairperson rapporteur of the Working Group on Arbitrary Detention; Leandro Despouy, rapporteur on the independence of judges and lawyers; Manfred Nowak, the rapporteur on torture and other cruel, inhuman or degrading treatment; Asthma Jahangir, the rapporteur on freedom of religion or belief; and Paul Hunt, the rapporteur on the right to physical and mental health.

[63] The Convention against Torture and Other Cruel, Inhuman or Degrading Treatment or Punishment, was adopted and opened for signature by General Assembly resolution 39/46 on December 10, 1984. The Convention entered into force on June 26, 1987, and the United States became party to it on November 20, 1994.

[64] U.N. document, E/CN.4/2006/120, Annex II, p. 53-54, February 15, 2006.

[65] Press Briefing by Scott McClellan, Spokesman, The White House, February 16, 2006.

[66] U.N. Press Release, "U.N. Rights Experts Ask International Community to Aid with Expeditious Closure of Guantanamo Detention Centre," July 6, 2006.

[67] In the inquiry letter, Scheinin expressed concern that the U.S. Military Commission Act may violate U.S. obligations under international human rights law.

[68] U.N. Press Release, "United States Accepts Visit Request of U.N. Expert on Human Rights and Counter-terrorism," January 16, 2007.

[69] Ibid. Scheinin also stated his intent to identify counter-terrorism measures and formulate conclusions and recommendations that balance human rights with the fight against terrorism.

[70] U.N. Press Release, "U.N. Special Rapporteur on Human Rights and Counter-terrorism to Visit United States," May 10, 2007. For an overview of the Special Rapporteur's mandate, see http://www.ohchr.org/english/issues/terrorism/ rapporteur/srchr.htm

[71] For more detailed information on Scheinin's findings, see U.N. Office in Geneva Press Release, "Preliminary Findings on the Visit to the United States by Special Rapporteur on Human Rights and Counter-Terrorism," May 29, 2007

[72] Ibid.

[73] Ibid. Scheinin also stated that U.S. labeling of prisoners in Guantanamo Bay as enemy combatants is a "description of convenience, without legal effect" since it is not a category under international law, where individuals are described as either "combatants" or "civilians."

[74] The International Covenant on Civil and Political Rights entered into force on March 23, 1976. It was signed by the United States on October 5, 1977, and was ratified on behalf of the United States on September 8, 1992. As of April 19, 2007, 160 countries were party to the Covenant. The text of the Covenant is available at http://www.unhchr.ch/html/ menu3/b/a_ccpr.htm.

[75] Evelyn Leopold, "U.N. Expert Faults U.S. on Human Rights in Terror Laws," The Washington Post, May 26, 2007.

[76] Ibid.

[77] More information on the mandate of the Council's Special Rapporteur on the Human Rights of Migrants is available at http://www.ohchr.org/english/issues/ migration/ rapporteur/.

[78] For a more detailed description on Bustamante's findings, see U.N. Office in Geneva Press Release, "Special Rapporteur on Human Rights of Migrants Ends Visit to the United States," May 21, 2007.

[79] Ibid.

In: Globalization

Editors: M. G. Massari and K. . Lutz, pp. 201-222

ISBN: 978-1-61470-327-3

© 2012 Nova Science Publishers, Inc

Chapter 9

THE UNITED NATIONS CONVENTION ON THE RIGHTS OF THE CHILD: BACKGROUND AND POLICY ISSUES[*]

Luisa Blanchfield

ABSTRACT

U.S. ratification of the United Nations (U.N.) Convention on the Rights of the Child (hereafter referred to as CRC or the Convention) may be a key area of focus during the 111th Congress, particularly if the Barack Obama Administration seeks the advice and consent of the Senate. CRC is an international treaty that aims to protect the rights of children worldwide. It defines a child as any human being under the age of 18, and calls on States Parties to take all appropriate measures to ensure that children's rights are protected—including the right to a name and nationality, freedom of speech and thought, access to healthcare and education, and freedom from exploitation, torture, and abuse. CRC entered into force in September 1990, and has been ratified by 193 countries, making it the most widely ratified human rights treaty in the world. Two countries, the United States and Somalia, have not ratified CRC. The President has not transmitted CRC to the Senate for its advice and consent to ratification.

Despite widespread U.S. support for the overall objectives of the Convention, some past and current policymakers have raised concerns as to whether it is an effective mechanism for protecting children's rights. The Clinton Administration signed the Convention in February 1995, but did not submit it to the Senate primarily because of strong opposition from several Members of Congress. The George W. Bush Administration opposed CRC and expressed serious political and legal concerns with the treaty, arguing that it conflicted with U.S. laws regarding privacy and family rights. The election of President Barack Obama in 2008 has focused renewed attention on the possibility of U.S. ratification. The Administration has stated that any decision to pursue ratification of CRC will be determined through an interagency policy review. Perhaps more than other human rights treaties, CRC addresses areas that are usually considered to be primarily or exclusively under the jurisdiction of state or local governments, including education, juvenile justice, and access to healthcare. Some of these conflicting areas will

---

[*] This is an edited, reformatted and augmented version of CRS Report R40484, dated December 2, 2009.

likely need to be resolved by the executive branch and the Senate before the United States ratifies the Convention.

The question of U.S. ratification of CRC has generated contentious debate. Opponents argue that U.S. ratification would undermine U.S. sovereignty by giving the United Nations authority to determine the best interests of U.S. children. Some are also concerned that CRC could interfere in the private lives of families, particularly the rights of parents to educate and discipline their children. Moreover, some argue that CRC is an ineffective mechanism for protecting children's rights. They emphasize that countries that are widely regarded as abusers of children's rights, including China and Sudan, are party to the Convention. Supporters of U.S. ratification, on the other hand, hold that CRC's intention is not to circumvent the role of parents but to protect children against government intrusion and abuse. Proponents emphasize what they view as CRC's strong support for the role of parents and the family structure. Additionally, supporters hold that U.S. federal and state laws generally meet the requirements of CRC, and that U.S. ratification would strengthen the United States' credibility when advocating children's rights abroad.

This report provides an overview of CRC's background and structure and examines evolving U.S. policy toward the Convention, including past and current Administration positions and congressional perspectives. The report also highlights issues for the 111th Congress, including the Convention's possible impact on federal and state laws, U.S. sovereignty, parental rights, and U.S. family planning and abortion policy. It also addresses the effectiveness of CRC in protecting the rights of children internationally and its potential use as an instrument of U.S. foreign policy.

INTRODUCTION

The 111th Congress may demonstrate an interest in U.S. ratification of the United Nations (U.N.) Convention on the Rights of the Child (hereafter referred to as CRC or the Convention), particularly if the Barack Obama Administration submits it to the Senate for its advice and consent. CRC is an international treaty that addresses the rights of children worldwide. It calls on States Parties to take all appropriate measures to ensure that children receive special rights, including the right to a name and nationality; access to healthcare, education, and parental care; and protection from exploitation, abuse, and neglect [1] CRC entered into force on September 2, 1990 and 193 countries are currently party to the Convention, making it the most widely ratified human rights treaty. The United States has signed, but not ratified, the Convention. One other country, Somalia, has not ratified CRC [2]

Past Administrations have generally supported the overall objectives of CRC, but have had concerns as to whether the Convention is the most effective mechanism for addressing children's rights domestically and abroad. The Ronald Reagan and George H.W. Bush Administrations played significant roles in negotiating the text of CRC; due to concerns regarding the Convention's possible impact on U.S. sovereignty and on state and federal laws, however, neither Administration signed or transmitted the treaty to the Senate for advice and consent to ratification. The Bill Clinton Administration supported CRC, and on February 16, 1995, then- Secretary of State Madeleine Albright signed the Convention on behalf of the United States. The Clinton Administration did not transmit the treaty to the Senate, however, because of opposition from key Members of Congress, including then-Senate Foreign Relations Committee Chairman Jesse Helms. The George W. Bush Administration did not support ratification of CRC, citing "serious political and legal concerns" with the treaty. It questioned the impact of U.S. ratification on state and federal laws and argued that the treaty was at odds with the emphasis of the United States on the duty of parents to protect and care for their children.

The election of President Barack Obama has focused renewed attention on the possibility of U.S. ratification of the Convention. During the 2008 presidential campaign, Obama stated that his Administration would review the treaty. Similarly, Susan Rice, appointed U.S. Permanent Representative to the United Nations, said at her January 2009 confirmation hearing that the Obama Administration supported CRC objectives and would conduct a legal review of the treaty. On November 24, 2009, a State Department spokesperson confirmed that the Administration is conducting an interagency policy review of CRC and other human rights treaties that the United States has not ratified [3].

This report provides a brief history of the Convention and outlines its objectives and structure, including the role and responsibilities of the treaty's monitoring body, the Committee on the Rights of the Child. It examines U.S. policy toward CRC, including the positions of past and current Administrations and congressional perspectives. The report also addresses selected policy issues that the 111th Congress may wish to take into account if considering ratification of CRC—including the treaty's possible impact on U.S. sovereignty, federal and state laws, and parental rights. Other issues for possible consideration include the effectiveness of the Convention in protecting children's rights, and its role as a U.S. foreign policy instrument.

EVOLUTION OF THE CONVENTION

U.N. member states first collectively recognized the rights of children in the Universal Declaration of Human Rights, a non-binding resolution adopted by the U.N. General Assembly in 1948 [4]. The Declaration states, "Motherhood and childhood are entitled to special care and assistance. All children, whether born in or out of wedlock, shall enjoy the same social protection." U.N. member states further enunciated children's rights by unanimously adopting the Declaration on the Rights of the Child in 1959. The Declaration, which incorporates language from the Universal Declaration of Human Rights, calls on governments, families, and individuals to ensure that all children enjoy certain rights, including appropriate legal protections, a name and nationality, access to healthcare, and protection from abuse and exploitation [5] The international community also acknowledged the special rights of children in the International Covenant on Economic, Social, and Cultural Rights (CESCR) and the International Covenant on Civil and Political Rights (CCPR), which both entered into force in 1976 [6]

The possibility of a Convention on the Rights of the Child was first raised by the government of Poland in 1978 as U.N. member states planned activities and programs that would take place during the International Year of the Child in 1979 [7]. For the next decade, U.N. member states participated in a U.N. Commission on Human Rights (now the Human Rights Council) working group to draft the CRC text. The Convention was adopted by the U.N. General Assembly after a decade of negotiations on November 20, 1989, and entered into force on September 2, 1990 [8].

OBJECTIVES AND STRUCTURE

CRC defines a child as "every human being below the age of eighteen years unless, under the law applicable to the child, majority is attained earlier." [9]. It states that the best interest of the child should be the primary consideration in all actions concerning children. Countries that are party to CRC agree to take all appropriate legislative, administrative, and other measures to ensure that all children in their jurisdiction have the rights set forth in the Convention. Such rights include life and development; name, nationality, and parental care; health and access to healthcare services; and education. They also include protection from abuse and neglect, freedom of expression, religion, association, and peaceful assembly. CRC also calls for the protection of children from economic, sexual, and other forms of exploitation, torture, and capital punishment for offenses committed before the age of 18. It also provides special protections for orphans, refugees, and the disabled.

Article 5 of CRC recognizes the role of parents, requiring that "States Parties shall respect the responsibilities, rights and duties of parents ... to provide ... appropriate direction and guidance in the exercise by the child of the rights recognized in the present Convention." The Convention also states that children have the right to know and be cared for by their parents, and recognizes that the "rights and duties" of parents should be taken into account when States Parties seek to ensure a child's well-being [10].

Committee on the Rights of the Child

The Committee on the Rights of the Child (the Committee) was established under Article 43 of CRC to examine progress made by States Parties in meeting their obligations under the Convention. It is comprised of 18 independent experts who serve four-year terms. Each State Party may nominate one candidate from among its nationals, and Committee members are elected by States Parties by an absolute majority, taking into account equitable geographic distribution [11]. The Committee generally meets in Geneva, Switzerland for three sessions per year—including a three-week plenary and a one-week pre-sessional working group. It may hold special sessions at the request of the Committee Chairperson in consultation with other Committee members.

Special sessions may also be convened at the request of a majority of Committee members or at the request of a State Party to the Convention [12]. Committee members elect a Chairperson, three Vice-Chairpersons, and a Rapporteur to serve two-year terms. The Chairperson, currently Yanghee Lee of the Republic of Korea, directs Committee discussions and decision making and ensures that Committee rules are followed. The Committee submits a report on its activities to the U.N. General Assembly through the U.N. Economic and Social Council every two years.

The Committee's primary responsibility is to monitor reports submitted by States Parties on national implementation of CRC. Countries are required to submit an initial report to the Committee within two years of ratifying or acceding to CRC, followed by regular reports every five years. According to the Convention, these reports should include any "factors and difficulties," affecting the fulfillment of the obligations under the Convention. States Parties present their reports at regular Committee meetings and engage in an open dialogue with

Committee members to address progress and challenges to implementing CRC, as well as priorities and future goals [13]. Committee members adopt concluding observations that include suggestions and observations, and may request further information from the reporting State Party as needed. The Committee also adopts general comments on articles, provisions, and themes of CRC to assist States Parties in fulfilling their obligations under the Convention. These comments address a range of issues—including juvenile justice, protection from corporal punishment and other forms of punishment, and HIV/AIDS prevention and treatment.

Optional Protocols on Children in Armed Conflict and the Sale of Children

The Convention has two optional protocols that provide specific protections for children: (1) the Optional Protocol on the Involvement of Children in Armed Conflict; and (2) the Optional Protocol on the Sale of Children, Child Prostitution and Child Pornography [14]. Though both Optional Protocols operate under CRC, they are independent multilateral agreements under international law [15]. The Optional Protocol on Children in Armed Conflict limits the recruitment of children under the age of 18 for armed conflict and requires parties to provide children who have participated in armed conflict with appropriate physical and psychological rehabilitation. It entered into force on February 12, 2002, and has been ratified by 120 countries. The Optional Protocol on the Sale of Children requires parties to criminalize child pornography and prostitution, close establishments that practice such activities, and seize any proceeds. It entered into force on January 18, 2002, and has been ratified by 126 countries.

Summary of Steps in the U.S.Process of Making Multilateral Treaties

The making of multilateral treaties for the United States involves a series of steps that generally include: (1) negotiation and conclusion; (2) signing by the President; (3) transmittal to the Senate by the President, which may include any proposed reservations, declarations, and understandings; (4) referral to the Senate Committee on Foreign Relations; (5) Committee consideration and report to the Senate recommending approval and a proposed resolution of ratification, which may include reservations, declarations, or understandings; (6) Senate approval of advice and consent to ratification by a two-thirds majority; (7) ratification by the President; (8) deposit of instrument of ratification; and (9) proclamation.

While the House of Representatives does not participate in the treaty-making process, legislation implementing any treaties requires action by both Houses of Congress [16]

U.S. Actions

The United States has signed, but not ratified, the Convention on the Rights of the Child, and the President has not transmitted CRC to the Senate for its advice and consent to ratification. In 2002, the United States ratified the CRC Optional Protocols on Children in Armed Conflict and the Sale of Children. The Optional Protocols to CRC were considered less controversial than the Convention itself because, in the view of many, existing U.S. laws generally met the standards of the agreements [17]

Obama Administration

President Obama has indicated his overall support for the objectives of CRC and has stated his intent to conduct a legal review of the treaty [18]. Susan Rice, appointed U.S. Permanent Representative to the United Nations, reiterated at her January 2009 confirmation hearing that the Obama Administration was committed to the objectives of CRC and would review the Convention. Rice acknowledged that CRC was a "complicated" treaty in many respects, particularly given the U.S. system of federalism. She remarked that the Administration needed to "take a close look at how we [the United States] manage the challenges of domestic implementation and what reservations and understandings might be appropriate in the context of ... ratification. Rice further stated that she could provide no information on how long it would take for the Administration to conduct a legal review of the Convention [19].

On November 24, 2009, a State Department spokesperson stated that the Administration is conducting an "interagency policy review" of CRC and other human rights treaties to which the United States is not a party [20]. The spokesperson further stated that the Administration supports the goals of CRC and is "committed to undertaking a thorough and thoughtful review of it." [21]

Previous Administrations

The Ronald Reagan and George H.W. Bush Administrations played a leading role in drafting the CRC. Neither Administration supported U.S. ratification, however, due to concerns regarding the Convention's impact on state and federal laws, parental rights, and U.S. sovereignty. As a result, the Convention remained under legal review during the George H.W. Bush presidency [22]

On February 16, 1995, then-U.S. Permanent Representative to the United Nations Madeleine Albright signed CRC on behalf of the Clinton Administration. The Administration announced that it would send the treaty to the Senate with a number of reservations, understandings, and declarations (RUDs) that are typically attached to treaties ratified by the United States.

It stated that it would ask for RUDs to protect states' rights and maintain "existing tools of the criminal justice system," a likely reference to CRC provisions that prohibit the death penalty for minors [23]. The Administration did not submit CRC to the Senate for advice and consent to ratification, however, due in part to strong opposition from members of the U.S. Senate, particularly Senator Jesse Helms, then-chairperson of the Senate Committee on Foreign Relations (SFRC) [24]

The George W. Bush Administration opposed the Convention, citing "serious political and legal concerns" with its impact on U.S. sovereignty and parental rights [25]

Administration officials acknowledged that while CRC may be a useful tool for protecting children in countries that have ratified it, it was "misleading and inappropriate" to use the Convention as a "litmus test" for measuring the United States' commitment to children [26]

Congressional Perspectives

Congressional perspectives on U.S. ratification of CRC have varied. Members who support U.S. ratification maintain that it would reaffirm the U.S. commitment to children's rights and enhance U.S. leadership in protecting children worldwide [27]. In September 1990, for instance, the House of Representatives passed a resolution supporting U.S. ratification, stating that "the issue of children's rights and their well-being is important to both the United States and the world at large." [28] Congressional opponents of U.S. ratification argue that the treaty would undermine U.S. sovereignty, particularly in the context of policy areas traditionally addressed by states— including education and juvenile justice [29]. Some Members of Congress have also expressed concern regarding the Convention's possible impact on parental rights and responsibilities.

In April 2009, for example, Representative Peter Hoekstra introduced a resolution proposing an amendment to the U.S. Constitution which states that the "liberty of parents" to raise and educate their children is a "fundamental right," and that no international treaty may "supersede, modify, interpret, or apply" this right [30]

POLICY ISSUES

The question of U.S. ratification of CRC has generated passionate debate. This section provides an overview of selected policy issues which have emerged during these discussions. These issues may continue to play a role in the ratification debate—particularly if the Obama Administration decides to seek the Senate's advice and consent [31]

Federal and State Laws

Perhaps more than other human rights treaties, CRC addresses areas that are usually considered to be primarily or exclusively under the jurisdiction of state or local governments. In general, both federal and state laws are consistent with the Convention's standards; however there are some key differences that may need to be resolved within the executive branch before CRC is transmitted to the Senate for its advice and consent to ratification. Areas where state and federal laws might conflict include juvenile justice, child labor, child education, welfare, custody and visitation, and adoption [32] State and local jurisdictions often address these issues differently and, according to some, U.S. ratification of CRC could, for the first time, apply federal laws to issues traditionally handled by individual states—thereby undermining the U.S. system of federalism [33] Some are also concerned that states may not adequately enforce implementation of U.S. laws that are in accord with the Convention.

Advocates of U.S. ratification contend that possible conflicts between state and federal laws may be addressed through reservations, understandings, and declarations (RUDs) that often accompany treaty ratifications. The use of a "non-self-executing" declaration, for example, would require implementing legislation to bring the Convention's provisions into use—thereby addressing any potential conflicts with U.S. laws or values. In addition, a "federalism" understanding would make clear that the federal government would fulfill U.S. treaty obligations where it exercises jurisdiction and take appropriate measures to ensure that states and localities fulfill the provisions.

Reservations, Understandings, and Declarations that may Accompany U.S. Ratification of Multilateral Treaties

The Senate Committee on Foreign Relations may recommend that the Senate approve a treaty conditionally, granting its advice and consent subject to certain stipulations that the President must accept before proceeding to ratification. These stipulations are generally referred to as "Reservations, Understandings, and Declarations" (RUDs). The President may also propose RUDs at the time he transmits the treaty to the Senate or during the Senate's consideration of the treaty.

"Reservations" are specific qualifications or stipulations that modify U.S. obligations without necessarily changing the treaty language.

"Understandings" are interpretive statements that clarify or elaborate, rather than change, the provisions of an treaty. They are generally deemed to be consistent with the obligations imposed by the treaty.

"Declarations" are statements of purpose, policy, or position related to matters raised by the treaty in question but not altering or limiting any of its provisions [34]

Other supporters of U.S. ratification, however, contend that the inclusion of such RUDs would demonstrate the United States' unwillingness to fully implement the Convention [35]. Some proponents argue that instead of placing limiting conditions on U.S. ratification, U.S. law should be brought into conformance with international standards when, in their view, the international standard is higher. Supporters of ratification also emphasize that countries with a system of federalism similar to the United States—such as Canada and Australia—ratified the Convention [36]

U.S. Sovereignty

Opponents of CRC argue that U.S. ratification would undermine U.S. sovereignty. They maintain that since ratified treaties are considered the "supreme Law of the Land" [37] under the U.S. Constitution, the Convention could supersede both national and local laws [38]. Some opponents hold that if the United States ratifies the Convention, the CRC Committee—a panel of 18 independent experts that monitors states' compliance with the treaty—would have authority over U.S. government and private citizens' actions toward children. A number of critics, for example, have taken issue with some CRC Committee decisions regarding parental rights, abortion, and the role of national governments in raising children [39]

Supporters of U.S. ratification maintain that federal and state laws generally meet the requirements of the Convention, thereby posing little threat to U.S. sovereignty. They also contend that the inclusion of RUDs—such as a non-self executing declaration that requires implementing legislation to bring the Convention's provisions into use—could address any additional sovereignty concerns. Proponents further emphasize that under the Convention, the CRC Committee may only comment on the reports of States Parties or make general recommendations. They emphasize that the Committee relies primarily on States Parties to comply with CRC obligations and has no established rules for treaty non-compliance [40] Supporters also contend that enforcement mechanisms under CRC are weaker than those of other human rights treaties ratified by the United States [41]

Parental Rights

A key area of debate regarding U.S. ratification of CRC is its possible impact on the rights of parents. Some critics have expressed strong concern that the Convention will give the U.N. Committee on the Rights of the Child or the U.S. government authority over the family structure and how parents choose to raise their children [42]. Many believe that parents should be able to raise their children in a way that reflects their morals and values without interference from outside parties, and some have argued that under CRC parental responsibility exists only in the context of its role in furthering the independent choices of children [43]. Moreover, CRC opponents argue that U.S. ratification would encourage children to disregard parental authority, possibly leading them to file complaints against or sue their parents [44]. Such actions, they argue, would undermine parental rights and give children inappropriate influence over their own lives [45]

In particular, some Convention opponents are concerned about how the CRC Committee may interpret the Convention's provisions on the "best interest of the child," which is referenced in several Articles, including 3, 9, 18, and 40. Critics maintain that allowing a U.N. Committee to interpret what is in the best interest of U.S. children severely undermines the role of U.S. parents to determine how to raise, educate, and discipline their children [46] Opponents have also taken issue with other CRC provisions that, in their view, could be interpreted to undermine parental rights and responsibilities:

- *Privacy—Article 16(1) states,* "No child shall be subjected to arbitrary or unlawful interference with his or her privacy.... " Some have interpreted this to mean that parents may not have the right to search their children's rooms or be notified if a child is arrested or undergoes an abortion.
- *Freedom of expression*—Article 13(1) provides that the child shall have the "right to freedom of expression," including "freedom to seek, receive, and impact information

and ideas of all kinds." Some contend that this could be interpreted to allow children to speak their minds at all times, regardless of parental authority or discipline.

- *Freedom of thought, conscience, and religion*—Some maintain that Article 14(1), which states that "States Parties shall respect the right of the child to freedom of thought, conscience and religion," might give children the right to object to their parents' religious beliefs or training.
- *Access to information*—Article 17 states that States Parties shall ensure that "the child has access to information and material from a diversity of national and international sources.... " Some interpret this to mean that children have a right to access any type of information regardless of their parents' preferences, including television, books, and other sources they find objectionable [47]
- *Education*—Critics assert that Article 28(1), which states that States Parties recognize "the right of the child to education," could lead to the government or CRC Committee mandating public schooling or interfering with the right of parents to home-school or send their children to private school. Some are concerned that Article 29(1), which addresses elements that shall be included in a child's education, could lead to government interference in private school and home-school curricula [48]
- *Corporal punishment*—Article 19(1) states, "no child should be subjected to physical or mental violence, injury or abuse, neglect or negligent treatment, maltreatment or exploitation," at school or by a parent or legal guardian. Some interpret this to mean that parents may not be allowed to discipline their children though corporal punishment, such as spanking [49]
- *Freedom of association*—Some are concerned that Article 15(1), which calls on States Parties to "recognize the rights of the child to freedom of association and to freedom of peaceful assembly" could give children the right to associate with people that his or her parents do not approve of, including cults or gangs [50]

Supporters of the Convention emphasize that CRC was established not to circumvent the role of parents but to protect children against government intrusion and abuse. They contend, for example, that Article 16 on the child's right to privacy is meant to protect children not from their parents but from government intrusion into the child's or family's privacy [51] Similarly, proponents maintain that Article 13 on a child's right to freedom of expression is intended to protect children from states that undermine parental authority by denying children the right to artistic, religious, or other forms of expression. Some also make a similar argument regarding Article 14 on a child's right to thought, conscience, and religion. In their view, the Article is not meant as a means for children to challenge their parent's religion or discipline, but to protect children from state interference in these areas, particularly if children are separated from their families. Some supporters have cited the experiences of Jewish children during the Holocaust and the plight of Christian children in China as examples of instances where children should be protected from government actions regarding religion [52]

Similarly, supporters emphasize that CRC provisions on children's access to information (Article 17) and freedom of association (Article 15) are meant to protect children not from parental authority, but from government intrusion in these areas [53]. CRC supporters also note that CRC provisions that address a child's right to education (Articles 28 and 29) are not intended to undermine the role of parents in choosing a child's education. Rather, they are meant to establish and protect children's rights in countries with poor or unbalanced educational systems. In some countries, for example, girls are forbidden or discouraged from receiving an education. In such cases, supporters argue, ratification of the Convention could play a role in ensuring equal access to education for both girls and boys.

Many CRC supporters also emphasize what they view as the Convention's strong support for the role of parents and the family structure. They contend that CRC's provisions— including those regarding education, corporal punishment, and references to the "best interest of the child"— should be balanced with what many perceive as the Convention's overall emphasis on the important role of parents in raising their children. Proponents support this view by citing Article 7, which states, "as far as possible, the child has a right to be known and be cared for by his or her parents," and Article 3, which states:

> States Parties undertake to ensure the child such protection and care as is necessary for his or her well-being, taking into account the rights and duties of his or her parents, legal guardians, or other individuals legally responsible for him or her [emphasis added].

Supporters also emphasize the Convention's references to the role of the family and parents in 18 other articles, as well as the CRC preamble, which states that the family is "the fundamental group of society," and recognizes, "... the child, for the full and harmonious development of his or her personality, should grow up in a family environment.... " [54] Advocates further emphasize that there is no language in the Convention that allows for prosecutions, lawsuits, or investigations of parents or guardians. Any such actions, they argue, would be based on existing U.S. laws rather than CRC provisions or recommendations of the CRC Committee [55]

To alleviate concerns regarding parental rights, some have suggested that if the United States were to ratify CRC, it may wish to include RUDs addressing the issue. When considering ratification of the U.N. Convention on the Elimination on All Forms of Discrimination Against Women (CEDAW), for instance, the Clinton Administration proposed a "private conduct" reservation which stated that the United States "does not accept any obligation under the Convention to regulate private conduct except as mandated by the Constitution and U.S. law." [56] Some have also suggested including RUDs that specifically address parental rights. One proposed understanding, for example, states that parents are primarily responsible for their children's upbringing and development and for making decisions related to the best interest of the child [57]

Abortion

There is significant debate regarding what impact, if any, U.S. ratification of CRC might have on domestic abortion policy. The ambiguous nature of some CRC provisions relating to these issues has left the door open for broad interpretation by both opponents and supporters of the Convention.

Critics of U.S. ratification have raised questions regarding the Convention's possible impact on state parental notification laws for children undergoing abortion. In particular, they are concerned about Article 16(1), which states, "No child shall be subjected to arbitrary or unlawful interference with his or her privacy, family, home, or correspondence.... " Some fear that this "right to privacy" could ultimately allow children to choose to have abortions without notifying or receiving guidance from their parents [58]. Opponents of the Convention express concern with CRC Committee decisions that appear to criticize countries that restrict abortion [59]. Additionally, some have argued that Article (24)(2)(d) of CRC, which states that States Parties "shall ... take appropriate measures ... to ensure appropriate pre-natal and post-natal health care for mothers," could be interpreted to mean that children may undergo abortions without parental notification.

Supporters of the Convention contend that the treaty does not take a position on abortion or when a child's life begins. They maintain that CRC text allows individual countries to interpret the treaty in a way that aligns with their national abortion policies. They note that countries with strict anti-abortion laws, such as the Holy See (Vatican), the Philippines, and Ireland, have ratified the Convention [60]. Proponents counter claims that the Convention encourages abortion by citing CRC Committee statements that appear to criticize countries for their high rates of abortion and teen pregnancy. In its report on Russia in 1993, for instance, the Committee expressed concern with "frequent recourse to abortion as what appears to be a method of family planning." [61]

Negotiating History of the Convention Addressing Abortion

The negotiating history of CRC's drafting leads many to conclude that the Convention is "abortion neutral." [62]. During negotiations on the treaty text, the issue of abortion and where life begins was debated among U.N. member states [63]. Ultimately, in the interest of compromise and to allow for the maximum number of ratifications, CRC drafters agreed to not address the issue in the main articles of the Convention. The intent was to leave the text purposefully vague so that ratifying countries could interpret the provisions to align with their own domestic law and policies on abortion [64]. For example, the Convention's definition of a child as "every human being below the age of eighteen years" intentionally does not set a lower age limit, leaving the States Parties to determine where life begins. This intentional ambiguity allows countries to apply their own interpretations to other provisions that address children's rights, particularly Article 6, which recognizes that "every child has the inherent right to life," and states that States Parties shall ensure "to the maximum extent possible the survival and development of the child."

Nevertheless, some States Parties to CRC, including China, France, Luxembourg, and Tunisia, attached reservations to CRC stating that Article 6 should not interfere with national legislation and policies regarding abortion.

The preamble of CRC has also raised some questions regarding the Convention's position on abortion [65]. It specifically mentions the needs of the child before birth, stating "the child ... needs special safeguards and care, including appropriate legal protection, before as well as after birth." Some maintain that this statement implies that CRC protects the rights of the so-called "unborn," which could require States Parties to outlaw abortion. [66] Though the preamble is not an operational paragraph of the Convention, some experts emphasize that under international law the preamble to a treaty could be relevant to its interpretation [67] Others contend, however, that preambular statements do not carry the same force as articles of the Convention [68]

The legislative history of CRC indicates that the drafters did not intend for the preambular sentence to protect the rights of children before birth. That sentence, which was originally included in the Declaration on the Rights of the Child, was reportedly included as a compromise during negotiations on Article 1 that sought to define a "child."[69] CRC drafters were concerned that it could be interpreted as protecting the rights of the "unborn," and in the official record of the negotiation included a statement clarifying that the preambular paragraph did not intend to prejudice States Parties' interpretation of Article 1 on the definition of a child or any other CRC provisions [70]

The United States generally agreed that the draft Convention should not aim to "institutionalize" a particular point of view on abortion because doing so would make the Convention "unacceptable from the outset to countries espousing a different point of view." During negotiations on the Convention text, the U.S. delegation insisted that CRC must be worded in such a way "that neither proponents nor opponents of abortion can find legal support for their respective positions in the draft Convention." [71]

Family Planning

Some CRC opponents are concerned that Article 24, which focuses on the right of the child to enjoy the highest attainable standard of health, could require parents to make or expose their children to family planning choices that contradict their values.

Specifically, Article 24(2)(f) states that States Parties "shall ... take appropriate measures ... to develop preventive health care, guidance for parents and family planning education and services." Some worry that this provision could require contraceptive distribution or "pornographic sex education" in schools [72] Similarly, some argue that it could allow children access to contraceptives without the knowledge of, or permission from, their parents.

Supporters of U.S. ratification argue that CRC provides for States Parties to make their own interpretations and decisions regarding family planning education and services. They emphasize that Article 24(2)(f) allows for States Parties to take "appropriate [emphasis added] measures ... to develop family planning education and services" thereby leaving it to individual countries to interpret what is appropriate in the context of their national policies and laws. Supporters also contend that concerns regarding the Convention's position on family planning should be balanced with the Convention's recognition of the role of parents in raising children [73]. They point out that countries with a wide range of family planning policies have ratified the Convention—including China, the Holy See (Vatican), Canada, Ireland, and the Philippines [74]

The Effectiveness of the Convention

A significant area of debate among CRC supporters and opponents is the effectiveness of the Convention, particularly in countries that have already ratified it. Some critics agree with CRC's overall goal of protecting children's rights internationally, but they do not believe that the treaty is an effective mechanism for achieving this goal. As evidence of this, they emphasize that countries that many regard as abusers of children's rights—including Sudan, Democratic Republic of the Congo, and China—are party to the Convention. Similarly, some argue that instead of helping children, ratification of CRC may serve as a facade for governments that abuse children's rights.

Critics have also asserted that reservations and declarations that some countries attached to the Convention are at odds with the purpose of the treaty, possibly undermining its intent and effectiveness [75]. A number of Islamic countries, for example, attached reservations stating that the Convention would not apply to provisions that they deem incompatible with Islamic Shari'a law or values [76]. Some are concerned that the ambiguity of such reservations could allow for broad interpretations of the Convention's provisions, particularly in the area of child marriage and education for girls. Other States Parties also included reservations that aim to apply CRC only when it is compatible with domestic laws. Holy See (the Vatican), for example, included a reservation stating that the application of the Convention [should] be "compatible in practice with the particular nature of the Vatican City State and of the sources of its objective law." Other countries, such as Sweden and Norway, have objected to the inclusion of these reservations. When filing their own reservations and declarations, they state that the reservations of some countries "may cast doubts on the commitments of the reserving state [to the Convention]" [77].

Supporters of CRC contend that it has enhanced children's rights in a number of countries that have ratified the Convention. Human Rights Watch, for example, reports that many countries have used CRC as a basis for enhancing existing legislation and improving children's rights [78]. Similarly, a 2004 U.N. Children's Fund (UNICEF) review of 62 States Parties to CRC found that more than half of the countries studied had incorporated Convention provisions into their domestic laws, and nearly one-third of the countries had incorporated provisions into their national constitutions [79]. UNICEF also reports that CRC played a role in establishing over 60 independent human rights institutions for children in 38 countries [80]. Ultimately, however, supporters generally acknowledge that while progress has been made, many countries still have a long way to go in implementing the Convention. The 2004 UNICEF review, for instance, found that while high-level political commitment to CRC is essential to developing new laws to protect children's rights, social change will occur only when high-level commitment is matched by "effective law enforcement, allocation of adequate resources and the engagement of all levels of society." [81]

The Convention as an Instrument of U.S. Foreign Policy

Many CRC supporters hold that ratification of the Convention would strengthen U.S. credibility abroad and give the United States additional fora in which to pursue the advancement of children's rights [82]. Specifically, they argue that U.S. non-ratification leads foreign governments to question the sincerity of the United States in addressing children's rights, thereby hindering the ability of U.S. diplomats to advocate child rights in countries with poor human rights records [83]. They contend that many countries view the United States as hypocritical because it expects other countries to comply with international standards that it does not itself follow [84]. Some, for example, point to U.S. statutes that require U.S. foreign assistance to be subject to a country's compliance with "internationally recognized human rights."[85] Further, some argue that U.S. ratification would provide the United States with an opportunity to influence international laws and standards in the area of children's rights. They maintain that the United States, with its history of democracy and policies that respect children, could share its experience and expertise with other countries that aim to protect children's rights [86]

Opponents of CRC argue that the United States is the international leader in advancing children's rights and that U.S. non-ratification does not impact its ability to advocate children's rights to foreign governments. They maintain that the United States has demonstrated its commitment to children by ratifying the Optional Protocols to the Convention and by implementing laws and policies that protect and preserve the rights of children in the United States. Some critics of ratification also contend that CRC and, more broadly, other international human rights treaties, are designed for countries with lesser human rights traditions [87]. They argue that U.S. laws far exceed the standards established in such agreements, and that ratifying the treaties would not benefit U.S. citizens. Moreover, some are reluctant to leave the question of U.S. obligations under international treaties to other countries—particularly those with low human rights standards. Critics have also expressed concern that U.S. ratification of CRC and other human rights treaties could be used as a basis for unfounded political criticisms of the United States in international for a [88]

REFERENCES

[1] The term "States Parties" refers to countries that have ratified or acceded to the Convention.

[2] The U.S. government is party to the CRC Optional Protocol on Children and Armed Conflict and the Optional Protocol on the Sale of Children. See the "Optional Protocols on Children in Armed Conflict and the Sale of Children" for more information.

[3] Department of State Daily Press Briefing by Ian Kelly, State Department Spokesperson, Washington, DC, November 24, 2009, at http://www.state.gov/r/pa/ prs/dpb/ 2009/nov/132362.htm.

[4] The Universal Declaration of Human Rights was not the first international document to address the rights of children. On September 16, 1924, members of the League of Nations agreed to the Geneva Declaration on the Rights of the Child. The Declaration recognized that children must be: given material and spiritual means for normal development; fed or nursed, reclaimed when delinquent, and sheltered when orphaned; the first to receive relief in times of distress; and put in a position to earn a livelihood and be sheltered from exploitation. It was adopted by U.N. General Assembly resolution 217 A (III) on December 10, 1948 by a vote of 48 in favor, zero against, and eight abstentions.

[5] U.N. General Assembly resolution 1386 (XIV), November 20, 1959.

[6] Article 10 of CESCR states, "Special measures of protection and assistance should be taken on behalf of all children and young persons without any discrimination for reasons of parentage or other conditions.... " Article 24 of CCPR states that every child shall have "the right to such measures of protection as are required by his status as a minor, on the part of his family, society and the State." CESCR entered into force on January 3, 1976, and CCPR entered into force on March 23, 1976. The United States ratified CCPR on October 21, 1994. It signed CESCR on October 5, 1997, but has not ratified it.

[7]   U.N. member states periodically designate years or decades to highlight special issues, events, or disadvantaged groups.

[8]   CRC was adopted and opened for signature, ratification and accession by General Assembly resolution 44/25 on November 20, 1989.

[9]   See Article 1, CRC. The text of the Convention is available at http://www.ohchr.org/english/law/crc.htm.

[10] See CRC Articles 7(1) and 3(2). For more information, see the "Parental Rights" section.

[11] Committee members are eligible for re-election if nominated. See Article 43 for more information on the Committee.

[12] U.N. document, CRC/C/4/Rev. 1, part I, rule 3, April 25, 2005

[13] For more information on Committee meetings, see "Committee on the Rights of the Child—Working Methods," at http://www2.ohchr.org/english/bodies/crc/workingmethods.htm.

[14] Both Optional protocols were adopted without a vote by U.N. General Assembly resolution 54/263 on May 25, 2000. Text of the Optional Protocols and a list of States Parties are available at http://www2.ohchr.org/english/law/crcsale.htm.

[15] See Article 13 of the Optional Protocol on the Sale of Children and Article 9 of the Optional Protocol on Children in Armed Conflict.

[16] For more information, see, *Treaties and other International Agreements: The Role of the United States Senate, A Study Prepared for the Committee on Foreign Relations by the Congressional Research Service*, S. Prt 106-7 1, 106th Congress, 2d Session, January 2001.

[17] The Clinton Administration signed the Optional Protocols on July 5, 2000, and transmitted both treaties to the Senate on July 25, 2000 (Treaty Doc. 106-3 7). The Bush Administration strongly supported the ratification of the Optional Protocols. The Senate provided its advice and consent to ratification of both agreements on June 18, 2002. The United States became party to the treaties on December 24, 2002, and they entered into force for the United States on January 23, 2003.

[18] When asked about the Convention during the 2008 presidential campaign Obama stated, "It is embarrassing to find ourselves [the United States] in the company of Somalia, a lawless land. I will review this [treaty] and other treaties to ensure that the United States resumes its global leadership in human rights." See Patrick Geary, "United States: Is Obama's Win also a Victory for Children's Rights?" Child Rights Information Network, November 7, 2008. A video of President Obama's statement is available at http://debate.waldenu.edu/video/question-12/.

[19] Congressional Transcripts, Congressional Hearings, "Senate Foreign Relations Committee Holds Hearing on the Nomination of Susan Rice to be the U.S. Permanent Representative to the United Nations," Congressional Quarterly, January 15, 2009.

[20] Department of State Daily Press Briefing by Ian Kelly, Spokesperson, Washington, DC, November 24, 2009, at http://www.state.gov/r/pa/prs/dpb/2009/nov/132362.htm.

[21] Ibid.

[22] The United States made recommendations on 38 of 40 substantive CRC articles. See Cynthia Price Cohen, "Role of the United States in Drafting the Convention on the Rights of the Child: Creating a New World For Children," *Loyola Poverty Law Journal*, Vol. 9, Spring 1998.

[23] U.S. Mission to the United Nations press release #26-(95), "Remarks by Ambassador Madeleine K. Albright to the United Nations on the Occasion of the Signing of the U.N. Convention on the Rights of the Child," February 16, 1995. In 2005, the Supreme Court found in *Roper v. Simmons* that the imposition of the death penalty on juvenile offenders is unconstitutional. See 543 U.S. 551 (2005).

[24] In 1995, Senator Jesse Helms warned President Clinton that as long as he was Chairperson of SFRC, "it is going to be very difficult for this treaty [CRC] even to be given a hearing." *Congressional Record*, Senate, Vol. 141, No. 97, p. S 8401, June 14, 1995.

[25] "United States Participation in the United Nations for 2002: Report by the Secretary of State to the Congress," October 2003, Part 2: Economic and Social Affairs, pp. 79-80.

[26] Statement by Ambassador E. Michael Southwick in the Preparatory Committee for the General Assembly Special Session on the Children's World Summit, U.S. Mission to the United Nations press release #15(01), February 1, 2001.

[27] See, for example, H.Res. 416 [111th], "Expressing the sense of the House of Representatives that the United States should become an international human rights leader by ratifying and implementing certain core international conventions," introduced on May 7, 2009, by Rep. John Lewis and referred to the Committee on Foreign Affairs.

[28] H.Res. 312 [101st], "Urging the President to submit the Convention on the Rights of the Child to the Senate for its advice and consent to ratification," passed/agreed to in the House by a voice vote on September 17, 1990. Similar legislation was introduced in the Senate and House during the 102nd, 103rd, and 105th Congresses.

[29] Former Senator Jesse Helms was a strong opponent of CRC, and in June 1995 he introduced a resolution in the 104th Congress that reflected the concerns of some CRC opponents. The resolution stated that CRC is "fundamentally flawed," and "incompatible with the God-given right and responsibility of parents to raise their children." (S.Res. 133 [104th], introduced June 14, 1995 and referred to the Committee on Foreign Relations.)

[30] See H.J.Res. 42 [111th], introduced on April 27, 2009 and referred to the Subcommittee on the Constitution, Civil Rights, and Civil Liberties. Similar legislation was introduced in the Senate, including S.J.Res. 13 [111th] by Sen. David Vitter on March 3, 2009, and S.J.Res. 16 [111th] by Sen. Jim DeMint on May 14, 2009. Both resolutions are entitled "A joint resolution proposing an amendment to the Constitution of the United States relative to parental rights," and were referred to the Committee on the Judiciary.

[31] Under Article II, section 2 of the U.S. Constitution, the President is responsible for making treaties by and with the advice and consent of the Senate. Once the President transmits a treaty to the Senate, it is, under the rules of the Senate, referred to the Committee on Foreign Relations. Thus, the issues for Congress discussed herein are issues that may be included in any consideration of the Convention by SFRC and/or the full Senate.

[32] For a detailed analysis of how U.S. state and federal laws may be affected by the Convention, see Cynthia Price Cohen and Howard A. Davidson, ed., *Children's Rights in America: U.N. Convention on the Rights of the Child Compared with United States Law*, American Bar Association, 1990.

[33] Sally J. Cummings and David P. Stewart, *Digest of United States Practice in International Law, 2002*, Office of the Legal Advisor, Department of State, p. 291.

[34] Drawn in part from *Treaties and other International Agreements: The Role of the United States Senate, A Study Prepared for the Committee on Foreign Relations by the Congressional Research Service*, S. Prt 106-7 1, 106th Congress, 2d Session, January 2001.

[35] RUDs accompanying U.S. ratification of human rights treaties are controversial among some analysts and policymakers due to concerns that they might undermine the effectiveness or intent of the treaty. See "U.S. Ratification of Human Rights Conventions: The Ghost of Senator Bricker," by Louis Henkin, *The American Journal of International Law*, Vol. 89:43 1, April 1995, pp. 341-350. Also see the "Effectiveness of the Convention" section.

[36] For more information on this issue, see Lawrence L. Stentzel, II, "Federal-State Implications of the Convention" in *Children's Rights in America: U.N. Convention on the Rights of the Child Compared with United States Law*, Cynthia Price Cohen and Howard A. Davidson, ed., American Bar Association, 1990, pp. 57-86. Parts of this section are drawn from archived CRS Report 96-736, *Human Rights Treaties: Some Issues for U.S. Ratification*, by Vita Bite.

[37] Article six of the U.S. Constitution states, "This Constitution, and the Laws of the United States which shall be made in Pursuance thereof; and all Treaties made, or which shall be made, under the Authority of the United States, shall be the supreme Law of the Land; and the Judges in every State shall be bound thereby, any Thing in the Constitution or Laws of any State to the Contrary notwithstanding."

[38] See, for example, Joseph Abrams, "Boxer Seeks to Erode Treaty that May Erode U.S. Rights," FoxNews.com, February 25, 2009. For further discussion of this issue, see Martin S. Flaherty, "History Right?: Historical Scholarship, Original Understanding, and Treaties as "Supreme Law of the Land," *Columbia Law Review*, Vol. 99, No. 8, December 1999, pp. 2095-2153.

[39] *An Analysis of the United Nations Committee on the Rights of the Child's Concluding Observations*, National Center for Home Education, November 11, 1999, updated March 2007.

[40] See Jonathan Todres, et al., *The U.N. Convention on the Rights of the Child, An Analysis of Treaty Provisions and Implications of U.S. Ratification*, Transnational Publishers, Inc., 2006, p. 28.

[41] Ibid. The International Covenant on Civil and Political Rights, for example, provides for "state-to-state" complaints. CRC, on the other hand, states that only the CRC Committee may comment on the report of a state party.

[42] See (1) Michael Smith, "Home-schooling: U.N. Treaty Might Weaken Families," *The Washington Times*, January 11, 2009, and (2) Andie Coller, "Parental Rights: The New Wedge Issue," *Politico*, April 8, 2009.

[43] "United Nations Special Session on Children Set to Meet," *National Center for Home Education*, May 3, 2002.

[44] When emphasizing these concerns, some opponents point to a 1997 CRC Committee report on Ethiopia, which recommended that "the limitation of the right to legal counsel of children be abolished as a matter of priority." (U.N. document, CRC/C/15/Add.67, January 24, 1997.) Some also reference the Committee's 1999 recommendation to

Belize expressing concern regarding "the absence of an independent mechanism to register and address complaints from children concerning violations of their rights under the Convention. The Committee suggests that an independent child-friendly mechanism be made accessible to children.... " (U.N. document, CRC/C/15/Add.99, May 10, 1999).

[45] Michael P. Farris, "Nannies in Blue Berets: Understanding the U.N. Convention on the Rights of the Child," parentalrights.org, December 15, 2008.

[46] "Congressional Action: The United Nations Convention on the Rights of the Child," Lifesite News, July/August 1993, at http://www.lifesitenews.com/waronfamily/unicef/homeschoolalert.html.

[47] CRC Article 17 further states that children should especially have access to sources "aimed at the promotion of his or her social, spiritual, and moral well-being and physical or mental health." Critics hold that Article 17 could also prevent parents from restricting children's access to pornographic material or other sources of information that contradict the parents' values.

[48] *Oppose the U.N. Convention on the Rights of the Child*, National Center for Home Education, November 1, 1999, updated March 2007.

[49] To support this point of view, critics point to a CRC Committee concluding observation for Canada in 2003 recommending "that the State party adopt legislation to remove the existing authorization of the use of 'reasonable force' in disciplining children and explicitly prohibit all forms of violence against children, however light, within the family in schools and in other institutions where children may be placed." (U.N. document, CRC/C/15/Add.215, October 27, 2003.)

[50] *Oppose the U.N. Convention on the Rights of the Child*, National Center for Home Education, November 1, 1999, updated March 2007.

[51] See (1) Opposition to the Convention on the Rights of the Child: Exploring Counterarguments and Seeking Clarification, presentation by the U.S. Fund for UNICEF, Voices for America's Children, Homeschooler's U.N. Club," at http://childrightscampaign.org/documents/OppositiontotheCRC.pdf; and (2) Barbara Bennett Woodhouse, "The Family Supporting Nature of the U.N. Convention on the Rights of the Child," in The U.N. Convention on the Rights of the Child, by Jonathan Todres et al., Transnational Publishers, Inc., 2006, p. 37.

[52] Barbara Bennett Woodhouse, "The Family Supporting Nature of the U.N. Convention on the Rights of the Child," in *The U.N. Convention on the Rights of the Child,* by Jonathan Todres et al., Transnational Publishers, Inc., 2006, p. 45.

[53] Some argue, for example, that CRC Article 17 is meant to encourage, and not discourage, states from providing children with access to information that may be beneficial to their well being. They emphasize, however, that parents must determine how much or what types of information to which their children are exposed.

[54] The parent-child role is referenced in the following CRC Articles: 2, 3, 5, 7, 8, 9, 10, 11, 14, 16, 18, 20, 21, 22, 23, 24, 27, 37, and 40. See "The United Nations Convention on the Rights of the Child: Answers to 30 Questions," by Cynthia Price Cohen and Susan H. Bitensky, *Child Rights International Research Institute,* 1994.

[55] *Myths and Facts on the Convention on the Rights of the Child (CRC),* The Campaign for U.S. Ratification of the Convention on the Rights of the Child, 2009.

[56] U.S. Congress. Senate. Committee on Foreign Relations, "Convention on the Elimination of All Forms of Discrimination Against Women," Report, September 12, 1994. Washington, D.C., Government Printing Office (Senate Exec. Rept. 103-38, 103d Congress, 2d Session), pp. 6-8. For more information, see CRS Report R40750, *The U.N. Convention on the Elimination of All Forms of Discrimination Against Women (CEDA W): Issues in the U.S. Ratification Debate*, by Luisa Blanchfield.

[57] David M. Smolin, "Overcoming Religious Objections to the Convention on the Rights of the Child," *Emory Law Journal*, Vol. 20, Spring 2006, pp. 81-110.

[58] Patrick F. Fagan, "How U.N. Convention on Women's and Children's Rights Undermine Family, Religion, and Sovereignty," *Heritage Foundation*, Backgrounder #1407, February 5, 2001.

[59] In a 1994 report on Chad, for example, the CRC Committee expressed its concern "at the impact that punitive legislation regarding abortion can have on maternal mortality rates for adolescent girls. The Committee suggests that a comprehensive and multi-disciplinary study be undertaken to understand the scope of adolescent health problems, including the negative impact of early pregnancy and illegal abortion." Some contend that the Committee was not criticizing Chad's abortion laws, but focusing on the plight of girls who fall ill or die because of illegal abortions. (U.N. document, CRC/C/15/Add. 107, August 24, 1999.)

[60] "Myths and Facts on the Convention on the Rights of the Child (CRC)," *The Campaign for U.S. Ratification of the Convention on the Rights of the Child*, 2009.

[61] U.N. document, CRC/C/15/Add.4, February 18, 1993. In the report, the Committee also noted with particular concern "the tendency towards the breakdown of family culture as regards abandoned children, abortion, the divorce rate ... "

[62] According to international law, a treaty may be interpreted by taking into account the preparatory work and negotiations related to the treaty text. Specifically, Article 32 of the 1969 Vienna Convention on the Law of Treaties states, "Recourse may be had to supplementary means of interpretation, including the preparatory work of the treaty and the circumstances of its conclusion, in order to confirm the meaning resulting from the application of article 31, or to determine the meaning when the interpretation according to Article 31: (a) leaves the meaning ambiguous or obscure; or (b) leads to a result which is manifestly absurd or unreasonable." The United States signed the Vienna Convention on April 24, 1970, but the Senate has not given its advice and consent to ratification. According to the State Department, the United States "considers many of the provisions of the Vienna Convention on the Law of Treaties to constitute customary international law on the law of treaties."

[63] For information on the history of CRC negotiations, see (1) Sharon Detrick, ed., *The United Nations Convention on the Rights of the Child: A Guide to the 'Travaux Preparatoires'*; Martinus Nijhoff Publishers, London, 1992; (2) Jonathan Todres and Louise N. Howe, "What the Convention on the Rights of the Child Says (and Doesn't Say) About Abortion and Family Planning," in *The U.N. Convention on the Rights of the Child*, by Jonathan Todres et al., Transnational Publishers, Inc., 2006, pp. 163-175; and (3) Sharon Detrick, *A Commentary on the United Nations Convention on the Rights of the Child*, Martinus Nijhoff Publishers, The Hague, 1999, pp. 133-136.

[64] Philip Alston, "The Unborn Child and Abortion Under the Draft Convention on the Rights of the Child," *Human Rights Quarterly*, Vol. 12, 1990, p. 163.

[65] For further discussion of the role of the preamble in the abortion debate, see "The Unborn Child and Abortion Under the Draft Convention on the Rights of the Child," *Human Rights Quarterly*, Vol. 12, 1990, pp. 165-172.

[66] William L. Saunders, The Convention on the Rights of the Child and the U.N. Special Session on Children, Family Research Council, 2001, available at http://www.worldfamilypolicy.org/New%20Page/forum/2001/saunders.pdf.

[67] Article 3 1(2) of the 1969 Vienna Convention on the Law of Treaties states, "The context for the purpose of the interpretation of a treaty shall comprise.... its preamble and annexes ... "

[68] Jonathan Todres and Louise N. Howe, "What the Convention on the Rights of the Child Says (and Doesn't Say) About Abortion and Family Planning," in *The U.N. Convention on the Rights of the Child,* Jonathan Todres et al.,Transnational Publishers, Inc., 2006, p. 166.

[69] Cynthia Price Cohen, "A Guide to Linguistic Interpretation of the Convention on the Rights of the Child" in *Children's Rights in America: U.N. Convention on the Rights of the Child Compared with United States Law,* Cynthia Price Cohen and Howard A. Davidson, ed., American Bar Association, 1990, p. 42.

[70] See U.N. document, E/CN.4/1989/48, March 2, 1989, paragraph 43. The record states, "In adopting this preambular paragraph, the Working Group does not intend to prejudice the interpretation of Article 1 or any other provision of the Convention by States Parties."

[71] U.N. document, E/CN.4/L. 1542, March 10, 1980.

[72] William L. Saunders, *The Convention on the Rights of the Child and the U.N. Special Session on Children,* Family Research Council, World Family Policy Forum, 2001.

[73] Article 3(2), CRC.

[74] The Holy See included a reservation stating that it "interprets the phrase 'family planning education and services' in Article 24(2), to mean only those methods of family planning which it considers morally acceptable, that is, the natural methods of family planning."

[75] For more information, see William A. Schabas, "Reservations to the Convention on the Rights of the Child," *Human Rights Quarterly*, Vol. 18.2, May 1996, pp. 472-491.

[76] States Parties that included similar reservations include Afghanistan, Algeria, Egypt, Iran, Iraq, Kuwait, Morocco, Saudi Arabia, and Syria. The full list of reservations and declarations by States Parties is at http://www.unhchr.ch/html/menu3/b/treaty15_asp.htm.

[77] The reservations of Sweden and Norway specifically state: "A reservation by which a state party limits its responsibilities under the Convention by invoking general principles of national law may cast doubts on the commitments of the reserving state to the object and purpose of the Convention and, moreover, contribute to undermining the basis of international treaty law." Ireland, Portugal, and Finland have also included reservations with similar wording.

[78] Human Rights Watch also reports that under CRC some countries have appointed special ombudspersons or envoys for children. It also reports that the CRC Committee has "developed new standards of protection and pressed governments for specific reforms." See *Promises Broken: An Assessment of Children's Rights on the 10th*

Anniversary of the Convention on the Rights of the Child, Human Rights Watch, November 1999.

[79] UNICEF press release, "Despite Progress, Children's Rights Far from Universal," November 20, 2004

[80] Ibid.

[81] Ibid. Also see, UNICEF press release, "Experts Discuss the Impact of CRC," November 20, 2007.

[82] *International Implications of the United States Ratifying the CRC*, presentation by Carl Triplehorn, Save the Children, May 20, 2005.

[83] In 1979, then-Secretary of State Christopher Warren stated that U.S. "... nonadherence to the [human rights] treaties prejudices our [the United States'] participation in the development of international law with respect to human rights." See, U.S. Congress. Senate. Committee on Foreign Relations. International Human Rights Treaties. Hearings, 96th Congress, 1st session. November 14-16, 19, 1979. Washington, U.S. Government Printing Office, 1979, pp. 19-20.

[84] The United States has called for countries to comply with CRC in U.N. fora even though the United States is not itself a party to the treaty. For example, in a November 2006 statement to the U.N. General Assembly, a U.S. representative stated, "The Government of Sudan, which is a party to the Convention on the Rights of the Child and the Optional Protocol to the Convention on the Rights of the Child on the Involvement of Children in Armed Conflict, must accept responsibility for the widespread problem of recruitment and use of child soldiers and take immediate steps to halt these practices." U.S. Mission to the United Nations Press Release #368(06), November 28, 2006.

[85] For example, Sec. 116(a) of the Foreign Assistance Act of 1961, as amended (P.L. 87-195) states, "No assistance may be provided ... to the government of any country which engages in a consistent pattern of gross violations of internationally recognized human rights.... " Similarly, Sec. 502B(a)(1) of that Act states, "a principal goal of the foreign policy of the United States shall be to promote the increased observance of internationally recognized human rights by all countries." Further, Sec. 502B(a)(2) states, " ... no security assistance may be provided to any country the government of which engages in a consistent pattern of gross violations of internationally recognized human rights."

[86] *Opposition to the Convention on the Rights of the Child: Counterarguments and Seeking Clarification*, presentation by U.S. Fund for UNICEF, Voices for America's Children, Homeschooler's U.N. Club.

[87] Chrisopher J. Klicka, Esq. And William A. Estrada, *Special Report: The U.N. Convention on the Rights of the Child, The Most Dangerous Attack on Parent's Rights in the History of the United States*, Home School Legal Defense Association, November 1, 1999, updated March 2007.

[88] See (1) Belinda Clark, "The Vienna Convention Reservations Regime and the Convention on Discrimination Against Women" *American Journal of International Law*, Vol. 85, April 1991, pp. 28 1-321; and (2) Rebecca J. Cook, "Reservations to the Convention on the Elimination of Discrimination against Women," *Virginia Journal of International Law*, Vol. 30, 1990, p. 643.

INDEX

D

E

J

K

L

M

N

Q

V

W

Y

Z